ROSEMARY STANTON'S

healthy eating

for families

Published in 2007 by Murdoch Books Pty Limited
www.murdochbooks.com.au

Murdoch Books Australia
Pier 8/9
23 Hickson Road
Millers Point NSW 2000
Phone: +61 (0) 2 8220 2000
Fax: +61 (0) 2 8220 2558

Murdoch Books UK LTD
Erico House, 6th Floor
93–99 Upper Richmond Road
Putney, London SW15 2TG
Phone: +44 (0) 20 8785 5995
Fax: +44 (0) 20 8785 5985

Chief Executive: Juliet Rogers
Publishing Director: Kay Scarlett

Project Manager: Rhiain Hull
Editor: Kim Rowney
Design concept, art direction and design: Alex Frampton
Production: Adele Troeger
Photographer: Steve Brown
Stylist: Saskia Hay
Food preparation: Grace Campbell

A catalogue record for this book is available from the British Library
ISBN 978 1 92125 927 2 (pbk.). ISBN 1 92125 927 2 (pbk.).

Printed by Midas Printing (Asia) Ltd. in 2007. PRINTED IN CHINA.

CONVERSION GUIDE: You may find cooking times vary depending on the oven you are using. For fan-forced ovens, as a general rule, set the oven temperature to 20°C (35°F) lower than indicated in the recipe. We have used 20 ml (4 teaspoon) tablespoon measures. If you are using a 15 ml (3 teaspoon) tablespoon, for most recipes the difference will not be noticeable. However, for recipes using baking powder, gelatine, bicarbonate of soda (baking soda), small amounts of flour and cornflour (cornstarch), add an extra teaspoon for each tablespoon specified.

The publisher thanks Bison Homewares, Bodum, Country Road, David Edmonds, Era is Evolution (distributed by Wild Oats Homewares), Iittala (distributed by Design Mode International), Maxwell & Williams, Mud Australia and The Ceramic Shed for their assistance with the photography of this book.

ROSEMARY STANTON'S
healthy eating

for families

MURDOCH BOOKS

CONTENTS

SPECIFIC DIETARY NEEDS

"Choosing healthy foods can leave us feeling more energetic, healthier and better able to cope with our busy lives. And it's not difficult to make better food choices — although it may require a little thought and some planning. Fortunately there are many deliciously healthy ingredients available and lots of easy, fast ways to prepare them. Let's make some simple changes to the way we think about the foods we choose and prepare for our families, so we can all reap the benefits of healthy eating. "

How to use this book

For each of the recipes in this book you will find an analysis of the energy and major nutrients in an average serve of the finished dish. The nutritional analysis does not include any serving suggestions or garnishes, unless listed in specific quantities in the ingredient list. Underneath the nutritional analysis for each serving is a list of specific vitamins and minerals contained in the recipe. This indicates that a serving contributes at least 10% of the recommended dietary intake for that nutrient.

All the recipes in this book are suitable for those with diabetes. The recipes have also been coded with an icon if they fit into one of the following categories.

quick and easy: If a meal can be prepared, cooked and on the table in 30–35 minutes, or less.

vegan: If the recipe is free from any animal foods and any foods that contain ingredients derived from animals, including honey. Vegans should also consider the recipes marked as vegetarian — with minor modifications, these may also be suitable. You may be able to use soy beverage in place of milk, soy yoghurt or tofu instead of regular yoghurt, brown sugar instead of honey, or you could simply omit the yoghurt or cheese in some of these recipes, particularly when used as a garnish.

vegetarian: If the recipe contains no meat, meat products, poultry or seafood.

gluten-free: If the recipe contains no gluten, which is derived from wheat or any wheat products, rye or barley.

Note also that the nutritional calculations for recipes that include stock have used figures for home-made stock. If you use ready-made stock, the sodium levels may be higher, and those who need a gluten-free diet should check that any purchased stock used is gluten-free.

These guidelines are designed to make the book easy to use. All questions related to medical problems or specific dietary requirements should be directed to your doctor.

Introduction

We are what we eat. It's an old adage, but it's true. Everything in our bodies was once in our food. Many people choose to ignore this fact and, fortunately, the human body is resilient, so some people appear to stay healthy even though they pay little attention to what they eat. There are also people who cross the road without looking and survive, but no sane person would teach a child to take such risks. Looking at all the

evidence, there is no doubt that for the majority of people, filling the body with junk food reduces the chances of the body staying healthy. However, if you feed your body well, don't smoke and get some exercise, the body is more likely to stay in good running order.

The effects of poor diet are not hard to see. In many wealthy countries throughout the world, the majority of adults are overweight and rates of childhood obesity have doubled or tripled in the last 20 years. Even in poor countries, excess weight now rivals malnutrition as a cause of ill-health. Type 2 diabetes is increasing so rapidly that it threatens future health budgets.

There is no mystery as to why we are growing fatter — we're eating more and moving less. Physical activity is valuable because it burns up kilojoules and also regulates the appetite. But the major cause of excess weight is too many kilojoules from foods and drinks consumed in ever-increasing portions.

Studies show clearly that we eat more than previous generations — not so much in the weight of food we consume, but mainly in the concentration of kilojoules in packaged foods. Our major problem is our high consumption of processed foods that are packed with fats, sugar and salt. Add the low consumption of fresh fruits and vegetables to the mix, and the cause of the problems is obvious.

The effects of a good diet are also very apparent. When you eat well, you have a lot more energy and that usually leads to a much greater enjoyment of life. There is also now good evidence that those who follow healthy eating habits (such as eating breakfast, including more vegetables, fruits and wholegrain products in their diet, choosing healthy fats from foods such as extra virgin olive oil, nuts and avocados, and avoiding too much sugar and salt) live longer, healthier and more active lives. Many of the studies showing such benefits have been done on people in various countries who have all followed a Mediterranean-style diet and all said they not only enjoyed the food but also felt better.

Most people are busy and extended travel times and other demands make us think we have no time to eat properly. Convenience foods therefore loom large in most people's lives. But, in fact, healthy cooking doesn't have to take a long time and is not difficult. A bit of planning also helps so that some foods can be prepared or partly prepared ahead. And cutting back a little on the two to four hours spent watching television each day would give time-poor people ample opportunity to cook and eat healthier foods.

Cooking fresh foods is a survival skill. It's also fun — especially if you don't have to do it all yourself. We all need to be able to cook and that includes men, women and children. If everyone can cook, the tasks can be shared, with various family members cooking a meal together — which can make for great camaraderie — or at least having a roster so that everyone shares the responsibility. Cooking skills mean less reliance on processed foods, and that benefits our health, as well as the enjoyment associated with eating quality meals.

A healthy diet rarely happens without some basic knowledge and planning, so the first section of this book includes some basic facts about nutrition and healthy eating and discusses the problem of excess weight. It also explains how to read food labels so you can choose wisely when shopping. The bulk of the book is healthy recipes — all delicious and easy to make. Lastly, there's a section on specialty areas of health, such as sports nutrition, pregnancy and lactation, vegetarian eating, feeding fussy children, diabetes and allergies.

All the recipes in this book are healthy and easy to prepare and the ingredients can be bought in any standard shopping centre. With only a few exceptions, all the recipes have less than 10 g of fat per serving, and this has been achieved without making the servings absurdly small. The recipes are also all suitable for those with diabetes (more information on page 276) and many are marked as suitable for those who must avoid wheat. However, it is always important that anyone with coeliac disease or a wheat allergy check to ensure that individual ingredients are suitable. For example, make sure you choose an icing (confectioners') sugar that does not contain wheat starch, and choose products such as mayonnaise or soy sauce that are gluten-free.

If you have been living on takeaway foods and restaurant meals, perhaps you could start with home-cooking some light meals, soups or dinners a few times a week.

Here's to happy and healthy eating!

(Dr) Rosemary Stanton OAM
Nutritionist

BASIC
NUTRITION

The basics of healthy eating

There are various pyramids and food groups that set out what we need to eat each day. My own preference is to consider three aspects of healthy eating.

1. The nutritional value of what we eat and drink.
2. Food literacy — which includes taste, understanding where foods come from, when foods are in season, and some of the processes that have been used in the modern food supply.
3. Environmental sustainability in our food choices.

1. Nutritional value

The pyramid approach tells us to:

eat most: vegetables, fruits, legumes, wholegrains and nuts

eat moderately: seafood, lean meat, poultry, eggs and dairy products (reduced-fat versions, where available)

eat least: sugar, fats, salt and alcohol.

It's an easy guide and as long as we choose a variety of foods from within these categories, we will get the nutrients our body needs, and keep the less nutritious ingredients in their correct place — which should be a small one.

More detail about quantities of healthy foods needed is given in the five food groups. These are:

1. Vegetables: five serves a day (a serving is $1/2$ cup of cooked vegetables or 1 cup of salad vegetables)
2. Fruit: two average pieces a day
3. Cereals, grains, breads, pasta and rice (including wholegrain choices where possible): quantity varies according to size and energy needs, but at least three to four serves a day
4. Dairy products: two serves a day for adults, three for children, and preferably low-fat choices for everyone over the age of two. A serving is a cup of milk, 40 g ($1^{1}/2$ oz) cheese or 200 g (7 oz) yoghurt
5. Lean meat, fish, poultry, eggs, nuts or legumes (including tofu): one serve a day

The benefits of a healthy diet

As the pyramid approach shows us, a healthy diet doesn't ban any food, but places greater emphasis on most of the diet being made up of healthy foods. The benefits of eating mainly healthy foods include:

- longer and healthier life span
- greater feelings of positive health
- plenty of energy for work and recreation
- correct weight — not too high and not too low
- healthy immune system, which helps to fight off infections
- better chance of strong bones and a straighter spine
- better chance of normal blood sugar levels
- better chance of normal blood fats

2. Food literacy

Many highly processed foods are developed to have no taste to which anyone will object. That seems a poor substitute for the delicious flavour of fresh foods consumed when they are in season and prepared with flavoursome and healthy ingredients. Most processed foods maximize the inclusion of cheap ingredients and minimize the real foods, giving us products such as chicken soup that contains less than 1% chicken, or fish products that contain only 25% fish. These foods then include flavour enhancers and lots of salt or artificial additives to boost the flavour that should have come from the major ingredient.

Many people are unaware of seasonality, partly because growers and large shops sell the products year round. Products sold as fresh foods, but out of season, may have similar levels of vitamin C to fresh produce if their storage conditions have been ideal. But consider the poor texture and flavour of apples sold in summer compared with the wonderful crispness and taste of apples straight from the tree, which are available in autumn and winter. Fruits also have their maximum levels of antioxidants when they have not been stored.

For some foods, we take pleasure in their seasonality. Who hasn't delighted at the aroma of mangoes and stone fruits in summer? We await their arrival and enjoy them with enthusiasm, knowing they won't be there all year round. Vegetables are much more likely to be sold only in season, as their quality deteriorates rapidly at other times.

We also need to know where our beef, pork, poultry and seafood come from. In some places, beef may come from feedlots where the animals are given steroid hormones from an implant placed in the animal's ear. This makes the animals grow faster and develop more muscle, as occurs in athletes who take steroid hormones. The animals are also kept in conditions equivalent to battery hens, with little room to move. Meat from these animals is not labelled, so you need to ask your butcher about the origins of the meat or buy beef that is labelled as organic. Meat from hormone-implanted animals is not acceptable in the European Union, so beef produced in, or designed for export to, Europe is free from any added hormones.

Healthy (and environmentally friendly) meals emphasize plant foods. Make sure your plate has a maximum of one-quarter animal foods and then fill the rest with vegetables or other plant-based foods.

Other animals (including chickens) are not given hormones, but pigs and chickens may be given antibiotics that function as growth promotants. The rationale is this: when any young animal (including humans) gets an infection, growth stops for a period. (Giving children antibiotics when they get an earache or other infection is also why the current generation of young people in many countries tends to be taller than their parents.) When pigs and chickens are kept in close quarters and the animals get little or no opportunity to exercise, infections occur and spread easily. By giving the animals regular doses of antibiotics, infections are curbed and there is no interruption to the animal's growth rate — hence the use of the term 'antibiotic growth promotants'.

If you wish to avoid antibiotic residues that will be present in pork and poultry, ask your butcher for free-range or organic products. Some supermarkets also stock these products.

3. Environmental sustainability in our food choices

The energy and water resources of the earth are finite. Many foods are produced in an environmentally sustainable way; others are not.

Sheep may be less problematic than beef cattle because the sheep eat grass and often are farmed in areas that are less suitable for cultivation of crops. Kangaroos are a wise environmental choice because they eat native grasses that grow in areas not suitable for cultivation of crops. Their long feet are also much less likely to cause erosion than the feet of sheep or cattle. By contrast, beef cattle in feedlots eat grain.

From an environmental perspective, it doesn't make sense to use valuable land and water to grow grain, feed the grain to animals and then eat the animals. My personal choice is thus to make up the diet with more plant-based foods and include meat less often. The recipes in this book reflect that balance, with more suggestions for non-meat meals.

There are also environmental concerns with genetically modified (GM) crops. Most of the GM crops currently in production in major areas such as the United States are used for animal feed — mainly soy and corn. These crops are genetically engineered to resist particular weedkillers so the farmer can plant the crop and then spray with weedkiller to kill everything but the crops. Many of us have doubts that sufficient tests have been carried out to show that GM crops are environmentally desirable. Already super-weeds that are resistant to the weedkillers are developing.

If you wish to avoid GM foods now and in the future, check products with the True Food Guide, available on http://sites.greenpeace.org.au/truefood/guide2.html

Before using artificial sweeteners, you may want to think of the environmental effects of using energy resources to produce these products. They contribute no energy and are manufactured so that overfed people can eat even more, while others in the world starve because they lack the energy resources to produce basic foods. Although sugar is basically a junk food and we should cut back on our consumption, I have not used artificial sweeteners in the recipes in this book. Even people with diabetes can have some sugar, as long as the quantity is not too great and the food contains dietary fibre or ingredients that slow down the absorption of the sugar.

To reduce energy use (and hence, global warming) associated with your food choices, try to buy foods grown close to where you live and shop. If that's not possible, at least aim to buy products that have not needed a plane journey to get to you.

The basics of good nutrition

Protein

Proteins are made up of amino acids that are vital for growth and repair of body tissues. Most people in developed countries such as Australia, the United States and Europe get more than enough protein. Rich sources of protein include lean meat, fish, chicken, eggs, milk, cheese, yoghurt, legumes, tofu, nuts and seeds. Breads and all grain and cereal foods also supply protein, contributing almost 30% of our intake.

Of the 23 amino acids that make up protein, eight are called essential amino acids because we can't make them ourselves. They must be supplied from the diet. Animal sources of proteins contain all the essential amino acids, whereas most vegetable sources of protein have a lower level of one or more.

Vegetarians were once advised to eat particular combinations of foods to supply all the essential amino acids. However, we now know that individual amino acids enter an amino acid 'pool' within the body and those protein foods that were eaten at adjacent meals can be used to meet the body's requirements. In reality, this means that those who do not eat animal products simply need to eat a variety of foods throughout the day, and do not need to engage in complicated mixing of foods at each meal.

The only time protein requirements may not be met occurs in vegan children who are fussy eaters. To supply enough protein for the rapid growth rate during infancy, it is advisable for children from vegan families to be breast-fed for the first two years of life, or breast-fed for the first 12 months (as is advised for all babies) and then given fortified soy beverages.

High-protein diets are currently enjoying a wave of popularity and are discussed in more detail on page 30.

AGE	PROTEIN (g)
1–3	14
4–8	20
9–13 (boys)	40
9–13 (girls)	35
14–18 (boys)	65
14–18 (girls)	45
19–70 (men)	64
19–70 (women)	46
>70 (men)	81
>70 (women)	57
pregnancy	60
lactation	67

How much protein?

Protein needs are highest (per unit of body weight) in children and gradually decrease as growth stops.

No protein requirement is set for breast-fed babies, but recommended protein intakes after breast-feeding stops are shown in the table above.

Surveys show that all age groups in developed countries consume much more protein than these quantities, but there is no evidence the current higher protein consumption is a problem. However, while there is no scientific support for even more protein in the diet, there is some potential for kidney problems with very high consumption of proteins in those with diabetes.

Fats — the good, the bad and the ugly

Babies need fat to fuel their rapid growth rate. Breast milk supplies half its kilojoules from fat and without this concentrated source of energy babies would not be able to triple their birth weight in their first 12 to 15 months of life. Infants continue to need more fat than other age groups until their appetite improves and they can consume enough kilojoules from a wider range of foods.

After two years of age, many people consume too much of the wrong kind of fat, and while all fats make the same high kilojoule contribution, some have benefits while others have undesirable effects on health.

Types of fat

Depending on their chemical structure, fats in foods can be described as mainly saturated, monounsaturated or polyunsaturated. Foods contain a mixture of different types of fat, but they are generally characterized by

Top protein tips

- There is no advantage in having huge portions of high protein foods, so keep to small quantities (about 100 g/3½ oz) of lean meat.

- Plant proteins are suitable and also contribute dietary fibre and many important nutrients.

- Amino acid supplements are a waste of money, even for athletes.

When nutritionists say that we need to eat some fat, they are not referring to fatty meats, cream, chips or fried foods but to the essential fats in foods such as avocado, olive oil, nuts and fish.

the predominant type. For example, butter is regarded as a saturated fat because about 65% of its fat is saturated (30% is monounsaturated and about 5% is polyunsaturated). Margarine has just as much total fat as butter, but those labelled 'unsaturated' have about half as much saturated fat and a higher percentage of unsaturated fat.

The good fats

We all need some polyunsaturated fats from two categories — the omega 3s and the omega 6s. These terms refer to their chemical structure. Both types are important in the structure of the membranes around every cell in the body and they also influence the production of various hormone-type substances that control inflammatory reactions in the body.

Omega 3 polyunsaturated fats are current favourites because they are an important structural component of the brain and the eye and they can also help prevent inflammatory reactions in the arteries, skin and joints.

There are different omega 3 fats and the best type are found in seafood. In Australia, all seafood has enough of the omega 3s to be legally classified as a good source, but this is not always the case in other areas. Top honours go to swordfish, salmon, sardines, mackerel, gemfish and bonito. Two servings of seafood a week will provide enough omega 3s and there is little benefit in more. Seafood may also contain mercury, with levels higher in long-lived large species of fish and also higher where there is industrial contamination. Most Australian seafood has low levels of mercury, but swordfish and shark may have higher levels and should not be consumed more than once a fortnight during pregnancy and no other fish should be eaten that fortnight.

For those who do not eat seafood, the meat from grass-fed (but not grain-fed) animals contains another omega 3 fat, while plant sources include linseeds (also called flaxseeds), canola oil, walnuts and green leafy vegetables. All omega 3 fats go rancid easily, and while most people know when fish has gone 'off', some may not realise when their linseed oil has turned rancid. It is difficult to find linseed oil that is not past its prime, and those who don't eat seafood are better off eating actual linseeds. Although some seeds will emerge from the intestine undigested, enough will stick to the intestine wall where helpful 'good' bacteria will gradually break down their coating and release their valuable fats.

Omega 6 polyunsaturated fats predominate in safflower, sunflower, grapeseed, corn, sesame and soya bean oils. Grains such as oats or wheat also contain omega 6 fat. One fat in this family, linoleic acid, is essential in small quantities for normal growth and development and also helps reduce blood cholesterol.

There is an ideal ratio of omega 6 to omega 3 fats. Breast milk is taken as the 'gold standard' and most people depart from this after infancy by consuming too many of the omega 6 fats and not enough of the omega 3s. This usually occurs because the omega 6-rich oils are widely used in spreads, salad dressings and for cooking. Those who rely on plant sources for their omega 3 fats need to be especially careful not to overdo the omega 6s, as these fats will use up the enzyme the body needs to convert plant-based omega 3s to the more useable form found ready-made in fish.

Monounsaturated fats also fit into the 'good' category because when they are substituted for saturated fats, they can lower blood cholesterol. These fats predominate in olive oil, avocado, canola and peanut oil, most nuts and chicken. Canola oil also contains some omega 3s. Extra virgin olive oil contains dozens of antioxidants and other components. Some of these help prevent blood cells sticking together and forming blood clots and may also help lower blood pressure. Avocado and nuts also contain a wide variety of antioxidants and provide vitamin E. However, if you consume too much of any 'good' fat, it will still make you fat.

The bad

Saturated fats have been damned for over 50 years because they increase levels of 'bad' LDL (low density lipoprotein) cholesterol in the blood. Many studies find them responsible for health problems. Some types of saturated fats are worse than others, but in general, it is best to cut back on all saturated fat. We could once identify saturated fat as animal fat in meat and dairy products. Over 40% of our saturated fat intake now comes from vegetable oils that have been processed to make them suitable for use as an ingredient in foods such as chips, crisps, crackers, sweet biscuits, pastries, snack foods, confectionery and anything crumbed or coated. The vegetable oil you buy as a liquid is still mainly unsaturated.

No more than 8–10% of our daily kilojoules should come from saturated fat. For most people, this equates to a daily total of 15–20 g.

Cholesterol is a waxy type of fat that is an essential part of our cell membranes and is also a building block for our body's production of hormones and vitamin D. Cholesterol is carried in the bloodstream attached to molecules called lipoproteins. Low density lipoprotein (LDL) forms a loose bond with cholesterol and may deposit the waxy fat in the arteries leading to the heart (or the penis in men), where it can form the basis for a fatty plaque from which an artery-blocking clot can detach. High density lipoproteins (HDL) pick up stray cholesterol and take it back to the liver so it can be used for essential functions.

There is some ready-made cholesterol in all animal foods, but we don't need to eat cholesterol to get what we need because the body can easily make its own. When we eat a lot of saturated fat, some people will make too much cholesterol. This contributes many times the amount of ready-made cholesterol we could get from foods such as eggs, and we need to exert vigilance over our intake of saturated fat rather than cholesterol itself. Food labels must now list saturated fat.

The ugly

The worst fat of all is called elaidic acid — usually referred to as 'trans' fat. Other trans fats occur in small quantities in meat and dairy products, but they are not harmful to health.

The trans fat elaidic acid doesn't occur in nature but is formed when liquid vegetable oils are converted to a more stable and solid form by a process called partial hydrogenation. Food manufacturers like trans fat because it has better keeping qualities than unsaturated vegetable oils from which it is made. This applies especially to canola oil, which goes rancid quite rapidly.

Some fats are good, some fats are bad, but whatever their virtues, all fats contribute 37 kilojoules per gram. However, take care when choosing low-fat foods, as these often include extra sugar or starches (just as low-carb foods often have extra fat). You can avoid them all by choosing more fresh foods.

Top fat tips

- We need some 'good' fats — from foods like seafood, nuts (not coconut), avocado, linseeds (flaxseeds), soya beans, olive oil, canola and other liquid vegetable oils. Try to eat two fish meals a week. If you can't eat seafood, choose breads and cereals with linseeds or foods with added omega 3-rich fish oils.

- Reduce animal fats by choosing reduced-fat milk, low-fat yoghurt, skinless chicken cuts and trimmed meats.

- Take care with reduced-fat foods where the fat has been replaced by sugar or refined starch. Many of these foods have little or no reduction in kilojoules.

- If you have little time, forget takeaway foods and think pasta with tomato and vegetable/seafood sauce, or grilled fish, steamed vegetables or green salad, or rice with stir-fried meat or chicken and vegetables.

- Low-fat fast foods include sushi, chargrilled chicken (pull the skin off), Asian foods that are not fried and do not include coconut milk, or a quality kebab. Say 'no' to 'fries with that?'

- Minimize fats in cooking by using a heavy-based saucepan and heat it so that a small amount of oil will spread over the base of the pan. Use olive oil spray on baked vegetables.

- Read labels and get a fat counter booklet. If you need to lose weight, keep to 30–40 g fat per day, with no more than one-third as saturated fat. If your weight is about right, avoid trans fats and keep saturated fat below 20 g per day.

Trans fat makes crisp biscuits, pastries, snack foods and anything with a crumb coating. The process that produces trans fat is also an easy way to make margarine or chocolate spreads.

Trans fat is similar to saturated fat in raising levels of 'bad' LDL cholesterol in the blood. But trans fat is worse, as it also reduces the protective 'good' HDL cholesterol and raises levels of several other undesirable fats linked to cardiovascular disease and type 2 diabetes. There is no safe level of trans fat and some Scandinavian countries have banned foods containing more than 2% trans fat. In countries such as the United States, many margarines are high in trans fats. Manufacturers in Australia changed their production methods a few years ago and made major brands of spreads with minimal trans fat. However, cheaper brands of margarine spreads, chocolate nut spreads, chicken nuggets, chips and many fast foods are high in trans fats.

Some countries, including the United States and some European nations, require trans fat content to be included on food labels. Such declarations have led the food industry to adopt other processing techniques that avoid production of trans fat. Australia currently requires labelling only where a claim about unsaturated fats or cholesterol is being made.

How much fat?

Saturated fats should be kept low — consume no more than 15–20 g per day. Consuming less than this is not a problem and a maximum of 10 g per day is appropriate for those who need to lose weight.

Total fat consumption depends on body weight. For those who are not overweight, there is no need to limit unsaturated fats. For those who need to lose weight, a total fat consumption of 30–50 g is recommended.

Carbohydrates and GI

Just as some fats are good and some are undesirable, so carbohydrates can be classified as 'good' or 'bad'. The 'good' carbohydrates come accompanied by other important nutrients in foods such as fruits, wholegrain breads and cereals (including pasta, brown rice and burghul/bulgur), legumes, low-fat milk and yoghurt, and a few vegetables such as peas, potatoes, sweet corn and sweet potatoes. Most other vegetables have very little carbohydrate.

Carbohydrates are broken down in the body to glucose. For those with diabetes, the slower the conversion of carbohydrate to glucose, the better. A flood of glucose can stimulate the body's production of insulin.

Carbohydrate foods can be classified according to how rapidly their carbohydrate is converted to glucose in the body compared with a similar quantity of straight glucose. This is called the glycaemic index (GI).

Foods with a low GI are more suitable for those with diabetes, although the concept of GI should only be taken into account after considering the overall nutritional effect of the food. A low GI does not make a food desirable. For example, some foods high in saturated fat, such as chocolate spread or ice cream, have a low GI but are undesirable because they have a high content of kilojoules and saturated fat (and trans fat in the case of chocolate spread).

The GI is best used to judge foods within a category. For example, cereals such as natural muesli or rolled (porridge) oats are better choices for those with diabetes than low-fibre, sugary cereals. Among breads, wholegrain or sourdough breads have a lower GI than other breads and are the best choice for those with diabetes.

Foods that have less than 10 g of carbohydrate in a serving do not (by definition) have a GI, as small amounts of carbohydrate do not exert any effect on blood glucose. So most vegetables and salads do not have a GI. Foods such as meat, fish, chicken or cheese also have no carbohydrate and so do not have a GI.

Low GI foods include legumes, wholegrain and sourdough breads, wholegrain cereals (such as rolled oats and muesli), pasta, most fruits, peas, sweet corn and sweet potatoes. Values vary for ordinary potatoes, with the waxy types that don't mash easily having a lower GI than mashed potatoes.

How much carbohydrate?

The amount of carbohydrate consumed varies with size and physical activity. An active athlete may need 350–400 g per day, whereas someone needing to lose weight may need half that amount. It's also important that carbohydrates come from healthy sources such as fruit, wholegrain breads and cereals, potatoes (not chips), wholegrain breakfast cereals, rice or pasta (without fatty sauces). The quantity of sugar consumed should be low, with those with diabetes having no more than 30–40 g per day. (For comparison, this entire quantity would be provided by a single can of soft drink.)

Top carbohydrate tips

-+- Get your carbs from low GI foods that are also high in nutrients, such as fruits, wholegrains, low-fat milk or yoghurt, pasta, peas, sweet corn and sweet potato.

-+- Use sugar only in small quantities.

-+- Dark brown sugar has a stronger flavour than white or light brown sugar and may be helpful when you're trying to cut back on sugar.

-+- If buying honey, choose a strongly flavoured type so you don't use too much.

-+- Have desserts, other than fruit, only occasionally.

-+- Make cakes a special-occasion food to share with family and friends.

-+- Remember that all carbohydrates act as food for bacteria in plaque in teeth and lead to dental decay, so brush your teeth, or at least rinse your mouth with water, after eating them.

Fibre

Dietary fibre is not digested by enzymes in the small intestine, as occurs with most carbohydrates, proteins and fats. Instead, dietary fibre passes through the small intestine to the large intestine (or colon) where 'good' bacteria break it down. One type of fibre, called lignin, defies even the strongest bacteria and passes straight through. Lignin was once the only kind of fibre that was recognized and it was called 'roughage'. That term is no longer used, as the term dietary fibre encompasses much more.

Dietary fibre is found only in plant foods — cereal grains and products made from them, vegetables (especially legumes), fruits, nuts and seeds. These foods contain many different types of fibre and just as we need different vitamins, so we need to consume a variety of plant-based foods to get different kinds of dietary fibre.

As they break down fibre, bacteria produce several organic acids. One is absorbed into the bloodstream and helps prevent cholesterol accumulating in the arteries. Another, called butyric acid (also known as butyrate), nourishes the cells in the colon. Butyrate may also make it more difficult for cancer cells to settle in the bowel.

Foods high in soluble fibre include: pectins in fruits and seeds; hemicelluloses in legumes, seeds, fruits, vegetables and nuts; mucilages in oats, barley and legumes; gums in seeds and psyllium; and algal substances in nori and other edible seaweeds. Insoluble fibres include cellulose found in vegetables, fruits, seeds and nuts; and lignins in wheat bran, wholegrains and in the seeds of fruits such as strawberries, passionfruit and pomegranates.

With the nourishment of dietary fibre, 'good' bacteria multiply profusely and when they finish their short life span, they are excreted, contributing up to one-third of our faeces.

The good work done by the bacteria also produces wind. This is not abnormal and healthy people on a mid-range intake of fibre pass wind an average of 8–12 times a day. A high-fibre diet may increase this to up to 20 times a day and is a sign of a healthy fibre intake.

Fibre produces gases, but they are odourless. When flatus has an aroma, it is related to other compounds present in foods such as onions, spices, red meat and beer. Those with excessive wind levels (passing wind 50 times a day) usually suffer from lactose intolerance and need to avoid large quantities of milk.

Fibre has many benefits. As well as keeping us regular and preventing constipation, a high-fibre diet reduces the risk of diverticulitis, haemorrhoids and bowel cancer. Dietary fibre also helps reduce the risk of obesity, type 2 diabetes and heart disease.

Perhaps the greatest benefit of dietary fibre is that it is filling and so acts as nature's obstacle to overeating. You can check this for yourself by comparing how full you feel after eating soft white low-fibre bread compared with the same quantity of a chewy grainy loaf.

How much fibre?

An average adult needs 30–40 g of dietary fibre a day. It's not difficult to achieve this if you include a high-fibre breakfast cereal and follow the guidelines to have at least two pieces of fruit and five serves of vegetables, plus plenty of wholegrain foods.

Vitamins

We need vitamins in very small quantities to act as catalysts in the many thousands of chemical reactions that occur in the body. Vitamins don't provide energy themselves, but they are essential for the release of energy from carbohydrates, fats and proteins.

There are 13 vitamins and they fall into two major categories: water soluble and fat soluble. Vitamin C and the eight vitamins that make up the B complex are water soluble. This means they dissolve in cooking water and if we take in excessive quantities, they are usually excreted in urine. Most are not stored in the body to any extent and need to be regularly supplied from the diet. However, excessive doses of some water-soluble vitamins can cause damage before they are excreted.

Vitamins A, D, E and K are soluble in body fat and can be stored in the body. They are also absorbed into the body in conjunction with fat. Fat-soluble vitamins are more stable to heat and cooking than most of the water-soluble ones. An excess of some can be harmful.

If you choose healthy foods, most people can easily get all the vitamins the body needs. It is untrue that today's fruits and vegetables lack vitamins and recent tests by independent laboratories confirm this. All most people need to do is to make healthy choices.

There are certain times when vitamin supplements are required. For example, some people have food sensitivities that preclude them eating some vegetables, fruits and grains. Some people do not eat a regular diet for a variety of reasons and need vitamins. Those who have had extensive surgery or must take particular medications may need larger quantities of some vitamins, while elderly people who no longer absorb some vitamins very well get great benefit from a concentrated source. In general, though, if the diet lacks vitamins, it is because of poor food choices and the ideal solution is to choose healthier foods.

Labels on foods and supplements may list the quantity of some vitamins, but this is only meaningful if you have some idea of how much you need. We need

> ## Top fibre tips
>
> - Choose wholegrain breakfast cereals and add a spoonful of wheatgerm.
>
> - Use wholemeal (whole-wheat) or multigrain breads instead of white.
>
> - Go for high-fibre vegetables such as peas, spinach, sweet corn, broccoli and Asian greens. Cooking does not destroy fibre, so you can enjoy these vegetables in soups or cooked and added to salads.
>
> - Choose fruits such as passionfruit, raspberries, pears, apples, oranges and bananas.
>
> - Use beans (home-cooked or tinned) in soups or add them to salads.
>
> - If you are hungry between meals, snack on fresh or dried fruit or nuts.
>
> - To reduce wind from legumes, soak them overnight, discard the soaking water (which will contain some of the indigestible sugars that cause extra wind) and cook until tender.

some vitamins in milligram (mg) quantities, while others are required only in micrograms (mcg) — a microgram is one-thousandth of a milligram. New government guidelines list the quantities of vitamins that are needed by each age group and give the estimated average requirements, the recommended dietary intake (RDI) and the upper limit that should be taken. A long document listing all the nutrient values is available at: www.nhmrc.gov.au/publications/synopses/n35syn.htm

Listed below are the major vitamins and why you need them.

Vitamin A (also called retinol)

This vitamin exists only in animal foods. After infancy, we can convert carotenes, especially betacarotene, in many fruits and vegetables into vitamin A. Infants do not convert carotene to vitamin A and need some animal food (such as breast milk) to supply it. The fact that vitamin A is found in full cream but not skim milk is the major reason why low-fat milks are recommended only after age two.

Why we need it Vitamin A is needed for vision in dim light and to defend the body against infections. It is also important for the body's immune system.

Can it be harmful? Yes, vitamin A is toxic in doses above 10 000 mcg (or 10 mg) a day. Symptoms include dry red skin, eczema, fatigue, irritability, loss of appetite, joint pains and liver damage.

Best sources For vitamin A: liver, salmon and other seafoods, butter or margarine, cheese, full-cream milk. For betacarotene: carrots, orange sweet potato, spinach, broccoli, pumpkin (winter squash), red capsicum (pepper), mango, apricots, papaya, yellow peaches and all green, red, orange or yellow fruits and vegetables.

Vitamin B

There are eight separate vitamins in this complex. Originally, nutritionists thought there were more members of the B complex but biochemistry later revealed that not all of these substances were vitamins. There are, therefore, gaps in the numbering of B vitamins and some that do not have numbers, as they were discovered after the numbering system had been put in place.

Thiamin (vitamin B1)

Why we need it The enzymes that release energy from carbohydrates require thiamin.

Can it be harmful? Excess is excreted and is unlikely to do any harm.

Best sources All wholegrain products (such as brown rice, wholemeal/whole-wheat pasta, burghul/bulgur), bread (especially wholemeal), rolled (porridge) oats, pork, Vegemite, Brazil nuts, peanuts, breakfast cereals, dried yeast, ham, sweet potato, milk and fish.

Riboflavin (vitamin B2)

Why we need it Riboflavin is essential for the body to use proteins and is important for maintaining healthy skin and eyes.

Can it be harmful? Excess is excreted in the urine and is unlikely to do any harm. This is the vitamin responsible for the greeny-yellow colour of urine after taking a multivitamin supplement.

Best sources Milk, yoghurt, liver, kidney, Vegemite, crab, fish, almonds, pork, chicken, mushrooms, eggs, breakfast cereals and green vegetables.

Niacin (vitamin B3)

Includes substances called nicotinic acid (no relationship to nicotine) and nicotinamide. This vitamin can also be made in the body from an amino acid called tryptophan.

Why we need it It is essential in the release of energy from proteins, fats and carbohydrates and is important for healthy skin. Large doses will lower blood cholesterol.

Can it be harmful? Doses higher than 1000 mg a day cause flushing and itchiness of the skin and may cause gout or diabetes in some people. High doses also increase the loss of glycogen from muscles, and so should not be used by endurance athletes.

Best sources Liver, tuna, chicken and all poultry, peanuts, sardines, fish and seafoods, beef, pork, lamb, Vegemite, peanut butter, wholemeal (whole-wheat) pasta, brown rice, wholegrain products and wholemeal bread, mushrooms, potatoes, peas, peaches and passionfruit.

Pantothenic acid (vitamin B5)

Why we need it Pantothenic acid takes part in reactions involving fats and carbohydrates, helps produce haemoglobin in red blood cells and is involved in reactions in nerves and muscles. Contrary to popular belief, it will not stop hair going grey.

Can it be harmful? Very large doses (over 10 000 mg) of pantothenic acid may cause diarrhoea.

Best sources Liver, kidney, broad (fava) beans, mushrooms, salmon, watermelon, peanuts, chicken, pork, red meat, avocado, broccoli, oats, milk and sweet potato. Royal jelly is a good source too, but not good enough to justify its high price. Some people have a severe allergic reaction to this product and a warning is supposed to be included on the label of all products containing royal jelly.

Pyridoxine (vitamin B6)

Like several other vitamins, this one comes in different forms: pyridoxine in vegetable foods and pyridoxal in animal foods.

Why we need it Pyridoxine is vital for the body to use amino acids in the repair of damaged tissues. It is also important in making red blood cells and in reactions in nerves and muscles.

If your diet is so poor that it lacks vitamins, the solution is to improve the diet. Adding vitamins to a poorly chosen diet won't overcome the basic problems that are due to eating foods with a high content of saturated fat, sugar and salt.

Sellers of supplements often claim that modern foods lack vitamins. Independent research shows this is untrue and vitamin levels in basic foodstuffs have not fallen.

Can it be harmful? Although excess pyridoxine is excreted in the urine, doses of 200 mg a day can damage the nerve endings in hands and feet. This has occurred in some people taking super B supplements, so check the label and do not exceed an upper limit of 50 mcg per day.

Best sources Fish (especially salmon), lentils and other legumes, bananas, pork, chicken, liver, red meats, avocado, walnuts, capsicums (peppers), green vegetables such as peas and broccoli, potatoes, bran cereals and wheatgerm.

Folate (folacin, folic acid)

This vitamin exists in several forms. Folic acid is the synthetic form that is often added to foods.

Why we need it Folate helps form new body cells and is vitally important from the moment of conception and for the first few months of pregnancy to reduce the risk of neural tube defects such as spina bifida. It is also involved in making red blood cells. Many of its actions are intertwined with that of vitamin B12.

Can it be harmful? High doses of folic acid may mask a deficiency of B12. This can be a problem in elderly people. Some new studies also suggest very large doses of synthetic folic acid may alter DNA synthesis and could increase the risk of certain cancers.

Best sources Liver (especially chicken liver), green leafy vegetables, peas, oats, avocado, oranges, peanuts, almonds and salmon. Many breakfast cereals and some breads are fortified with folic acid.

Vitamin B12 (Cyanocobalamin)

This is the most recently discovered of the vitamins. It occurs in several forms and its absorption requires adequate acid and pepsin in the stomach and a substance called intrinsic factor that is produced in the upper part of the small intestine. After removal of parts of the stomach, B12 must be given by injection. Some elderly people also fail to absorb vitamin B12 and need supplements or regular injections every three months.

Why we need it Vitamin B12 is essential for making the body's DNA and red blood cells. A deficiency leads to pernicious anaemia.

Can it be harmful? There are no reports of danger.

Best sources This vitamin only occurs in animal foods, including liver, kidney, oysters, fish, red meat, chicken, rabbit, milk, cheese, yoghurt and eggs. A small amount may be found in mushrooms grown in compost. A related substance in comfrey and spirulina is not absorbed by the body. Vegans need supplements.

Biotin (once called vitamin H)

This vitamin is made by bacteria living in the intestine. Prolonged use of antibiotics may inadvertently wipe out these good bacteria, and a substance called avidin found in raw egg white also destroys biotin.

Why we need it Biotin helps produce various essential fatty acids in the body and is needed in breaking down proteins to glucose, which occurs during starvation or extreme carbohydrate restriction.

Can it be harmful? No toxic effects are known.

Best sources Bacterial synthesis in the intestine, chicken livers, liver, peanuts, eggs, seafood, soya beans, oats and artichokes.

Vitamin C (ascorbic acid)

Captain James Cook was one of the first people to recognize the need for fresh foods on his ships so his sailors would not get scurvy. On his voyages, he used limes and sprouted wheat grains to produce a fresh source of the vitamin at sea.

Why we need it Vitamin C is needed to make connective tissue, which is important in bones, blood capillaries, cartilage, gums and teeth. It also helps iron to be absorbed from foods and functions as an antioxidant to help the body's immune system. Many people take extra vitamin C to prevent the common cold, but 30 studies have now failed to confirm its value, although one found a reduction in the duration of a cold by half a day.

Can it be harmful? Taking more than 1000 mg a day may cause diarrhoea and they may also decrease the body's stores of copper and selenium. Excess vitamin C may damage the body's DNA. Chewable vitamin C supplements are highly acidic. Whether they are sugar-free or not, they damage tooth enamel. Chewable vitamin C should not be given to children and should also be avoided by adults.

Best sources Breast milk, liver and fruits and vegetables are the only sources. Highest levels occur in guava, red capsicum (pepper), brussels sprouts, broccoli, papaya,

RECOMMENDED DIETARY INTAKE (RDI) OF VITAMINS

	Children 1–3 years	Children 4–8 years	Children 9–13 years	Adolescents 14–18 years	Women *pregnancy #lactation	Men
Vitamin A (retinol) mcg	300 UL 600	400 UL 900	600 UL 1700	900 (boys) 700 (girls) UL 2800	700 *800 #1100 UL 3000 (all)	900 UL 3000
Thiamin (vitamin B1) mg	0.5 (NP)	0.6 (NP)	0.9 (NP)	1.2 (boys) 1.1 (girls) (NP)	1.1 *#1.4 (NP)	1.2 (NP)
Riboflavin (vitamin B2) mg	0.5 (NP)	0.6 (NP)	0.9 (NP)	1.3 (boys) 1.1 (girls) (NP)	1.1 (<70 yr) 1.3 (>70 yr) *1.4 #1.6 (NP)	1.3 (<70 yr) 1.6 (>70 yr) (NP)
Niacin (vitamin B3) mg	6 UL 10	8 UL 15	12 UL 20	16 (boys) 14 (girls) UL 30	14 *18 #17 UL 35 (all)	16 UL 35
Pantothenic acid (vitamin B5) mg	3.5 (NP)	4 (NP)	5 (boys) 4 (girls) (NP)	6 (boys) 4 (girls) (NP)	4 *5 #6 (NP)	6 (NP)
Pyridoxine (vitamin B6) mg	0.5 UL 15	0.6 UL 20	1.0 UL 30	1.3 (boys) 1.2 (girls) UL 40	1.3 (<50 yr) 1.5 (>51 yr) *1.9 #2.0 UL 50 (all)	1.3 (<50 yr) 1.7 (>51 yr) UL 50
Folate mcg	150 UL 300	200 UL 400	300 UL 600	400 UL 800	400 *600 #500 UL 1000 (all)	400 UL 1000
Vitamin B12 (Cyanocobalamin) mcg	0.9 (NP)	1.2 (NP)	1.8 (NP)	2.4 (NP)	2.4 *2.6 #2.8 (NP)	2.4 (NP)
Biotin mcg	8 (NP)	12 (NP)	20 (NP)	30 (boys) 25 (girls) (NP)	25 *30 #35 (NP)	30 (NP)
Vitamin C (ascorbic acid) mg	35 (NP)	35 (NP)	40 (NP)	40 (NP)	45 (NP) *60 (NP) #85 (NP)	45 (NP)
Vitamin D mcg	5 UL 80	5 UL 80	5 UL 80	5 UL 80	5 (<50 yr) 10 (51–70 yr) 15 (>70 yr) UL 80 (all)	5 (<50 yr) 10 (51–70 yr) 15 (>70 yr) UL 80 (all)
Vitamin E mg	5 UL 70	6 UL 100	9 (boys) 8 (girls) UL 180	10 (boys) 8 (girls) UL 250	7 #11 UL 300 (all)	10 UL 300
Vitamin K mcg	25 (NP)	35 (NP)	45 (NP)	55 (NP)	60 (NP)	70 (NP)

UL = upper limit   NP = not possible to set, due to insufficient studies green capsicum (pepper), oranges and other citrus, cauliflower, kiwi fruit, rambutans, strawberries, mangoes, custard apples and cabbage. A serving of any one of these foods will provide more than you need for the entire day.

Vitamin D

This is another vitamin that exists in several forms and actually functions as a hormone within the body.

Why we need it This vitamin is essential for the absorption of calcium into bones. Cases of rickets due to vitamin D deficiency are appearing in infants of women who lack this vitamin. Vitamin D may also provide protection against some types of cancers.

Can it be harmful? This is the most toxic of all vitamins. Taking five to ten times the normal daily requirement can be dangerous, allowing calcium to be absorbed into soft tissues such as the kidneys and spleen.

Best sources Sunlight acts on a substance in the skin, which forms vitamin D. Just 10–15 minutes exposure of the face and arms to sunlight three to four times a week is sufficient. To take in enough vitamin D but reduce the risk of skin cancer, exposure before 10 a.m. or after 3 p.m. is advised. Food sources include fish liver oils (such as cod liver oil), herrings, mackerel, salmon, sardines, tuna, eggs, butter and margarine.

Vitamin E

There are eight forms of this vitamin in natural foods and all seem to be important. Supplements often contain only one or two forms.

Why we need it Vitamin E is an important antioxidant that prevents the fatty acids in cell membranes being damaged by oxygen. It's also important in red blood cells. Clinical trials have not found any reduction in cardiovascular disease or cancers in those taking vitamin E compared with a placebo, but natural sources may be protective.

Can it be harmful? This vitamin is stored in the body but it is generally considered fairly safe. At high doses (200–800 mg/day) it can cause bleeding after surgery, so vitamin E supplements should not be taken before or after surgery.

Best sources Plant foods are the best sources of vitamin E, especially wheatgerm oil and other vegetable oils (more in cold-pressed oils), seeds (such as sunflower, sesame, poppy), avocado, wheatgerm, nuts and seafoods.

Vitamin K

This is another vitamin that exists in several forms, some in plants, others made by bacteria in the intestine and also present in some animal tissues.

Why we need it It is essential for the normal clotting of blood.

Can it be harmful? Large doses of vitamin K may cause a type of anaemia.

Best sources As well as the vitamin K made by bacteria in the intestine, food sources include soya beans, spinach, silverbeet (Swiss chard), cauliflower, cabbage, lettuce, broccoli and calf liver.

Minerals

Low levels of minerals are more common in developed countries than vitamin deficiencies. Calcium and iodine are the minerals most likely to be low, with sub-optimal levels of zinc and iron also occurring occasionally.

Teenage girls are the group most likely to lack calcium and iron. These nutrients are found in many foods but the richest sources are dairy products (for calcium) and meat (for iron). Many girls reject these foods but fail to seek other sources of these nutrients.

Iodine deficiency is the most common deficiency throughout the world and it is becoming more common in children and pregnant women in many parts of Australia and New Zealand.

Iron

Iron is needed for making haemoglobin — a pigment in red blood cells that carries oxygen to every cell in the body. If you do not have enough haemoglobin, less

Don't be taken in by merchants trying to sell you vitamins F, B-T, P, B13, B15 or B17. These are not true vitamins and there is no evidence that we need them as supplements. Some of the non-genuine B vitamins contain cyanide and can be deadly.

oxygen is delivered to each cell. The cells are then unable to produce their full potential energy level and a feeling of constant fatigue may then occur.

Iron deficiency occurs much more commonly in women because even a small woman needs more iron than a large man. This is because women lose blood each month with menstruation and iron is then needed to make new red blood cells. During pregnancy and lactation, the baby takes iron from the mother and if the mother's diet is not adequate, this leads to low iron levels.

Traditionally, women have eaten less meat than men and most women also eat smaller quantities of other sources of iron such as wholemeal (whole-wheat) bread, cereals and grain foods.

If you feel constantly tired and irritable, you should ask your doctor to check your iron levels. This requires a simple blood test.

It is easy to keep iron levels normal with a good diet but if they drop too low, it is best to take an iron supplement to get the blood levels back to normal as soon as possible. However, do not take iron tablets without confirmation that you are actually lacking iron, since excess iron is undesirable. Approximately one in every 300 people suffers from an excess of iron with a condition called haemochromatosis, and taking extra iron can lead to severe problems with the pancreas and liver. The initial symptoms of excess iron are also constant fatigue and lack of energy, although the condition sometimes develops so slowly that some sufferers do not realize it is not normal to feel this way.

For those who are low in iron and need a supplement, the usual one prescribed is ferrous sulphate. Many people find it causes constipation, sometimes alternating with loose black bowel motions. Some can overcome the constipation by eating more high-fibre foods. Others find a different iron supplement (usually containing ferrous fumarate) may be less constipating. Another alternative is to take the supplement only every four or five days rather than taking it daily. Overall absorption is usually similar and the gastrointestinal problems do not occur.

At the same time you should upgrade the iron content of your diet. Iron comes in two forms — haem iron in meat, fish and chicken, and non-haem iron in vegetables, grains, legumes, nuts, seeds and eggs. We absorb haem iron better than non-haem iron and including even a small amount of haem iron will increase the amount of non-haem iron absorbed. So a small quantity of meat, fish or chicken in a meal consisting mainly of vegetables means you get some haem iron from the animal food and also absorb more of the non-haem iron from the vegetables. We can

	RDI FOR IRON (mg)	UPPER LIMIT (mg)
Men, all ages	8	45
Women		
19–50 years	18	45
over 50 years	8	45
pregnancy	27	45
lactation	9	45
Children		
1–3 years	9	20
4–8 years	10	40
9–13 years	8	40
14–18 years (boys)	11	45
14–18 years (girls)	15	45

also absorb more iron when we need more and during pregnancy, when absorption may be up to six times greater than usual.

Consuming a source of vitamin C with a meal also increases the quantity of iron absorbed. This means it is wise to have a piece of fruit or some vegetables at each meal, especially if you do not eat meat. Good examples would be fruit with wholegrain breakfast cereal; salad on a sandwich made with wholemeal (whole-wheat) bread, and a tomato-based sauce with pasta, with a green salad. **Sources of haem iron** Kidney, liver, oysters, beef, lamb, veal, scallops, sardines, fish, tinned salmon, tinned tuna, pork and chicken.

Sources of non-haem iron Lentils, dried beans or peas, cashews, fortified breakfast cereals, green peas, almonds, dried apricots, sunflower seeds, rolled (porridge) oats, wheatgerm, tahini, peanuts, walnuts, wholemeal (whole-wheat) bread, broccoli and other vegetables.

Calcium

Bones need many minerals and some vitamins, but the one most likely to be low is calcium. Our bones are not stable structures and the calcium they contain moves in and out of the bone structure. The calcium in your wrist today may not be the same as was there last week. In fact, the body uses the bones as a kind of calcium bank, withdrawing what it needs to keep blood levels constant, to ensure normal functioning of nerves and muscles.

As children grow, high levels of calcium are needed for their bone growth. Once growth stops, the bones continue to become more dense to reach their peak density by about age 30. Around the time of menopause, hormonal changes cause less calcium to be retained by bones and the bones begin to thin. If bones were not very dense to start with, or if withdrawal of calcium increases because the diet of the woman does not provide sufficient calcium to restore blood levels, so much calcium may be withdrawn from the bones that they become porous and liable to break with even a small fall.

As people live to older ages and generally decrease their physical activity, osteoporosis has become much more common. About 60% of women and nearly 30% of men have bones showing porous changes. There is also great concern that younger people consume less calcium than earlier generations and do not achieve their full peak bone density. As they age and calcium is lost from bone, their risk of osteoporosis will be even worse.

Other factors are necessary for calcium to be deposited into bone. These include:

- vitamin D (from sunlight on skin)
- vitamin K
- magnesium
- protein (but excess protein can have the opposite effect)
- weight-bearing exercise (calcium goes into bones when muscles exert a pull on the bones during exercise or when carrying goods)

Other factors work against calcium absorption. These include:

- nicotine (from cigarette smoking)
- falling levels of hormones that occur after menopause in women, and in men as they age
- a high intake of sodium from salt (increases losses of calcium in urine)
- intake of cola drinks (it is thought that the phosphoric acid added to both sugar-sweetened and artificially sweetened cola drinks interferes with calcium absorption)
- a very high intake of protein
- very high levels of caffeine (in excess of 8 cups of coffee or cans of cola drink per day)
- high levels of alcohol (more than 2–3 standard drinks per day)

Small light women are at high risk of porous bones simply because they do not carry enough weight for their bones to become strong. Carrying weights or weight-training programs (usually in a gym) are helpful to overcome this problem.

Sources of calcium Milk, yoghurt and cheese are excellent sources of calcium, and you can reduce their fat by using low-fat varieties. Other good sources include soy or rice beverages with added calcium, fish with edible bones (such as tinned sardines or salmon), almonds and tofu (if set with a calcium salt — check the label). Smaller amounts are found in tahini, oranges and green vegetables.

	RDI FOR CALCIUM (mg)
Men	
19–70 years	1000
>70 years	1300
Women	
19–50 years	1000
>50 years	1300
pregnancy	1000
lactation	1000
Children	
1–3 years	500
4–8 years	700
9–13 years	1000–1300
14–18 years	1300

The upper limit for all ages is 2500 mg/day.

Zinc

Like many other minerals, zinc is a vital part of many enzymes that catalyze various reactions in the body. It is important in wound healing, in the storage of insulin in the pancreas, in growth and reproduction, and it is required for the manufacture of some proteins and the structure of membranes around all body cells. A zinc-containing protein in saliva is also important in taste.

As is the case with iron, the more zinc you need, the greater the amount you absorb from foods. After a period of starvation, large amounts of zinc can be absorbed, so supplements can be hazardous at this stage. Phytic acid in wheat and phosphates in soya beans and some cereal products can reduce zinc absorption, but yeast added to breads breaks down the phytic acid complex so wholegrain yeasted breads are a good source of zinc. Very high doses of unprocessed bran can also reduce the absorption of zinc, but 1–2 tablespoons of bran a day will not cause problems.

	RDI FOR ZINC (mg)	UPPER LIMIT (mg)
Men		
all ages	14	40
Women		
all ages	8	40
pregnancy	11	40
lactation	12	40
Children		
1–3 years	3	7
4–8 years	4	12
9–13 years	6	25
14–18 years (boys)	13	35
14–18 years (girls)	7	35

Deficiencies of zinc, leading to poor growth and sterility in men, have occurred in parts of the world where malnutrition is rife, zinc intake is low and breads are made without yeast. A lack of zinc also occurs in heavy drinkers. Symptoms of a zinc deficiency include a lack of taste sensation, slow healing of sores and wounds, failure to grow and reduced sperm count. Hair analysis to estimate zinc levels in the body is unreliable.

Excessive amounts of zinc are dangerous and just 10 times the recommended dietary intake can present a health hazard. Symptoms of zinc toxicity include dehydration, diarrhoea, nausea, abdominal pains, dizziness and lethargy.

Sources of zinc Oysters, beef, crab, prawns (shrimp), sardines, rolled (porridge) oats, wholegrain cereals, lamb, chicken, dried beans, nuts (especially Brazil nuts and almonds), peanuts and dairy products.

Iodine

The total amount of iodine we need throughout our life is less than one teaspoon, but if we don't get enough iodine while in the uterus and during infancy and childhood, the brain can be adversely affected for life. Iodine is vital for the thyroid gland and too much or too little can have adverse effects on the thyroid. Iodine deficiency is the most common micronutrient deficiency in the world and recent studies show that a mild deficiency is becoming common in pregnant and lactating women and in young children in some parts of Australia. In general, levels in the United States and the United Kingdom are adequate, although those who avoid dairy products in the United Kingdom may have iodine levels bordering on deficient.

Iodine levels are low in poor soils and it is easily leached out of soils in mountainous areas with a heavy downpour of rain, ending up in rivers and the ocean.

Where soils contain enough iodine, vegetables will contain it and cows will take iodine from grass and pass it into their milk. Until recently, milk contained the iodine from grass plus extra traces of iodine left from iodine solutions used to clean dairies. Low iodine levels were rare under these conditions. Dairies now use different cleansers and a mild iodine deficiency is now occurring in some Australian states.

Sources of iodine The best natural source of iodine is seafood, with seaweed being the richest source. Milk continues to provide some iodine, and dairy cows in Australia are usually farmed in areas where the soil and rainfall produce rich green grass for the cows to eat. However, iodine levels in milk vary from farm to farm. In the United Kingdom, dairy cows are usually given an iodine supplement.

	RDI FOR IODINE (mcg)	UPPER LIMIT (mcg)
Men		
all ages	150	1100
Women		
all ages	150	1100
pregnancy	220	1100
lactation	270	1100
Children		
1–3 years	90	200
4–8 years	90	300
9–13 years	120	600
14–18 years	150	900

Iodized salt also supplies iodine, but it is rarely used in the processed foods that supply over 80% of our salt intake. Salt can also raise blood pressure, so nutritionists are reluctant to recommend salt, even if it is iodized. Mandatory use of iodized salt in a staple food such as bread is an option.

You can meet your daily requirement of iodine by eating seafood twice a week or a couple of sushi or nori rolls once a week. Eggs, vegetables, citrus fruits, cereals and cashews also have small amounts.

Anyone who is lacking iodine will absorb greater quantities and is at risk of excess iodine. Since too much iodine depresses the action of the thyroid gland, it's important never to take more than the recommended dose of any iodine supplement.

Magnesium

Like most minerals, magnesium plays many roles within the body. It is essential for normal muscle function, including the way the heart contracts. Magnesium is also needed for the biochemical reactions that produce energy within the body.

Low magnesium levels were never a problem when people cooked and ate fresh foods, but many highly processed foods lack magnesium. It is also found in hard water and some experts believe that people living in areas where the water is hard have less heart disease. Others dispute this theory.

A deficiency of magnesium causes disturbances in heart rhythm. Prolonged diarrhoea leads to deficiency and it may also develop in those who drink large quantities of alcohol, especially if their diet is mainly junk foods.

Sources of magnesium This mineral is distributed widely in foods. The best sources of magnesium include nuts (especially Brazil nuts and almonds), all types of wholegrains, seafood (especially prawns/shrimp),

	DAILY MAGNESIUM REQUIREMENTS (mg)	UPPER LIMIT (mg)*
Men		
19–30 years	400	350
over 30 years	420	350
Women		
19–30 years	310	350
>30 years	320	350
19–30 years (pregnancy)	350	350
>30 years (pregnancy)	360	350
19–30 years (lactation)	310	350
>30 years (lactation)	320	350
Children		
1–3 years	80	65
4–8 years	130	110
9–13 years	240	350
14–18 years (boys)	410	350
14–18 years (girls)	360	350

* The upper limits refer to magnesium in supplements. High doses from supplements cause stomach cramps and diarrhoea.

spinach and other green vegetables, fruit, legumes and chicken. Highly processed foods lack magnesium.

Potassium

Potassium works in conjunction with sodium to maintain the correct concentrations of fluid inside cells and in the spaces outside cells. It also regulates the levels of acidity in the blood, with ultimate control of this coming from the kidneys. Potassium is also needed for the transmission of impulses along nerves and muscles. Low levels of potassium can alter the normal rhythm of

	DAILY POTASSIUM REQUIREMENTS (mg)
Men	
all ages	3800
Women	
all ages	2800
pregnancy	2800
lactation	3200
Children	
1–3 years	2000
4–8 years	2300
9–13 years (boys)	3000
9–13 years (girls)	2500
14–18 years (boys)	3600
14–18 years (girls)	2600

No upper limit has been set, but supplements should only ever be taken under medical supervision. An excess usually only occurs in kidney failure or as a result of shock after severe injury.

the heart as well as causing muscle weakness. This usually occurs only as a result of vomiting and diarrhoea or in those who take laxatives or diuretics.

The modern diet is high in sodium from salt. Ideally, we should reduce our intake of sodium to reduce damage within the arteries of the body, but increasing potassium helps balance things to some extent.

Sports people often need to increase their intake of potassium during endurance events, so sports drinks have added potassium. In general, we can get ample quantities of potassium from foods.

Sources of potassium Potassium is widely distributed in vegetables, fruits, dairy products, grains and meat. It is present only in small quantities in most processed foods, especially those that contain salt.

Salt

Salt is sodium chloride and it was once highly valued and used as salary (*sal* means salt). Some foods contain sodium naturally, and the body can handle a small amount of salt added to foods, but the modern food supply with many processed foods contains far more than is good for our health.

Sodium is vital for nerves and muscle cells (including the heart muscle) and helps maintain fluid balance in the body. But once we have enough sodium, more is not better. Most people consume five to six times as much sodium as the body can safely handle.

When babies are given their first taste of salt, most screw up their noses in distaste. Gradually they learn to like it and then they crave it. Excess sodium can lead to high blood pressure (hypertension) and a high salt intake during childhood, or possibly even before birth, can cause high blood pressure later in life, which then increases the risk of heart attack and stroke.

It is not normal for blood pressure to rise as we grow older. In primitive societies, such as the bushmen of the Kalahari, the Yanomama Indians of Brazil and various tribes in New Guinea where no salt is added to foods, blood pressure does not increase as people grow older and high blood pressure is unknown. This is not due to these people's genes, because if they are given salt, their blood pressure rises, just like the rest of us.

One of our dietary guidelines is to 'avoid too much salt and salty foods'. Many people no longer add salt to meals, and so do not realize how much salt they consume. Our salt intake is high because over 80% of the salt we eat has already been added to foods before we buy them.

Many products contribute salt, but they don't taste salty. Who would guess that some breakfast cereals have more salt than potato crisps? Or that commercial ice creams, cakes and even apple pies have salt added to

	DAILY SODIUM REQUIREMENTS (mg)	UPPER LIMIT (mg)
Men all ages	460–920	2300
Women all ages	460–920	2300
Children		
1–3 years	200–400	1000
4–8 years	300–600	1400
9–13 years	400–800	2000
14–18 years	460–920	2300

them? Salt also plays a role in making foods such as bread and cheese, and it is a major flavour component of sauces, soups, stocks, dressings, flavoured noodles and fast foods. Most chefs also add more salt to restaurant meals than home cooks would use.

Processing destroys the natural flavour in food and many processed foods contain very little of any real ingredients to contribute their flavour. Instead they rely on salt to provide flavour. Once you get used to the more complex natural flavours of fresh foods, salty processed foods gradually lose their attraction.

Reducing salt A classic study involved a colony of chimpanzees living in long-standing, socially stable small groups for three years. Their diet was rich in fruits and vegetables and their blood pressure was normal. Over a period of 20 months, half of the chimps had a small amount of salt gradually added to their diet. Their blood pressure rose. The salt was then removed and six months later, their blood pressure returned to normal. As occurs with humans, some of the chimps had much greater increases in blood pressure than others, even though they all consumed the same diet.

In some human studies when people have been asked to restrict their salt intake, they find no fall in their blood pressure. The reason is that most people did not actually reduce their salt intake.

One study, Dietary Approaches to Stop Hypertension (DASH), had two stages. Initially, participants increased their fruit, vegetables and low-fat dairy products but were not asked to restrict salt. Their blood pressure fell and pro-salt advocates claimed this showed we do not need to give up salt. In stage 2, moderate salt restriction was added, and blood pressure fell much more.

The trick in cutting down salt is to do it gradually and give your taste buds time to adjust. Here's a guide:
1. Do not add salt in cooking (most people won't notice).
2. Choose more fresh foods.
3. Check ingredient lists on labels and choose products with less salt, such as unsalted tinned tomato or tomato paste, unsalted pasta rather than flavoured noodles, curry pastes without added salt, natural muesli or lower salt processed cereals (the sodium range for cereals is 20–850 mg/100 g).
4. Be frugal with salty sauces such as fish sauce or soy sauce (reduced-salt soy sauce is slightly better, but is still high in salt).
5. Only add salt where it really matters to you — for example, if you love salt on tomatoes or eggs, then use it only on those foods and buy large crystal sea salt so that a small quantity is more apparent to your taste buds.

Low-salt and reduced-salt To be labelled as *low-salt*, a product must contain less than 120 mg sodium/100 g. *Reduced-salt* means the product has at least 25% less salt than regular products. For high-salt foods, reduced-salt versions may still be high in salt.

Sea salt All salt comes from the sea, whether it is evaporated from sea water or mined from salt deposits left from extinct seas. Internet sites make claims about sea salt, especially from the Celtic Sea (off the coast of Brittany). Some salts have flavour from clay or algae from the evaporation ponds and one brand has added powdered lava.

All sea salt is basically sodium chloride. Sea salt does not contain the anti-caking additives used in regular table salt, but its content of nutrients is so low as to be negligible. Some brands claim to contain 85 minerals, but they fail to mention that the quantities are insignificantly tiny. A teaspoonful will provide barely 1% of daily calcium requirements and even less of other minerals. Sea salt has virtually no iodine.

The flavour of the large crystals of sea salt may be more apparent to the taste buds than regular salt, but don't kid yourself it is good for you. Sprinkle sea salt onto a tomato, and the tomato will contribute hundreds of times the quantity of minerals in the sea salt.

The 'proof' offered on internet sites promoting sea salts come as testimonials from satisfied users. This does not equal scientific proof and there is no evidence that sea salt lowers blood pressure or has other benefits.

Lose weight and keep it off

Populations in most countries of the world are getting fatter. People of all ages and both sexes are eating more and moving less, and have the excess kilos to prove it.

Hardly a week goes by without a new diet appearing. Some are pushed by celebrities, others are supposedly backed by science. Most diets will work as long as you follow them, but research shows that most people who follow the latest diet will regain their lost weight within a year or so. It is relatively easy to lose weight — keeping it off is the real challenge.

All diets work on the basic principle of cutting kilojoules. They may claim otherwise with headlines that you can eat as much as you like. But when you read the fine print, what is permitted is so restricted that the total kilojoule content of the diet is limited.

Studies of people following popular diets show that they reduce their energy intake. Diets such as the low-carbohydrate diets may say you can eat as much butter and cream as you like, but they restrict everything you would normally put butter or cream on. Few people can eat much butter or cream on its own! One diet promised unlimited pasta, but the fine print forbade anything with it. How much plain boiled pasta could anyone eat?

The most popular diets at the moment are not new. The Atkins Diet was popular in the 1970s and 80s. Like any diet, it works initially but the long-term results are poor. Almost everyone regains their lost weight — many collecting a few bonus kilos for their efforts.

Any evidence?

Until recently, there were few studies comparing low-carbohydrate diets with more conventional low-fat diets. Few researchers were keen to subject people to what they knew were unbalanced diets. Several studies have now been completed. They show that the initial weight loss with a low-carbohydrate diet is good — better, in fact, than other diets, with weight loss at three months exceeding that for more conventional diets. At six months, low-carb dieters still have a slight advantage, but by 12 months, there was no significant difference between the few people still following either of the two diets. This is not quite the resounding success trumpeted by many newspapers!

For those sticking with the low-carbohydrate diet, side effects are common and affect over 90% of dieters. Most common are constipation, other gastrointestinal problems, headaches, bad breath, muscle cramps and general weakness. Cholesterol levels fall initially, but rise in about a third of those following the diet for 12 months. No longer term results have yet been reported.

Australia's Commonwealth Scientific and Industrial Research Organisation (CSIRO) has developed a diet that is better balanced than the Atkins Diet. It is very low in fat and has some carbohydrate from healthy sources, such as servings of high-fibre cereal, two slices of wholemeal (whole-wheat) bread, some fruit and low-fat dairy products. The diet also includes lots of vegetables and features large quantities of lean red and processed meats. The diet is promoted by the red meat industry and is labelled as a high-protein diet.

There is no doubt this diet works to help people lose weight in the short term. What gets less publicity is the fact that this diet was trialled against a diet with the same low-fat and low-kilojoule count but with less meat and a little more of the carbohydrate foods, and showed exactly the same weight loss. Claims that the high meat diet was more popular also failed scientific scrutiny, with the same number of drop-outs occurring with both diets. Although most of the trials lasted 12–16 weeks, some longer follow-up found there was still no difference in weight loss after 12 months. Both diet groups were severely depleted, again with equal numbers failing to stick to either diet.

Too much too soon?

Many people expect too much from weight loss. Excess weight accumulates slowly over a period of years. It takes time to disappear, but many people have unrealistic ideas about how fast the body can burn fat.

Low-carbohydrate diets are popular because they produce a rapid weight loss in the first couple of weeks. Most of it is water, some is lean muscle tissue and a little is from carbohydrate stored in the muscles. The average adult has about 600 g of carbohydrate stored in muscles as glycogen, ready for physical activity. Each gram of carbohydrate is stored with almost 3 g of water. Cut out carbs and the body uses up the stored carbohydrate and excretes the accompanying water, accounting for a rapid loss of about 2 kg (4 lb 8 oz).

The body must have glucose (it is the only fuel that the brain can use) and glucose can only come from carbohydrates or proteins. It is physiologically impossible to convert fat to glucose. So when the diet lacks carbohydrate, proteins are broken down to glucose. Protein can come from the body's own muscle or from high-protein foods. Either way, when the body breaks down protein to form glucose, the leftover part of the protein molecule must be excreted by the kidneys. This takes water and the result is a reduction in the body's water content — and a drop in the scales. If you continue

with the low-carbohydrate diet, its restrictions ensure you consume fewer kilojoules and this results in some fat loss. Since carbohydrate is a major source of fuel for physical activity, exercise becomes too tiring.

Unless you are very obese and exercise strenuously for many hours a day, it is virtually impossible to lose more than a kilogram of fat in a week. Even that is difficult for the average person. This is because you must create a deficit of 32 300 kJ (7700 Calories) to lose 1 kg of body fat. Even those who overeat usually only consume a maximum of 12 500 kJ (3000 Calories) a day — and often much less. And if you stop eating altogether, the body cuts its metabolic rate back to survival level, as well as breaking down its own muscle. Few people can manage a daily energy deficit of more than about 2500 kJ (600 Calories) and if they maintain this, it should result in a loss of about a kilogram of fat every two weeks. In practice, studies that last at least six months (including those on the Atkins diet) show an average weight loss of about 1 kg (2 lb) a month. Fast weight loss is almost always followed by regaining the lost weight — usually with a few bonus kilos.

The real cause of obesity

There is no disputing the laws of thermodynamics: if we take in more energy than we use for growth, metabolism and physical activity, we gain weight. Conversely, if we take in fewer kilojoules of energy than we use, we lose weight. A very small percentage of people have a metabolic defect that leads to weight gain, but research shows clearly that most people gain weight because they eat more than their body requires.

The reasons why we eat so much and use so little energy are important, but they don't change the basic facts. However, it's helpful to look at why our energy balance is so out of kilter.

Portion sizes

Soft drinks once came in 170 ml (5½ fl oz) bottles. These were replaced by 250 ml (9 fl oz) bottles, then 370 ml (13 fl oz) cans, and now a 600 ml (21 fl oz) bottle is considered an individual-sized serving. Similarly, potato crisps increased from 30 g (1 oz) to 50 g (1¾ oz), with 100 g (3½ oz) or 200 g (7 oz) packets now commonly bought for individual consumption. Typical Australian hamburgers in the 1970s had less than half the fat of many of the larger fast-food burgers that are available today, partly because they were smaller. We are also offered 'king size' confectionery bars that are 50% larger for only 10% extra cost. To many people, this seems like good value.

Bucking the trend towards larger sizes, some biscuits appear to have down-sized. However, this is because the entire smaller packet is designed to be eaten as a snack. Crackers are also sold as 'nibbles' and eaten by the handful, similar to potato crisps.

The size of plates also influences portion sizes. Modern dinner plates are larger than previously considered normal, while pasta, rice, soups and breakfast cereals are served in bowls that would once have been considered serving bowls.

Serving bowls are larger too and studies show that people take more food from a larger bowl. Researchers in Chicago showed that movie-goers ate around 50% more popcorn from big buckets compared with smaller buckets. However, both groups reported consuming similar quantities.

In another study, people ate more from 'super huge' than 'very large' packets of sweets. And when asked to cook spaghetti, and offered the same quantity of raw spaghetti in either a large or medium box, everyone cooked more when given the bigger box. We also tend to eat foods by the unit, with little consideration of changing sizes. For example, the modern sandwich made with a large piece of focaccia may weigh three times as much as a regular sliced bread sandwich.

Frequent snacking

Supermarkets now stock about 1800 different snack foods. Most are eaten in addition to meals. Indeed many people now snack so often that they do not know what a hunger pang feels like. Food companies aim to make as many foods as possible into quick snacks so they can be consumed in the car, on public transport, before, during or after physical activity and in front of the television. A breakfast cereal bar has many more kilojoules than the bowl of cereal it replaces.

Some research shows that dividing the day's meals into a series of smaller portions (or snacks) can help regulate blood glucose and cholesterol levels. But in every one of these studies, the researchers controlled the total amount of food consumed. Subjects usually kept half their meal to consume as a snack later; they did not add snacks to their regular meals, as usually occurs outside a laboratory setting.

Lack of physical activity

The majority of children still play sport, although adults are more likely to watch sport than participate in it. A recent study in Australia found that children's sporting activity has increased, without any beneficial effect on their weight. Even though children increased their sport,

their body fat levels increased. There was no mystery to this: the children more than made up for the kilojoules used in sport with the drinks and snack foods that they consumed afterwards.

The major problem is the decrease in incidental physical activity. Children are less likely to play outdoors, due partly to parental fear of danger. Computers and television are considered safer, which indicates that parents do not understand the danger of obesity. Indeed, parents often fail to recognize obesity in their children. And both adults and children travel in cars rather than walking, cycling or using public transport (which always involves some walking).

Most people cite lack of time as their major reason for lack of physical activity. Poor time management may be more relevant since the average person watches television for several hours a day.

More takeaway food, less home cooking

Foods cooked at home have less fat and salt and fewer kilojoules than most fast foods or meals consumed in cafés or restaurants. With most women working outside the home, some men have taken a turn in the kitchen. However, most responsibility for meals remains with women. Not surprisingly, people who work outside the home all day want to relax when they arrive home, so they are more likely to buy ready-prepared meals and takeaway foods.

Many parents also believe that their children will leave the kitchen in a mess if they cook, and rather than teach them to clean up the kitchen, they banish children from food preparation.

Liquid kilojoules

After eating solid foods, we feel full — and usually stop eating. But when we consume liquids that contain kilojoules there is no feeling of satisfaction, and studies show that liquid kilojoules slip in under our radar and do not result in any decrease in intake of foods. Serving sizes for juices and soft drinks are getting bigger, super-sized takeaway cups for coffee are now common and healthy-sounding drinks such as smoothies come with an enormous kilojoule load.

An English study found that avoiding energy-containing drinks at, and between, meals was the behaviour most likely to have a beneficial effect on

Before eating something, ask yourself if it's really worth the kilojoules. If it isn't of the best quality, wait for something better.

women's weight loss. Danish studies have also found that sugar in drinks is more likely to produce weight gain than solid sugar found in foods because the liquid-sugar kilojoules don't register on the brain's satiety centre. And an Australian study found no difference in young men's energy intake from food after they had consumed 375 ml (13 fl oz) of either regular cola, sugar-free cola or mineral water. Several studies in children show that curtailing consumption of soft drinks prevents weight gain.

Alcohol also fails to reduce food intake. In fact, several studies show that when elderly people are not eating, some alcohol before a meal encourages them to eat more.

The solution

There is no magic diet that will cure obesity. Prevention is probably the best approach, but if it's too late for that, there are other approaches that can help.

Following popular diets is a good way to set yourself up for failure. Any diet will 'work' to bring about weight loss, but as soon as you go off the diet, the lost weight returns. Diets don't work for weight maintenance. Instead we need to change our eating and exercise habits to something that we can live with and is healthy.

The single strongest evidence for long-term success in weight loss comes from the United States National Weight Control Registry, which began in 1993 and now holds the dieting records of over 4000 people. Eligible registry entrants must lose at least 13.6 kg (30 lb) and maintain their weight loss for at least a year. The average registrant has lost 32 kg (70 lb) and kept it off for six years. The successful habits of these people have been identified as:

- they eat breakfast
- they use a low-fat/moderately high-carbohydrate diet (with emphasis on fruits, vegetables, breads and cereals rather than sugar)
- they exercise daily for at least 45 minutes
- they monitor their weight to detect any straying off track

Many other long-term studies also show that when people genuinely reduce their fat intake, which in turn reduces their kilojoule intake, they lose weight. If fat is removed from foods such as milk or meat, it assists us to eat less fat and fewer kilojoules. But many processed foods labelled as low-fat have replaced the fat with sugar and refined starches. These foods sometimes have as many kilojoules as the regular product. Studies also show that when a label says a product is low- or reduced-fat, most people consume a larger portion.

A *different approach*

There is no doubt that we must reduce the number of kilojoules we consume and increase our output. However, many people find that too much thinking about weight increases their desire to eat. A better approach may be to think about health rather than weight. A recent study found that when people concentrated on being healthy, whatever their size — which meant making healthier food choices and getting much more exercise — they weighed less after 12 months than another group who thought more about weight.

We eat for various reasons, and my own approach is to look at why someone overeats and deal with that rather than encouraging people to follow any particular diet. For some people, eating too much and failing to exercise are just bad habits. Focusing on getting more enjoyment from high-quality foods (which may simply mean choosing more truly fresh foods) and thinking whether so much food is really needed will help. Establishing regular activities is also important.

For others, eating and drinking is a comfort or release from stresses, and eating or drinking less will only be effective if the reasons for the stress or discomfort are dealt with. Yoga, tai chi or meditation and greater understanding of problem-solving tactics may help.

For everyone, greater attention to what we eat and drink is important. The recipes in this book are designed to make that process easier.

Underweight

Many people who are very thin are annoyed by the attention given to excess weight. Genes play a part in our body size and shape and some people are naturally lean. There is no medical problem with this, but for aesthetic reasons, some people want to gain weight.

Studies show that every person will gain weight if they eat more than they currently consume, but some gain more than others. This is the effect of genetic differences. When some people eat more, they move more and burn up some extra energy in metabolism; others don't. But the point is that eating more will result in some weight gain for everyone.

In gaining weight, it is important not to eat lots of junk. Thin people can still develop clogged arteries that will impede blood flow to the heart and other organs. Healthy foods that will help with weight gain include:

- avocado
- nuts
- olive oil — use it in cooking and on salads

It may also be safe to eat more cheeses. The French and Swiss eat large quantities of cheese and have relatively low rates of coronary heart disease.

Reading food labels

Reading all the information on food labels may give you the feeling you are in a library rather than a supermarket, but labels contain a lot of useful information. All food labels must provide:

- the name of the product
- the name and address of the manufacturer, packer, importer or vendor
- the country of origin
- identification of where the food was produced and a 'lot' or 'batch' number so the food can be traced to its packaging plant
- a 'use by' or 'best before' date, or, for foods with a long shelf life, the date of packaging
- an ingredient list
- a nutrition information panel

Genetically modified ingredients are not listed in the United States but must be listed in Australia, New Zealand and the European Union. However, oils, sugars and products from animals fed GM ingredients are exempted. This means most GM material in foods currently escapes labelling. Any food that has been subjected to irradiation must contain this information on the label.

The ingredient list

The ingredients in all products must be listed in descending order according to their weight in the product. The ingredient present in the greatest quantity must come first, followed by the next most abundant ingredient, and so on.

The ingredient list won't always tell you everything you need to know, but it will provide some clues. The position in the ingredient list helps to establish if an ingredient is a major one or not. For example, sugar near the top of the list in a breakfast cereal will indicate the product has a lot of sugar and is not particularly healthy, whereas the sugar in a loaf of bread listed below minor ingredients such as salt or yeast indicates that the sugar content is low and can be ignored.

There are some subtleties to watch out for. For example, if a muesli bar is high in sugar, the manufacturer may choose to use several different types of sugar (perhaps raw sugar, honey, glucose and maltose) so that other ingredients will be listed before the sugars. Watch out for ingredients ending in 'ose', as this indicates a sugar (for example, glucose, fructose, sucrose, maltose or mannose).

Food labels in some countries, including Australia and New Zealand, must list the percentage of any ingredient that is included in the name of the product. For example, a tin of chicken soup must list the percentage of chicken present, an avocado dip will state how much avocado is present, and fish fingers (with fish listed as 40%) let you know you are not getting much fish for your money!

Percentage labelling also helps you discover how many additives go into a product. A brand of freshly crushed garlic lists garlic (56%), salt, sugar, food acid and water. You therefore know that 44% of the product is not garlic. A better buy would be found in the vegetable section, where you could just buy a bulb of garlic, with no additives.

Standards also apply for foods that Australian authorities judge to be 'icon' foods. For example, a meat pie must contain 25% meat (offal can be added but must be identified), sausages must have 50% meat flesh, jam must contain at least 40% of the fruit mentioned on the label, and ice cream must have 10% milk fat or it cannot use the words 'ice cream' on the label. Other countries do not impose such regulations.

The nutrition information panel

Manufacturers must list prescribed nutritional factors per 100 g and per serving (the number of servings is arbitrary but must also be listed):

- energy in kilojoules (calories can also be given if desired and are used in the United States and United Kingdom)
- protein
- fat
- saturated fat
- total carbohydrate
- sugars (which does not distinguish between added sugars and the naturally occurring ones in fruits or milk)
- sodium

Any other nutrient for which a claim is made must also be included. For example, if bread mentions dietary fibre, the quantity must be listed. Margarine described as 'polyunsaturated' would need to include its content of monounsaturated, polyunsaturated and trans fats. Breakfast cereals that add vitamins or minerals must also include the quantity on the nutrition information panel. Food authorities also limit which foods may have added vitamins and minerals and the quantity.

Some countries insist the trans fat content must be included on food labels. Australia and New Zealand currently only require this on products making a claim about their unsaturated fat or cholesterol content. Recent changes in the United States requiring trans fats to be included on the label have led some manufacturers to remove trans fats from food products. There are calls for labelling of trans fats in the European Union, while Denmark insists on full labelling and prohibits the sale of any food with more than 2% trans fat.

Before placing too much value on the information for the designated serving size, check it corresponds with what you would eat. Some desserts and yoghurts sold in 200 g (7 oz) containers list a serving as 150 g (5½ oz). Few people would leave the small amount in the container. Margarine servings will not usually scrape over a slice of toast, and breakfast cereal servings may be more appropriate for a 3 year old than a teenager or adult.

% free

Food companies use 'x% free' claims because they help sell products. A code of practice gives manufacturers guidelines for using such marketing strategies, but these are often flouted and most countries are replacing such codes with legislation. A food that states it is 92% fat-free actually contains 8% fat, which may be a lot, especially if a consumer is likely to eat large quantities.

'Cholesterol-free' claims can be misleading, since most excess blood cholesterol is produced within the body and this occurs when the diet is high in saturated fat. Some tea declares it is '97% caffeine-free'. In fact, regular tea has only 3% caffeine, so this tea is not different on that score and the implication that caffeine has been removed could be considered misleading. In general, it is more important to note what a food contains rather than looking for % free claims.

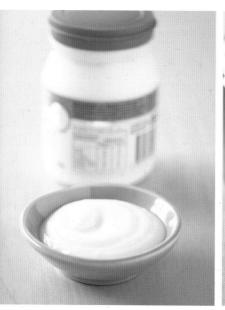

Check the percentage of the major ingredient in a food and do a rough calculation of how much you are really paying. For example, if a 250 g (9 oz) packet of fish fingers contains only 50% fish, you are getting only one-eighth of a kilogram (4½ oz) of fish — multiply the price by eight, and you will probably find that fresh fish is a better buy.

A good rule of thumb when choosing packaged foods is to reject anything that has more than five ingredients (muesli is the exception), contains numbered additives or is not naturally produced.

'Use by' date

All packaged foods that have a shelf life of 2 years or less and are sold in shops or for catering purposes in restaurants, canteens or self-catering institutions must carry a 'best before' statement, unless the food needs to be eaten within a certain period for health or safety reasons, in which case it must carry a 'use by' date.

Foods that have a 'use by' date may not be sold after this date, as consumption could carry a health or safety risk. Foods that have a 'best before' date can be sold after the date has passed, as long as the food is still fit for human consumption.

Additives

The use of food additives in foods is controlled by law and food authorities evaluate additives and publish lists of those that are permitted.

For most people, food additives do not pose health problems, but they can be a problem for people with food allergies or sensitivities. In such cases, you need to know which foods or additives you react to and which foods contain the relevant additives.

All approved additives have a number which must appear on the food label, along with the class of additive, such as emulsifier, thickener, preservative, colouring or food acid. If a product contains monosodium glutamate, for example, the ingredient list will state 'flavour enhancer (621)'. The manufacturer may also add 'MSG' or 'monosodium glutamate', but is not required by law to do so.

Types of food additives

Colourings 100–181, 579 are used to add or restore colour to foods.
Preservatives 200–252, 282, 1105 are used to stop food deteriorating due to the action of microorganisms.
Antioxidants 300–322, 1102 are used to stop foods such as fats going rancid.
Food acids 260–270, 296–304, 325–381, 507, 541 are used to maintain a constant level of acid in foods.
Mineral salts 339–343, 450–452, 500–529 are added to give texture and stability to foods such as processed meats.

Thickeners and vegetable gums 400–416, 440, 461–466, 1400–1450 give uniform consistency to foods.
Humectants 420–422, 914, 953, 965–967, 1200, 1518, 1520 are added to stop foods drying out.
Emulsifiers 322, 433–444, 470–492, 541, 900, 1001, 1518 keep fat distributed evenly through a food.
Anti-caking agents 460, 504, 535, 536, 542–570, 900 ensure powdered foods don't clog or clump together.
Artificial sweeteners 420–421, 950–967 provide sweetness and, in some cases, added bulk.
Flavour enhancers 620–641, 957, 1101, 1104 strengthen flavours.
Bleaching agents 925–928, 1100, 1011 can be used at some stage in manufacturing a food to remove colour.
Glazes or waxes 901–905 give a shine to fruits.
Stabilizers 577, 965, 1201, 1202, 1521 are used to hold a foam or colour in a food product.

Where gaps occur in the numbering list, it is usually because no manufacturer has applied to use the particular additive, or the substance may have been deleted from the list because of research showing the potential for harm.

Some additives fit into more than one of these categories. There are also additives approved as 'flour treatment agents', and others are permitted as propellants for aerosol products.

Foods sold in restaurants need not list their additives, so if you are sensitive to MSG, you will need to ask about its use in Asian restaurants.

Allergens

Substances that may cause allergic reactions must be listed on food labels. These include wheat (gluten-containing cereals and their products), eggs and egg products, fish and fish products, milk and milk products, nuts and sesame seeds (including their products), peanuts and soya beans (including their products), and added sulphites (in concentrations of 10 mg per kg or more). In practice, this means that a sauce or a cake or any other food that contains a thickener derived from a cereal must list the cereal used (for example, wheat, rye, barley or oats).

RECIPES

BREAKFAST

The old adage that breakfast is the most important meal of the day is true. It gets your metabolism going and helps you burn kilojoules throughout the morning. Breakfast eaters also have a higher intake of nutrients throughout the day and are less likely to be overweight.

SERVES 1
PREPARATION TIME: 5 minutes
COOKING TIME: nil

NUTRITIONAL
INFORMATION/SERVING:
14 g protein, 2.5 g fat (1.5 g
saturated fat), 40 g carbohydrate,
3.5 g dietary fibre, 135 mg sodium,
1000 kJ (240 Cals)

A source of vitamins B1, B2, C and
E, and also potassium, magnesium,
calcium, iron and zinc.

Banana smoothie

It's tempting to skip breakfast when we're busy and have hundreds of things to do. If you can't find the time to sit down for breakfast, at least take a few minutes to whip up this nutritious drink.

1 banana
100 g (3½ oz) low-fat natural yoghurt
125 ml (4 fl oz/½ cup) reduced-fat milk
1 teaspoon honey
2 teaspoons wheatgerm*
2 ice cubes

* Omit the wheatgerm for a gluten-free smoothie.

1. Place all ingredients in a blender and process until smooth and frothy.

SERVES 1
PREPARATION TIME: 5 minutes
COOKING TIME: nil

NUTRITIONAL
INFORMATION/SERVING:
16 g protein, 5.5 g fat (2.5 g
saturated fat), 37 g carbohydrate,
2 g dietary fibre, 215 mg sodium,
1085 kJ (260 Cals)

A source of vitamins A, B1, B2,
B3 and C, and also potassium,
magnesium, calcium, iron and zinc.

Peach soy smoothie

Soy beverages are often called soy milk. Choose one with added calcium — 120 mg per 100 ml is ideal.

125 g (4½ oz/½ cup) tinned peaches in juice
250 ml (9 fl oz/1 cup) light soy beverage
1 egg
125 ml (4 fl oz/½ cup) orange juice

1. Place all ingredients in a blender and process until smooth and frothy.

HINT

If there isn't time in the morning to whip up a smoothie, grab a carton of yoghurt and a banana or some other fruit.

Winter fruit salad

This fruit salad is not only delicious for breakfast but it can also be served as a snack or a healthy dessert. Leaving the fruit in the refrigerator allows the flavours to develop and also gives the fruit time to soften.

35 g (1¼ oz/½ cup) dried apples
50 g (1¾ oz/½ cup) dried peaches or nectarines
110 g (3¾ oz/½ cup) pitted prunes
30 g (1 oz/¼ cup) raisins
250 ml (9 fl oz/1 cup) apple juice
1 cinnamon stick
1 teaspoon honey
1 teaspoon finely grated orange zest
200 g (7 oz) natural yoghurt
1 tablespoon flaked almonds, toasted

1. Combine the dried fruits, apple juice, cinnamon stick, honey and orange zest in a saucepan. Bring to the boil, then remove from the heat. Transfer to a bowl, cover and refrigerate overnight.

2. Remove the cinnamon stick before serving. To serve, top the fruit salad with the yoghurt and almonds.

SERVES 4
PREPARATION TIME: 5 minutes
COOKING TIME: 3 minutes
+ overnight refrigeration

NUTRITIONAL
INFORMATION/SERVING:
4.5 g protein, 3.5 g fat (1 g saturated fat), 47 g carbohydrate, 5 g dietary fibre, 55 mg sodium, 975 kJ (235 Cals)

A source of vitamins B2, B3, C and E, and also potassium, magnesium, calcium and iron.

 HINT

Getting up even 10 minutes earlier in the morning will give you enough time to sit down for a quick breakfast.

Buttermilk pancakes with berries

Pancakes are an easy dish to prepare for weekend breakfasts. These are made with buttermilk, which makes the pancakes deliciously fluffy.

SERVES 4

PREPARATION TIME: 10 minutes
+ at least 15 minutes standing time

COOKING TIME: 15 minutes

NUTRITIONAL
INFORMATION/SERVING:
11 g protein, 4.5 g fat (1.5 g
saturated fat), 32 g carbohydrate,
6 g dietary fibre, 75 mg sodium,
890 kJ (215 Cals)

A source of vitamins B1, B2, B3
and C, and also magnesium,
calcium and iron.

375 ml (13 fl oz/1¹/₂ cups) buttermilk
2 eggs
125 g (4¹/₂ oz/1 cup) plain (all-purpose) flour
2 tablespoons wheatgerm
1 teaspoon finely grated lemon zest
1 tablespoon lemon juice
light olive oil or macadamia oil, to grease
300 g (10¹/₂ oz) mixed fresh berries or thawed frozen berries

1. Put the buttermilk, eggs, flour, wheatgerm, lemon zest and lemon juice into a blender and process until smooth. Leave to stand for 15 minutes, or refrigerate the batter overnight.

2. Heat a heavy-based frying pan over medium heat and lightly grease with the oil. Pour about one-eighth of the mixture into the pan, swirl to spread the mixture over the base of the pan, and cook until bubbles appear on the surface and the underside is lightly browned. Turn the pancake over and cook the other side until brown. Stack the pancakes on a plate and keep warm while cooking the remainder.

3. Serve the pancakes topped with berries.

French fruit toast

SERVES 1
PREPARATION TIME: 10 minutes
COOKING TIME: 5 minutes

NUTRITIONAL
INFORMATION/SERVING:
14 g protein, 8.5 g fat (3 g
saturated fat), 39 g carbohydrate,
2 g dietary fibre, 220 mg sodium,
1195 kJ (285 Cals)

A source of vitamins A, B1 and B2,
and also calcium, iron and zinc.

*Here's a new twist on an old favourite that is popular with all ages. Using fruit loaf
instead of regular white bread tastes great and also lowers the overall glycaemic
index (GI) of the meal.*

for each person
60 ml (2 fl oz/¼ cup) reduced-fat milk
pinch of ground cinnamon
½ teaspoon finely grated lemon zest
1 egg
2 slices of fruit loaf
melted butter or oil, to grease
½ teaspoon icing (confectioners') sugar

1. Beat together the milk, cinnamon, lemon zest and egg. Dip the fruit loaf slices into
   the milk mixture, allowing the liquid to soak into the bread.

2. Heat a heavy-based frying pan over medium heat, brush the pan with a little
   melted butter or oil and cook the bread until brown on both sides. Sprinkle with
   icing sugar and serve immediately.

HINT

When buying a packaged
cereal, look for one that
does not have any type of
sugar listed in its first
three ingredients.

Wholemeal banana and orange pancakes

For weekdays, make the pancake batter the night before and refrigerate it overnight, so it's ready for a quick and easy breakfast the next day.

500 ml (17 fl oz/2 cups) skim milk
1 large banana
150 g (5½ oz/1 cup) wholemeal (whole-wheat) flour
1 teaspoon finely grated orange zest
2 eggs, separated
light olive oil or macadamia oil, to grease
60 ml (2 fl oz/¼ cup) orange juice

1. Place the milk, banana, flour, orange zest and egg yolks into a blender and process until smooth. Leave to stand for 15 minutes, or refrigerate overnight.

2. When ready to cook the pancakes, beat the egg whites until stiff, then fold gently into the pancake batter using a metal spoon.

3. Heat a heavy-based frying pan over medium heat and lightly grease with the oil. Pour about one-sixth of the batter into the pan, swirl to spread it over the base of the pan, and cook until bubbles appear on the surface and the underside is lightly browned. Turn the pancake over and cook the other side until brown. Stack the cooked pancakes on a plate and keep warm while cooking the remainder.

4. Serve the pancakes sprinkled with orange juice.

MAKES 6
PREPARATION TIME: 10 minutes
+ at least 15 minutes standing time
COOKING TIME: 15 minutes

NUTRITIONAL INFORMATION/PANCAKE:
8.5 g protein, 2.5 g fat (0.5 g saturated fat), 23 g carbohydrate, 3.5 g dietary fibre, 61 mg sodium, 620 kJ (150 Cals)

A source of vitamins B1, B2 and B3, and also calcium and iron.

 HINT

If you don't feel hungry at breakfast, it's because your body is still in its slow overnight mode. Go for a walk or a swim or do some other exercise to get your body going and then eat breakfast.

Toasted muesli

This recipe is not difficult to make and the toasted oats and nuts release a delicious aroma — but take care you don't burn them.

750 g (1 lb 10 oz/7½ cups) rolled (porridge) oats
90 g (3¼ oz/1 cup) flaked almonds
40 g (1½ oz/¼ cup) sesame seeds
30 g (1 oz/½ cup) flaked coconut
100 g (3½ oz/¾ cup) pepitas (pumpkin seeds)
90 g (3¼ oz/¾ cup) sunflower seeds
90 g (3¼ oz/1 cup) wheatgerm
140 g (5 oz /1 cup) chopped dried apricots
125 g (4½ oz/1 cup) sultanas (golden raisins)
60 g (2¼ oz/½ cup) dried cranberries (craisins)

1. Preheat oven to 180°C (350°F/Gas 4). Spread the oats on two ungreased baking trays and bake for 8–10 minutes, stirring several times until the oats are golden brown (take care they don't burn). Tip into a large basin and allow to cool.

2. Toast the almonds and sesame seeds by the same method, watching carefully as they take only 2–3 minutes. Set aside to cool.

3. Toast the coconut in the same way, leaving it in the oven for a maximum of 1–2 minutes only (it burns easily). Cool.

4. Combine all ingredients and store in an airtight container.

MAKES 25 SERVES
PREPARATION TIME: 10 minutes
COOKING TIME: 15 minutes
+ 30 minutes cooling time

NUTRITIONAL INFORMATION/SERVING:
7.5 g protein, 10 g fat (2 g saturated fat*), 29 g carbohydrate, 5.5 g dietary fibre, 10 mg sodium, 980 kJ (235 Cals)

*The small amount of coconut adds flavour and only a small amount of saturated fat. If omitted, saturated fat is 1 g.

A source of vitamins B1, B3, folate and E, and also magnesium, iron and zinc.

Swiss muesli

Muesli is a filling and healthy start to a weekend breakfast or brunch. This recipe is suitable for gluten-free if the oats are guaranteed free from contamination from wheat flakes, and you do not have an adverse reaction to oats.

200 g (7 oz/2 cups) rolled (porridge) oats*
250 ml (9 fl oz/1 cup) reduced-fat milk
2 apples, unpeeled, cored and grated
30 g (1 oz/¼ cup) chopped hazelnuts
200 g (7 oz) low-fat honey yoghurt

* Check the oats are gluten-free.

1. Combine the oats and milk in a bowl. Cover and refrigerate overnight.

2. In the morning, add the grated apple, hazelnuts and yoghurt and mix well.

Toasted muesli (back) and Swiss muesli (front)

SERVES 4
PREPARATION TIME: 10 minutes
+ overnight refrigeration
COOKING TIME: nil

NUTRITIONAL INFORMATION/SERVING:
12 g protein, 9 g fat (2 g saturated fat), 52 g carbohydrate, 5.5 g dietary fibre, 35 mg sodium, 1450 kJ (350 Cals)

A source of vitamins B1, B2 and E, and also magnesium, calcium, iron and zinc.

SOUPS

Home-made soups are great for good health. A bowl of hot soup is filling and deliciously warming in winter, and chilled soups are excellent for restoring a jaded summer appetite. Many can be made ahead and frozen, or refrigerated in individual portions for lunches. The nutritional value for all the soups in this chapter assume you use home-made stock. If using commercial stock, the sodium content will increase by 600–900 mg per serving.

Avocado and lemon chilled soup

This is an ideal quick soup for a summer dinner party or easy brunch.

SERVES 4

PREPARATION TIME: 5 minutes
+ 30 minutes refrigeration

COOKING TIME: nil

NUTRITIONAL
INFORMATION/SERVING:
5.5 g protein, 14 g fat (3 g
saturated fat), 6.5 g carbohydrate,
1 g dietary fibre, 85 mg sodium,
740 kJ (175 Cals)

A source of vitamins B2, B3,
B6, folate, C and E, and also
potassium, calcium and iron.

1 large ripe avocado
750 ml (26 fl oz/3 cups) cold chicken or vegetable stock*
60 ml (2 fl oz/¼ cup) lemon juice
1 teaspoon grated lemon zest
250 g (9 oz/1 cup) low-fat natural yoghurt
1 small handful mint, plus extra mint leaves, to serve

* Use vegetable stock for a vegetarian meal.

1. Place the avocado flesh into a food processor or blender with the remaining ingredients and process until smooth.

2. Cover and refrigerate for 30 minutes, or place in the freezer for 15 minutes to chill. Serve garnished with mint.

French onion soup

Using reduced-fat cheddar cheese makes this a healthier version of an old favourite.

SERVES 4

PREPARATION TIME: 15 minutes

COOKING TIME: 30 minutes

NUTRITIONAL
INFORMATION/SERVING:
13 g protein, 7.5 g fat (2 g
saturated fat), 30 g carbohydrate,
5 g dietary fibre, 440 mg sodium,
1000 kJ (240 Cals)

A source of vitamins B1,
B3 and C, and also potassium,
calcium, iron and zinc.

1 tablespoon olive oil
1 kg (2 lb 4 oz) onions, thinly sliced
1 teaspoon dried thyme
1 teaspoon soft brown sugar
2 teaspoons balsamic vinegar
1.25 litres (44 fl oz/5 cups) chicken or vegetable stock*
4 bay leaves
4 slices of sourdough baguette
2 tablespoons dijon mustard
60 g (2¼ oz/½ cup) grated cheddar cheese (7% fat)

* Use vegetable stock for a vegetarian meal.

1. Place the oil, onions, thyme and sugar in a heavy-based saucepan and cook over gentle heat, stirring occasionally, for 20 minutes. Do not allow the onions to brown.

2. Add the vinegar, stock and bay leaves, bring to the boil, then cover and simmer for 10 minutes.

3. Meanwhile, preheat oven to 180°C (350°F/Gas 4). Spread the bread with mustard and place on a baking tray. Bake for 7–8 minutes, or until crisp. Sprinkle with cheese and return to the oven for 1–2 minutes until the cheese melts.

4. Ladle the soup into bowls and top each with a slice of the toast.

Mushroom soup

For the best results, try to find field mushrooms for this soup because they have a strong, almost 'meaty' mushroom flavour. If unavailable, use the more delicately flavoured button mushrooms.

2 teaspoons olive oil
1 red onion, chopped
2 garlic cloves, crushed
2 teaspoons dijon mustard*
1 teaspoon dried tarragon
600 g (1 lb 5 oz) flat or field mushrooms, roughly chopped
750 ml (26 fl oz/3 cups) vegetable or chicken stock**
125 ml (4 fl oz/½ cup) red wine or use extra stock
2 tablespoons natural yoghurt
1 tablespoon snipped chives

* Check the mustard is gluten-free.
** Use vegetable stock for a vegetarian meal.

1. Heat the oil in a saucepan over low heat, add the onion and garlic and cook for 3–4 minutes, allowing the onion to brown slightly.

2. Add the mustard, tarragon and mushrooms and cook for a further 2–3 minutes, stirring gently.

3. Add the stock and wine, bring to the boil, then cover and simmer for 10 minutes. Leave the soup to cool a little, then purée in a food processor or blender. Serve topped with yoghurt and sprinkled with chives.

SERVES 4
PREPARATION TIME: 10 minutes
COOKING TIME: 20 minutes

NUTRITIONAL INFORMATION/SERVING:
7.5 g protein, 4 g fat (1 g saturated fat), 7 g carbohydrate, 5 g dietary fibre, 100 mg sodium, 520 kJ (125 Cals)

A source of vitamins B2 and B3.

 HINT

To make a creamy-tasting soup without using any cream, mix skim milk powder with a little water until you achieve a thick, cream-like consistency. Stir this into the hot soup just before serving.

Carrot and orange soup

Vegetable soups are an easy way to get some vegetables into reluctant eaters. Make your own stocks and avoid the high levels of salt and other additives found in many ready-made stocks.

750 g (1 lb 10 oz) carrots, sliced
1 large potato, peeled and sliced
500 ml (17 fl oz/2 cups) vegetable or chicken stock*
1 teaspoon chopped fresh ginger
250 ml (9 fl oz/1 cup) orange juice
125 g (4½ oz/½ cup) natural yoghurt
1 handful coriander (cilantro) leaves

* Use vegetable stock for a vegetarian meal.

1. Place the carrots, potato, stock and ginger into a saucepan, bring to the boil, then cover and simmer for 15–20 minutes, or until the vegetables are tender. Leave the soup to cool a little, then purée in a food processor or blender until smooth, adding the orange juice as you purée.

2. Reheat the soup. Sprinkle with freshly ground black pepper if desired, and top with a dollop of yoghurt. Sprinkle with coriander.

SERVES 4
PREPARATION TIME: 10 minutes
COOKING TIME: 20 minutes

NUTRITIONAL INFORMATION/SERVING:
5.5 g protein, 2 g fat (1 g saturated fat), 25 g carbohydrate, 7 g dietary fibre, 135 mg sodium, 580 kJ (140 Cals)

A source of vitamins A, B1, B2, B3, folate and C, and also potassium, magnesium, calcium and iron.

HINT

After you've enjoyed roast chicken, make a richly flavoured chicken stock, great for soups, sauces or risottos. Place all bones and remaining chicken carcass into a large saucepan. Pour boiling water into the roasting tin and stir to dissolve any drippings. Add this to the chicken bones and cover with more water. Bring to the boil, cover and simmer for 30–40 minutes. Cool, then strain the stock into a bowl, discard the bones and refrigerate or freeze the stock.

Tomato soup

There's no need to skin the tomatoes for this soup because the soup is passed through a sieve before serving. If you prefer, you can first skin the tomatoes by covering them with boiling water for 1 minute. The skins should then slip off easily.

SERVES 4
PREPARATION TIME: 15 minutes
COOKING TIME: 15 minutes

NUTRITIONAL
INFORMATION/SERVING:
4 g protein, 3 g fat (0.5 g
saturated fat), 10 g carbohydrate,
4 g dietary fibre, 75 mg sodium,
345 kJ (80 Cals)
A source of vitamins A, B1, B3, C
and E, and also potassium and iron.

2 teaspoons olive oil
1 onion, diced
1 garlic clove, crushed
1 teaspoon sugar
1 kg (2 lb 4 oz) ripe tomatoes, roughly chopped
1 tablespoon tomato paste (concentrated purée), no added salt
750 ml (26 fl oz/3 cups) vegetable or chicken stock*
1 bunch of fresh herbs (tie together stalks of parsley, thyme, mint and rosemary)

* Use vegetable stock for a vegetarian or vegan meal.

1. Heat the oil in a large saucepan, add the onion and garlic, then cover and cook over low heat for 3–4 minutes, stirring occasionally.

2. Add the sugar, tomatoes and tomato paste and cook for a further 2–3 minutes. Add the stock and herbs, bring to the boil, then cover and simmer for 5 minutes (do not overcook). Remove and discard the herbs.

3. Leave the soup to cool a little, then purée. Push the purée through a sieve to remove any pieces of tomato skin. Season with freshly ground black pepper.

Creamy cauliflower soup

Using skim milk powder instead of cream or whole milk gives a surprisingly creamy result — without adding any fat.

SERVES 4
PREPARATION TIME: 10 minutes
COOKING TIME: 20 minutes

NUTRITIONAL
INFORMATION/SERVING:
16 g protein, 1 g fat (0.5 g
saturated fat), 22 g carbohydrate,
5 g dietary fibre, 200 mg sodium,
680 kJ (165 Cals)
A source of vitamins B1, B2, B3,
folate, C and E, and also potassium,
calcium, iron and zinc.

1 kg (2 lb 4 oz) cauliflower, roughly chopped
1 litre (35 fl oz/4 cups) chicken or vegetable stock*
1 onion, roughly chopped
3 bay leaves
1 mint sprig
100 g (3½ oz/1 cup) skim milk powder
1 tablespoon snipped chives

* Use vegetable stock for a vegetarian meal.

1. Place all ingredients, except the milk powder and chives, in a large saucepan. Bring to the boil, cover and simmer for 12–15 minutes, or until the cauliflower is tender.

2. Remove and discard the bay leaves and mint. Leave the soup to cool a little, then purée in a food processor or blender, gradually adding the milk powder. Reheat the soup. Serve in deep soup bowls sprinkled with chives.

Bean soup

Using tinned white beans makes this a quick meal, but they need to be rinsed in a sieve under cold running water to remove some of the salt.

  1.5 litres (52 fl oz/6 cups) vegetable or chicken stock*
  2 x 400 g (14 oz) tins butterbeans (lima beans) or white beans, drained and rinsed
  2 garlic cloves, crushed
  1 teaspoon dried thyme
  4 bay leaves
  1 large onion, diced
  1 large carrot, diced
  2 celery stalks, thinly sliced
  2 tablespoons tomato paste (concentrated purée), no added salt
  1 teaspoon chilli sauce
  1 tablespoon white wine vinegar
  2 tablespoons chopped parsley

  * Use vegetable stock for a vegetarian or vegan meal.

1. Place all the ingredients, except the vinegar and parsley, in a large saucepan. Bring to the boil, cover and simmer for 10 minutes. Stir in the vinegar.

2. Serve in deep bowls sprinkled with parsley.

SERVES 4
PREPARATION TIME: 10 minutes
COOKING TIME: 15 minutes

NUTRITIONAL INFORMATION/SERVING:
12 g protein, 2 g fat (0.5 g saturated fat), 26 g carbohydrate, 13 g dietary fibre, 350 mg sodium, 715 kJ (170 Cals)

A source of vitamins A, B1, B2, B3, C and E, and also potassium, magnesium, calcium, iron and zinc.

 HINT

Make your own vegetable stock and avoid high levels of salt and other additives found in ready-made stocks. Place a chopped onion (no need to peel), a roughly chopped carrot, a few sliced celery stalks, a few sprigs of fresh parsley and thyme (or 1 teaspoon of dried herbs) and 3–4 bay leaves into a large saucepan with 1.5 litres (52 fl oz/6 cups) water. Bring to the boil, cover and simmer for 1 hour. Cool, then strain stock into a bowl. Discard the vegetables and herbs and refrigerate or freeze the stock.

Farmhouse soup

The flavours of this hearty soup intensify after standing, so make the soup one day and serve it the next, or freeze any leftovers for another time. This is a thick soup and can be thinned with extra water or stock, if desired. You don't need to stick to the exact vegetables listed here — replace them with whatever you have on hand. For a vegetarian soup, simply omit the osso bucco.

200 g (7 oz) dried chickpeas

400 g (14 oz) osso bucco

1 onion, sliced

2 rosemary sprigs

2 bay leaves

3 large parsley sprigs

1 large carrot, sliced

1 large potato, peeled and diced

1 parsnip, peeled and sliced

1 leek, white part only, washed and sliced

800 g (1 lb 12 oz) tin tomatoes

100 g (3½ oz/½ cup) long-grain brown rice

125 g (4½ oz/½ cup) tomato paste (concentrated purée)

300 g (10½ oz) broccoli florets

200 g (7 oz) sliced green beans

1. Place the chickpeas and 1.5 litres (52 fl oz/6 cups) water into a large saucepan, bring to the boil, then cover and cook for 1 minute. Turn off the heat and leave to stand for 1 hour. (If leaving for a longer period, place in the refrigerator.)

2. Drain the chickpeas and add 1.5 litres (52 fl oz/6 cups) fresh water. Bring to the boil, add the osso bucco, onion and herbs, cover and simmer gently for 1½ hours. Remove and discard the bay leaves and herbs. Cool the soup and refrigerate it so that any fat will rise to the surface for easy removal.

3. Remove fat from the top of the soup and remove the osso bucco. Remove the meat from the bones and set aside.

4. Return the soup to the stovetop, add the carrot, potato, parsnip, leek, tomatoes, brown rice and tomato paste. Bring to the boil, then reduce the heat, cover and simmer for 30–40 minutes, or until the rice is cooked.

5. Add the osso bucco meat, broccoli and beans and cook for a further 5 minutes. Serve in large bowls.

SERVES 6

PREPARATION TIME: 15 minutes

COOKING TIME: 2¼ hours
+ 1 hour standing time

NUTRITIONAL
INFORMATION/SERVING:
21 g protein, 3 g fat (0 g saturated fat), 46 g carbohydrate, 13 g dietary fibre, 225 mg sodium, 1235 kJ (295 Cals)

A source of vitamins A, B1, B2, B3, folate, B12, C and E, and also potassium, magnesium, calcium, iron and zinc.

 HINT

It is not always necessary to peel all your vegetables when making soups and stews. Vegetables such as carrots, parsnips and potatoes can all be left unpeeled if you like, as long as they have been washed first. However, if using carrots in a salad, it is always best to peel them first, as the skin will quickly turn brown when exposed to the air.

Beetroot soup

No one will guess this is low in kilojoules. If desired, replace the raw beetroot with the drained contents of an 800 g (1 lb 12 oz) tin of beetroot. Look for a brand that has no added salt.

SERVES 4

PREPARATION TIME: 15 minutes

COOKING TIME: 20 minutes
+ at least 2 hours refrigeration
if serving cold

NUTRITIONAL
INFORMATION/SERVING:
8.5 g protein, 1 g fat (0.5 g
saturated fat), 29 g carbohydrate,
8 g dietary fibre, 245 mg sodium,
680 kJ (160 Cals)

A source of vitamins A, B1, B2, B3,
folate and C, and also potassium,
magnesium, calcium, iron and zinc.

4 beetroot (beets), peeled and grated
1 litre (35 fl oz/4 cups) vegetable or chicken stock*
90 g (3¼ oz/2 cups) shredded Chinese cabbage (wong bok)
1 large apple, peeled, cored and sliced
400 g (14 oz) tin chopped tomatoes, no added salt
2 tablespoons lemon juice
200 g (7 oz) low-fat natural yoghurt
2 tablespoons chopped parsley

* Use vegetable stock for a vegetarian meal.

1. Place the grated beetroot and stock into a saucepan, bring to the boil, then cover and simmer for 10 minutes.

2. Add the cabbage, apple and tomatoes, cover and continue cooking for 10 minutes.

3. Just before serving, add the lemon juice and season with freshly ground black pepper. If serving cold, leave the soup to cool, then refrigerate for at least 2 hours.

4. Serve in bowls topped with a dollop of yoghurt — swirl the yoghurt into the soup with a fork to produce a spiral effect. Sprinkle with parsley.

HINT

Peeling and grating beetroot can be quite messy, as the beetroot 'bleeds' when cut and can easily stain your hands and chopping board. It may be a good idea to wear gloves when handling cut beetroot, although the purple juice stains will come off after a few washes in warm soapy water. Alternatively, grate the beetroot in a food processor.

Lentil and vegetable soup

This is a great meal for vegetarians. Lentil cooking times can vary between brands and types of lentils, so check the lentils towards the end of cooking time — you want the lentils to be soft, but not turned to lentil mash.

2 teaspoons olive oil
1 teaspoon ground cumin
2 teaspoons ground coriander
1 small chilli, finely chopped
1 large onion, diced
1.5 litres (52 fl oz/6 cups) vegetable stock or water
1 large carrot, peeled and sliced
125 g (4¹/₂ oz/1 cup) sliced celery
800 g (1 lb 12 oz) tin tomatoes in tomato juice
200 g (7 oz) mushrooms, sliced
1 red capsicum (pepper), diced
250 g (9 oz/1¹/₃ cups) green lentils
60 ml (2 fl oz/¹/₄ cup) red wine
2 tablespoons chopped parsley

1. Heat the oil in a large saucepan and cook the cumin, coriander, chilli and onion over low heat for 3–4 minutes.

2. Add the stock or water, carrot, celery, tomatoes, mushrooms, capsicum, lentils and wine. Bring to the boil, then cover and simmer for 25–35 minutes, or until the lentils are cooked.

3. Serve the soup into large bowls and sprinkle with parsley.

SERVES 6
PREPARATION TIME: 10 minutes
COOKING TIME: 35–45 minutes

NUTRITIONAL INFORMATION/SERVING:
14 g protein, 2.5 g fat (0.5 g saturated fat), 34 g carbohydrate, 9.5 g dietary fibre, 160 mg sodium, 900 kJ (215 Cals)

A source of vitamins A, B1, B2, B3, folate and C, and also potassium, magnesium, calcium, iron and zinc.

SERVES 4

PREPARATION TIME: 20 minutes
+ 2 hours chilling time

COOKING TIME: nil

NUTRITIONAL
INFORMATION/SERVING:
4.5 g protein, 0.5 g fat (0 g
saturated fat), 10 g carbohydrate,
5 g dietary fibre, 55 mg sodium,
290 kJ (70 Cals)

A source of vitamins A, B1,
B3, folate, C and E, and also
potassium and iron.

Chilled tomato soup

This is a no-cook rustic soup that is perfect for a hot evening. Tomatoes are at their best in late summer to early autumn. The best flavoured are those that have been vine-ripened or those with a strong, sweet tomato aroma.

1 kg (2 lb 4 oz) ripe tomatoes
2 Lebanese (short) cucumbers
1 small red onion
1 red capsicum (pepper)
2 garlic cloves, crushed
500 ml (17 fl oz/2 cups) vegetable or veal stock*
2–3 lemon thyme sprigs
1 tablespoon lemon juice
2 tablespoons torn basil or parsley
4 ice cubes

* *Use vegetable stock for a vegetarian or vegan meal.*

1. Skin the tomatoes by removing the cores and cutting a small cross in the end of each tomato. Place in a heatproof bowl, cover with boiling water, leave for 1 minute and drain. Transfer to a bowl of cold water, then peel off the skins. Cut into quarters and squeeze out the seeds, then dice the tomato flesh finely.

2. Dice the cucumbers, onion and capsicum (some food processors will do this well). Combine with the tomatoes, garlic, stock and thyme sprigs. Refrigerate for at least 2 hours. Remove the thyme.

3. Just before serving, stir in the lemon juice and basil and season with freshly ground black pepper. Divide the soup among serving bowls and place an ice cube on top of each soup.

Scandinavian fruit soup

⊘ ❀

SERVES 4

PREPARATION TIME: 10 minutes
+ at least 1 hour soaking time

COOKING TIME: 20 minutes
+ at least 2 hours chilling time if
serving cold

NUTRITIONAL
INFORMATION/SERVING:
5.5 g protein, 1.5 g fat (0.5 g
saturated fat), 86 g carbohydrate,
7.5 g dietary fibre, 70 mg sodium,
1560 kJ (375 Cals)

A source of vitamins A, B3, folate,
C and E, and also potassium,
magnesium, calcium and iron.

Served hot, this fruit soup is wonderfully warming in winter. Served cold in summer for lunch, it is refreshingly different. This soup is suitable to freeze.

500 ml (17 fl oz/2 cups) apple juice
500 ml (17 fl oz/2 cups) orange juice
140 g (5 oz/1 cup) dried apricots
100 g (3^1/$_2$ oz/1 cup) dried peaches
35 g (1^1/$_4$ oz/^{1}/$_2$ cup) dried apples
60 g (2^1/$_4$ oz/^{1}/$_2$ cup) raisins
6 cm (2^1/$_2$ inch) piece cinnamon stick
3–4 cardamom pods
80 g (2^3/$_4$ oz) sago, or use white rice
125 g (4^1/$_2$ oz/^{1}/$_2$ cup) natural yoghurt
1 teaspoon finely grated orange zest

1. Place the juices, dried fruits, spices and sago into a large saucepan and leave to soak for at least 1 hour.

2. Bring the mixture to the boil, cover and simmer gently for 15 minutes. Remove the cinnamon stick and cardamom pods. Serve topped with a swirl of yoghurt and a sprinkle of orange zest. If serving cold, leave to cool, then refrigerate for at least 2 hours.

Leek and potato soup

This is a rich and creamy-tasting soup, but surprisingly it's low in fat.

2 teaspoons olive oil
1 white onion, sliced
2 leeks, white part only, washed and sliced
500 g (1 lb 2 oz) all-purpose potatoes, such as pontiac or desiree,
    peeled and quartered
1 litre (35 fl oz/4 cups) vegetable or chicken stock*
3 bay leaves
75 g (2¹/₂ oz/³/₄ cup) skim milk powder
pinch of ground nutmeg
finely grated zest and juice of 1 lemon

* Use vegetable stock for a vegetarian meal.

1. Heat the oil in a large saucepan over medium heat and add the onion and leeks.
   Cover and allow the vegetables to 'sweat' for 4–5 minutes, stirring occasionally.

2. Add the potatoes, stock and bay leaves, bring to the boil, then cover and simmer
   for 15–20 minutes, or until the potatoes are tender. Remove the bay leaves.

3. Leave the soup to cool a little, then purée in a food processor or blender, gradually
   adding the milk powder. Add the nutmeg and lemon zest.

4. Serve into bowls and sprinkle with lemon juice.

SERVES 4
PREPARATION TIME: 15 minutes
COOKING TIME: 25 minutes

NUTRITIONAL
INFORMATION/SERVING:
12 g protein, 3.5 g fat (0.5 g
saturated fat), 33 g carbohydrate,
4.5 g dietary fibre, 150 mg sodium,
900 kJ (215 Cals)

A source of vitamins B1, B2, B3,
folate and C, and also potassium,
magnesium, calcium, iron and zinc.

 HINT

Soups usually freeze well.
Freeze individual portions
so you can take some
to work and heat it in
the microwave.

Seafood soup

This soup is a complete meal and is ideal for a special occasion. Ask your fishmonger for fish bones to use for the fish stock. If preferred, use ready-made fish stock (check it is gluten-free) or substitute water.

fish stock
300 g (10^1/$_2$ oz) raw prawns (shrimp)
750 g (1 lb 10 oz) fish bones, trimmings or fish heads (optional)
1 carrot, roughly chopped
250 ml (9 fl oz/1 cup) white wine
a few parsley sprigs
^{1}/$_2$ teaspoon dried tarragon
^{1}/$_2$ lemon, flesh and skin roughly chopped

soup
2 teaspoons olive oil
1 onion, sliced
1 garlic clove, crushed
500 g (1 lb 2 oz) potatoes, peeled and diced
1 leek, white part only, washed and sliced
300 g (10^1/$_2$ oz) boneless fish fillets, cut into 4 cm (1^1/$_2$ inch) pieces
300 g (10^1/$_2$ oz) scallops
chopped parsley, to serve
lemon wedges

1. To make the fish stock, peel and devein the prawns and set them aside, reserving the shells. Place the prawn shells into a large saucepan with the fish trimmings (if using), 1.5 litres (52 fl oz/6 cups) water, carrot, wine, parsley sprigs, tarragon and lemon. Bring to the boil, cover and simmer for 15 minutes. Strain the fish stock and reserve the stock.

2. To make the soup, heat the oil in a large wok or saucepan and gently sauté the onion and garlic until softened but not brown.

3. Add the potatoes, leek and fish stock, bring to the boil, then cover and simmer for 15 minutes.

4. Add the fish, simmer for 3 minutes, then add the scallops and prawns and continue cooking for about 2 minutes, or until the prawns turn pink. Ladle the soup into deep bowls, sprinkle with parsley and serve with lemon wedges.

SERVES 6
PREPARATION TIME: 20 minutes
COOKING TIME: 40 minutes

NUTRITIONAL
INFORMATION/SERVING:
26 g protein, 4 g fat (1 g saturated fat), 13 g carbohydrate, 2.5 g dietary fibre, 250 mg sodium, 810 kJ (195 Cals)

A source of vitamins B1, B3, B12 and C, and also potassium, magnesium, calcium, iron, zinc and iodine.

SERVES 4

PREPARATION TIME: 20 minutes

COOKING TIME: 1¼ hours

NUTRITIONAL
INFORMATION/SERVING:
8.5 g protein, 5.0 g fat (1.5 g
saturated fat), 30 g carbohydrate,
5 g dietary fibre, 60 mg sodium,
805 kJ (195 Cals)

A source of vitamins A, B1, B2,
B3, folate and C, and also
potassium, calcium and iron.

Roast pumpkin, orange and rosemary soup

Roasting the pumpkin produces a much better flavour than if the pumpkin is boiled, and the sweetness of the orange adds an extra dimension to this popular soup.

1.5 kg (3 lb 5 oz) pumpkin (winter squash)
olive oil spray
2 teaspoons olive oil
1 onion, chopped
2 teaspoons finely chopped rosemary or 1 teaspoon dried rosemary
1 teaspoon finely grated orange zest
1 litre (35 fl oz/4 cups) vegetable or chicken stock*
125 ml (4 fl oz/½ cup) orange juice
natural yoghurt, to serve (optional)

* Use vegetable stock for a vegetarian or vegan meal.

1. Preheat oven to 180°C (350°F/Gas 4). Cut the pumpkin into large chunks and remove the seeds. Place on a flat baking tray, spray lightly with olive oil and bake for 50–60 minutes, or until the pumpkin is tender. When cool enough to handle, peel and discard the skin.

2. While the pumpkin is cooking, heat the olive oil in a large saucepan and cook the onion and rosemary over low heat until the onion is soft but not brown. Add the orange zest and stock, bring to the boil, then cover and simmer for 15 minutes.

3. Add the roasted pumpkin flesh and simmer for a further 5 minutes.

4. Leave the soup to cool a little, then purée in batches in a food processor or blender, adding the orange juice. Reheat the soup. If desired, top each serving with a dollop of yoghurt and swirl it into the soup with a fork.

HINT

For extra flavour in
soups or stocks, add
plenty of herbs or spices
as well as grated lemon
or orange zest.

Laksa

The fat content of light coconut milk varies between brands. Check the label before buying and choose one with less than 6 grams fat per 100 grams. For gluten-free, make sure you choose rice noodles.

200 g (7 oz) fresh rice noodles
2 teaspoons sesame oil
1 red onion, sliced
1 garlic clove, crushed
2 tablespoons laksa paste*
300 g (10½ oz) boneless fish fillets, cut into 2.5 cm (1 inch) cubes
180 g (6 oz/4 cups) shredded Chinese cabbage (wong bok) or any Chinese greens
200 g (7 oz/½ bunch) snake (yard-long) beans, cut into 3 cm (1¼ inch) lengths
1 red capsicum (pepper), sliced
300 g (10½ oz) raw prawns (shrimp), peeled and deveined
250 ml (9 fl oz/1 cup) light coconut milk
250 g (9 oz/3½ cups) mung bean sprouts
8 Vietnamese mint leaves
1 large handful coriander (cilantro) leaves

* Check the laska paste is gluten-free.

1. Put the rice noodles in a bowl and cover with boiling water. Leave to soak for 3 minutes, or follow the directions on the packet, then drain and keep warm.

2. Heat the oil in a large wok or saucepan over medium heat. Add the onion, garlic and laksa paste and stir for 3–4 minutes.

3. Add 1.5 litres (52 fl oz/6 cups) water, fish, Chinese cabbage, beans and capsicum. Bring to the boil, then reduce the heat and simmer for 3–4 minutes. Add the prawns and coconut milk and cook for 2 minutes, or until the prawns turn pink.

4. Divide the bean sprouts among four large serving bowls. Top with the rice noodles and then ladle the hot soup over the noodles. Garnish with Vietnamese mint and coriander leaves.

SERVES 4
PREPARATION TIME: 20 minutes
COOKING TIME: 15 minutes

NUTRITIONAL INFORMATION/SERVING*:
42 g protein, 10 g fat (4 g saturated fat), 24 g carbohydrate, 8.5 g dietary fibre, 740 mg sodium, 1490 kJ (355 Cals)

* Values may vary a little and fat may be lower depending on the brand of laksa paste and coconut milk used.

A source of vitamins A, B1, B2, B3, folate and C, and also potassium, magnesium, calcium, iron, zinc and iodine.

Watercress vichyssoise

SERVES 4

PREPARATION TIME: 10 minutes

COOKING TIME: 20 minutes
+ 2 hours chilling time

NUTRITIONAL
INFORMATION/SERVING:
8.5 g protein, 3.5 g fat (0.5 g
saturated fat), 21 g carbohydrate,
5.5 g dietary fibre, 115 mg sodium,
665 kJ (160 Cals)

A source of vitamins A, B1, B2, B3,
folate, C and E, and also potassium,
magnesium, calcium, iron and zinc.

With its peppery, mustard-like flavour, watercress teams wonderfully with potato to make this classic soup. Watercress is available year-round, and its dark green leaves are packed with vitamins and minerals. This chilled soup can be prepared ahead of time and enjoyed on a summer evening.

2 teaspoons olive oil
1 onion, roughly chopped
2 garlic cloves, crushed
2 leeks, white part only, washed and sliced
2 large potatoes, peeled and sliced
1 litre (35 fl oz/4 cups) vegetable or chicken stock*
finely grated zest and juice of 1 lemon
400 g (14 oz/1 large bunch) watercress, washed, coarse stems removed
   (to give about 200 g/7 oz trimmed watercress)
200 g (7 oz) low-fat natural yoghurt
4 thyme sprigs

* Use vegetable stock for a vegetarian meal.

1. Heat the oil in a large saucepan, add the onion and garlic and gently cook for 3–4 minutes.

2. Add the leeks, potatoes, stock and lemon zest and simmer, covered, for 15 minutes. Add the watercress and cook for 2 minutes.

3. Leave the soup to cool a little, then purée in a food processor or blender. Swirl in the yoghurt and then chill until ready to serve. Just before serving, season with freshly ground black pepper, then add some lemon juice and a thyme sprig to each serving.

STARTERS

These recipes are great to serve with drinks or as part of a simple lunch with bread and a salad. Many of the starters in this chapter are dips, which are a healthy and inexpensive alternative to many prepared dips. Making your own dips is especially useful for those who need to avoid saturated fat or salt.

SERVES 4

PREPARATION TIME: 10 minutes

COOKING TIME: 1 hour
+ 1 hour standing

NUTRITIONAL
INFORMATION/SERVING:
13 g protein, 9.5 g fat (1 g
saturated fat), 28 g carbohydrate,
10 g dietary fibre, 30 mg sodium,
1030 kJ (245 Cals)

A source of vitamins A, B1, B3 and
E, and also potassium, magnesium,
calcium, iron and zinc.

Hummus

Use hummus as a spread, dip or serve with tabouleh salad. If you are short on time, you may prefer to use tinned chickpeas. If using cooked chickpeas, use 2½ cups or 2 x 400 g (14 oz) tins and start the recipe from step 3.

220 g (7¾ oz/1 cup) dried chickpeas
2 garlic cloves, peeled
2 tablespoons tahini
60 ml (2 fl oz/¼ cup) lemon juice

1. Place the chickpeas and 1 litre (35 fl oz/4 cups) water into a large saucepan, bring to the boil, then cover and cook for 1 minute. Turn off the heat and leave to stand for 1 hour. (If leaving for a longer period, place in the refrigerator.)

2. Drain the chickpeas and cover with fresh water. Bring to the boil, cover and simmer gently for 1 hour. Do not discard the cooking liquid.

3. In a food processor or blender, process the chickpeas with the garlic, tahini and lemon juice, adding enough of the chickpea cooking liquid (or use water if using tinned chickpeas) to make a thick paste.

Baba ghanoush

*This is an easy dip to make and it is also great to serve with falafel and tabouleh.
If you are not on a gluten-free diet, serve with seeded crispbread (page 79) or pieces
of toasted pitta bread.*

1 eggplant (aubergine), about 500 g (1 lb 2 oz)
2 garlic cloves, peeled
60 ml (2 fl oz/¼ cup) lemon juice
2 tablespoons tahini
1 teaspoon paprika
1 teaspoon olive oil

1. Preheat oven to 200°C (400°F/Gas 6). Place the whole eggplant on the oven shelf,
   placing a baking tray on the shelf below, and bake for 40 minutes. Remove from
   the oven and leave for 10 minutes to cool a little.

2. Peel the eggplant and place the flesh into a food processor. Add the garlic, lemon
   juice and tahini and season with freshly ground black pepper. Purée until smooth,
   then place into a bowl.

3. Combine the paprika and oil and drizzle over the top. Serve with vegetable
   crudités or rice crackers.

SERVES 6
PREPARATION TIME: 10 minutes
COOKING TIME: 40 minutes

NUTRITIONAL
INFORMATION/SERVING:
2.5 g protein, 5.5 g fat (0.5 g
saturated fat), 2.5 g carbohydrate,
3 g dietary fibre, 10 mg sodium,
295 kJ (70 Cals)

A source of vitamins B3, C and E,
and also magnesium.

 HINT

Serve raw vegetables
with dips — carrot sticks,
celery curls, broccoli florets
or different coloured
capsicums (peppers) cut
into strips.

NUTRITIONAL
INFORMATION/SERVING:
2 g protein, 3.5 g fat (0.5 g
saturated fat), 5 g carbohydrate,
2.5 g dietary fibre, 5 mg sodium,
250 kJ (60 Cals)

A source of vitamins A, B3 and C.

Roasted eggplant and red capsicum dip

*This is delicious as a dip or sauce for chicken or lamb and also makes a great
topping for steamed or baked whole potatoes. Roasting the vegetables gives the dip
a delicious smoky flavour.*

1 eggplant (aubergine), about 450 g (1 lb)
2 red capsicums (peppers)
2 garlic cloves, peeled
1 teaspoon ground coriander
1 teaspoon paprika
2 tablespoons lemon juice
1 tablespoon extra virgin olive oil

1. Preheat oven to 200°C (400°F/Gas 6). Place the whole eggplant and capsicums on
   the oven shelf, placing a baking tray on the shelf below, and bake for 30 minutes,
   or until the capsicum skin puffs and blackens. Using kitchen tongs, place the
   capsicums into a bowl, cover and leave until cool enough to handle. Place the
   eggplant onto a plate and cool.

2. Peel off the capsicum skins, holding the capsicums over a bowl to catch any juices.
   Discard the skins and remove the seeds. Reserve the capsicum juice.

3. Place the eggplant flesh and capsicum in a blender. Add the garlic, spices, lemon
   juice and oil and process until smooth. Add the reserved juice from the capsicum
   if any more liquid is needed, and process to combine.

HINT

Purchased avocado dips
often have very little
avocado. Make your own
by mashing the flesh of
an avocado with tofu or
natural yoghurt. Add chilli
and freshly ground black
pepper to taste.

*(from left to right) Tzatziki, Roasted eggplant and red capsicum dip
and Beetroot dip, served with Seeded crispbread*

SERVES 6
PREPARATION TIME: 10 minutes
COOKING TIME: nil

NUTRITIONAL
INFORMATION/SERVING:
3.5 g protein, 1.5 g fat (0.5 g
saturated fat), 7 g carbohydrate,
2 g dietary fibre, 80 mg sodium,
230 kJ (55 Cals)

A source of vitamins folate and C.

Beetroot dip

Whip this up in a few minutes and serve with sticks of celery or other raw vegetables, or with rice crackers. It's also excellent to use as a topping on barbecued steak or lamb.

3 beetroot (beets)
2 teaspoons horseradish sauce*
1 tablespoon lemon juice
200 g (7 oz) low-fat natural yoghurt
1 tablespoon sesame seeds, toasted

* Check the horseradish sauce is gluten-free.

1. Wearing rubber or disposable gloves, peel the beetroot. Grate the beetroot, either by hand or using a food processor.

2. Combine the beetroot, horseradish, lemon juice and yoghurt and put into a serving bowl. Sprinkle with the toasted sesame seeds.

SERVES 4
PREPARATION TIME: 10 minutes
COOKING TIME: nil

NUTRITIONAL
INFORMATION/SERVING:
3.5 g protein, 0 g fat (0 g
saturated fat), 4.5 g carbohydrate,
1 g dietary fibre, 50 mg sodium,
155 kJ (35 Cals)

A source of vitamin C and calcium.

Tzatziki

Serve as a dip or a delicious topping for baked potatoes or as an accompaniment to grilled lamb in pitta bread (don't use pitta bread if following a gluten-free diet).

3 Lebanese (short) cucumbers
1 garlic clove, crushed
200 g (7 oz) low-fat natural yoghurt
1 large handful mint, finely chopped

1. Grate the cucumbers and squeeze out as much liquid as possible.

2. Combine the cucumber with the remaining ingredients.

Seeded crispbread

These crispbreads are a delicious alternative to crackers and one which children can help prepare. The seeds are rich in nutrients, including vitamin E, iron and zinc. Serve the crispbread with a variety of dips, such as those on pages 76 and 78.

4 wholemeal (whole-wheat) pitta breads
1 egg white
2 tablespoons sesame seeds
2 tablespoons poppy seeds
1 tablespoon fennel seeds

1. Preheat oven to 180°C (350°F/Gas 4).

2. Separate the layers of pitta bread and lay each piece out flat on a baking tray.

3. Beat the egg white and 2 tablespoons water with a fork until combined.

4. Using a pastry brush, brush the surface of the pitta breads lightly with the egg white mixture and then sprinkle with the combined seeds. Bake for 5–7 minutes until crisp, taking care the bread does not burn. When cool, break into pieces and serve with dips.

SERVES 6
PREPARATION TIME: 5 minutes
COOKING TIME: 10 minutes

NUTRITIONAL INFORMATION/SERVING:
7 g protein, 5 g fat (0.5 g saturated fat), 26 g carbohydrate, 5 g dietary fibre, 430 mg sodium, 730 kJ (175 Cals)

A source of vitamins B1, B3 and E, and also magnesium, calcium, iron and zinc.

Smoked salmon pinwheels

These pretty pinwheels can be made in advance and are an ideal party fingerfood.

200 g (7 oz) low-fat ricotta cheese
2¹/₂ tablespoons natural yoghurt
1–2 teaspoons wasabi paste
2 teaspoons finely grated lemon zest
2 tablespoons finely chopped mint
4 slices of mountain or lavash bread
150 g (5¹/₂ oz) smoked salmon

1. Combine the ricotta, yoghurt, wasabi, lemon zest and mint. Mix well.

2. Spread the bread with the ricotta mixture and top with salmon. Roll up the bread and wrap in plastic wrap. Refrigerate for 1 hour (or up to 6 hours). When ready to serve, unwrap and slice each roll into 10 pinwheels.

MAKES 40
PREPARATION TIME: 20 minutes + 1 hour refrigeration
COOKING TIME: nil

NUTRITIONAL INFORMATION/2 PINWHEELS:
4 g protein, 1.5 g fat (0.5 g saturated fat), 6.5 g carbohydrate, 0.5 g dietary fibre, 220 mg sodium, 235 kJ (55 Cals)

A source of vitamins B3 and B12.

Pesto-stuffed cherry tomatoes

The bright colours make these morsels an attractive starter to serve with drinks. The size of the cherry tomatoes may vary from what we've used here, so you may end up with slightly more or less filled tomatoes than the quantity listed.

40 cherry tomatoes
200 g (7 oz) basil
2 garlic cloves, peeled
2 tablespoons pine nuts, toasted
2 tablespoons lemon juice
3 tablespoons olive oil

1. Cut a thin slice off the top of each tomato and, using a small spoon or a melon baller, scoop out the seeds. Turn the tomato 'shells' upside down on a clean tea towel (dish towel) and leave to drain.

2. To make the pesto, place the remaining ingredients into a food processor and blend until combined. Using a small spoon, fill the drained tomato shells with the pesto mixture.

MAKES 40
PREPARATION TIME: 30 minutes
COOKING TIME: nil

NUTRITIONAL
INFORMATION/2 TOMATOES:
0.5 g protein, 4 g fat (0.5 g saturated fat), 1.5 g carbohydrate, 1.5 g dietary fibre, 5 mg sodium, 180 kJ (45 Cals)

A source of vitamins C and E.

HINT

If you don't have time to make a starter, serve slices of perfectly ripe melon.

LIGHT MEALS

There is no reason why light meals should or should not contain meat, but none of the recipes in this section do. The aim is to demonstrate the range of delicious and healthy meals that can be prepared using vegetarian ingredients. Suggestions for the inclusion of meat have been made, where appropriate.

SERVES 4
PREPARATION TIME: 30 minutes
COOKING TIME: 45 minutes

NUTRITIONAL
INFORMATION/SERVING:
11 g protein, 6 g fat (0.5 g
saturated fat), 22 g carbohydrate,
9.5 g dietary fibre, 95 mg sodium,
790 kJ (190 Cals)

A source of vitamins A, B1, B2, B3,
folate, C and E, and also potassium,
magnesium, iron and zinc.

Barbecued vegetables with romesco sauce

*Transform ordinary barbecued vegetables with this delicious sauce, based on an old
Spanish recipe.*

16 mushroom caps
4 zucchini (courgettes), sliced lengthways
16 spring onions (scallions), trimmed
16 asparagus spears

romesco sauce
1 onion, peeled and cut into quarters
4 garlic cloves
2 teaspoons olive oil
2 red capsicums (peppers)
1 tablespoon slivered almonds
2 large tomatoes, roughly chopped
1 teaspoon paprika
1 thick slice of sourdough bread, roughly broken up
2 tablespoons red wine vinegar
1 teaspoon soft brown sugar

1. Preheat oven to 250°C (500°F/Gas 9). To make the romesco sauce, place the onion
   and garlic cloves onto one half of a baking tray and drizzle with the oil. Place the
   capsicums directly onto the oven shelf and put the baking tray on the shelf below
   so that the capsicums sit over the empty part of the tray (to catch any juices).
   Reduce the oven temperature to 220°C (425°F/Gas 7) and bake for 35 minutes (the
   garlic will probably only take 20 minutes to cook, so it may need to be removed
   from the oven before the capsicums).

2. Transfer the capsicums to a bowl, cover and leave until cool enough to handle.
   Peel off the capsicum skins, holding them over a bowl to catch any juices. Discard
   the skins and remove the seeds. Reserve the capsicum juice.

3. While the capsicums are roasting, toast the almonds in a dry frying pan, shaking
   over medium heat until they brown, taking care they do not burn. Set aside.

4. Skin the tomatoes by removing the core and cutting a small cross in the end of
   each tomato. Place in a bowl, cover with boiling water, leave for 1 minute and
   drain. Transfer to a bowl of cold water, then peel off the skins. Cut into quarters
   and squeeze out the seeds.

5. Place the capsicum flesh in a food processor with the onion, the flesh squeezed
   from the garlic cloves, almonds, tomatoes, paprika, bread, vinegar and sugar.
   Season with freshly ground black pepper. Process until smooth, adding the
   reserved capsicum juice to thin the sauce. Store in the refrigerator until required.

6. Cook the mushrooms, zucchini, spring onions and asparagus on the barbecue for
   about 10 minutes, or until just tender. Serve with the sauce.

Dal

Serve dal with curry and rice, or scoop up with poppadoms. Most poppadoms use lentil flour as their main ingredient and so are ideal for those following a gluten-free diet, but it is always advisable to check the label, as some brands may contain flour.

- 200 g (7 oz/1 cup) red lentils
- 2 potatoes, peeled and cut into large dice
- 250 g (9 oz/1 cup) tinned tomatoes, no added salt, roughly chopped
- 1/2 teaspoon turmeric
- 1 teaspoon ground cumin
- 2 teaspoons ground coriander
- 1 garlic clove, crushed
- 2 teaspoons garam masala

1. Place the lentils, potatoes, tomatoes, turmeric, cumin, coriander, garlic and 750 ml (26 fl oz/3 cups) water into a saucepan. Bring to the boil, cover and simmer for 20 minutes, or until the lentils are cooked.

2. Stir in the garam masala, cover and leave the dal for 2–3 minutes for the flavours to blend.

SERVES 4
PREPARATION TIME: 10 minutes
COOKING TIME: 20 minutes

NUTRITIONAL
INFORMATION/SERVING:
14 g protein, 0.5 g fat (0 g saturated fat), 40 g carbohydrate, 7.5 g dietary fibre, 20 mg sodium, 920 kJ (220 Cals)

A source of vitamins B1, B3, folate and C, and also potassium, magnesium, iron and zinc.

 HINT

Instead of pan-frying poppadoms in oil, avoid extra fat by cooking them in the microwave.

Barbecued vegetable kebabs

Vegetables are often given only token attention at barbecues. Enjoy these vegetable kebabs on their own for a vegetarian meal, or serve them with barbecued fish, chicken or lamb.

SERVES 4

PREPARATION TIME: 15 minutes

COOKING TIME: 10 minutes

NUTRITIONAL
INFORMATION/SERVING:
6 g protein, 0.5 g fat (0 g
saturated fat), 14 g carbohydrate,
5 g dietary fibre, 20 mg sodium,
370 kJ (90 Cals)

A source of vitamins A, B2,
B3, folate, C and E, and also
potassium and iron.

8 small onions, peeled and cut in half
1 red capsicum (pepper), cut into 16 squares
1 green capsicum (pepper), cut into 16 squares
2 zucchini (courgettes), each cut into 8 pieces
16 button mushrooms

marinade
1 tablespoon honey
2 tablespoons balsamic vinegar
2 teaspoons finely chopped fresh ginger
1 garlic clove, crushed
2 tablespoons lemon juice
2 tablespoons chopped fresh herbs, such as parsley, chives or rosemary

1. Soak some bamboo skewers in cold water for 15 minutes (so they won't burn on the barbecue).

2. Arrange the vegetables on the skewers.

3. Combine all ingredients for the marinade and brush over the vegetables. Barbecue the vegetable skewers for about 10 minutes, turning several times until cooked, and brushing with the remaining marinade.

HINT

Light meals are ideal for weekend lunches, but are also great on hot summer evenings when a heavy meal is unappetizing.

Lentil and carrot patties

SERVES 6
PREPARATION TIME: 5 minutes
COOKING TIME: 40 minutes

NUTRITIONAL
INFORMATION/SERVING:
12 g protein, 5 g fat (1 g
saturated fat), 29 g carbohydrate,
8 g dietary fibre, 115 mg sodium,
890 kJ (215 Cals)

A source of vitamins A, B1, B3,
C and E, and also potassium,
iron and zinc.

Tuck these vegetable patties inside a pitta bread with some salad, or serve with steamed vegetables or salad.

200 g (7 oz/1 cup) red lentils
2 bay leaves
500 ml (17 fl oz/2 cups) vegetable or chicken stock*
400 g (14 oz) carrots
1 tablespoon snipped chives
2 tablespoons chopped almonds
1 egg
2 slices of wholemeal (whole-wheat) bread, made into crumbs
1 teaspoon olive oil

sauce
400 g (14 oz) tin chopped tomatoes, no added salt
1 teaspoon dried oregano
1 garlic clove, crushed
60 ml (2 fl oz/¼ cup) red wine

* Use vegetable stock for a vegetarian meal.

1. Place the lentils, bay leaves and stock into a saucepan. Bring to the boil, cover and cook over low heat for 20 minutes.

2. While the lentils are cooking, grate the carrots (a food processor makes this easy) and then combine with the chives, almonds, egg and breadcrumbs.

3. Place all the sauce ingredients in a saucepan, bring to the boil and simmer, uncovered, for 10 minutes, stirring occasionally.

4. Combine the lentils and carrot mixture and form into six patties.

5. Heat a non-stick frying pan, add the oil and cook the patties over medium heat for 3–4 minutes on each side. Serve with the sauce.

HINT

The slicing and grating blades on a food processor make food preparation fast and easy.

Vegetables with crumble topping

This dish is an ideal way to use up small quantities of different vegetables.

2 teaspoons olive oil

1 onion, sliced

1 garlic clove

800 g (1 lb 12 oz/6 cups) diced vegetables, such as a combination of broccoli, cauliflower, zucchini (courgette), carrot, asparagus, whole button mushrooms, green beans

400 g (14 oz) tomato passata (puréed tomatoes) or tinned chopped tomatoes, no added salt

crumble topping

100 g (3½ oz/1 cup) rolled (porridge) oats

20 g (¾ oz) butter or margarine

45 g (1½ oz/½ cup) wheatgerm

1 tablespoon sunflower seeds, toasted

1 teaspoon dried basil

60 g (2¼ oz/½ cup) grated cheddar (7% fat)

1. Preheat oven to 180°C (350°F/Gas 4).

2. Heat the oil in a large saucepan over low heat, add the onion and garlic, cover and cook for 3–4 minutes.

3. Add the vegetables and tomato passata or chopped tomatoes. Bring to the boil, then reduce the heat and simmer for 3–4 minutes. Spoon into a casserole dish.

4. Put all the ingredients for the crumble topping in a food processor and process until large crumbs form. Sprinkle the crumble topping over the vegetables. Bake for 20–30 minutes until the crumble is golden and the vegetables are cooked.

SERVES 4

PREPARATION TIME: 20 minutes

COOKING TIME: 30–40 minutes

NUTRITIONAL INFORMATION/SERVING:
17 g protein, 9.5 g fat (4 g saturated fat), 27 g carbohydrate, 10 g dietary fibre, 135 mg sodium, 1090 kJ (260 Cals)

A source of vitamins A, B1, B2, B3, folate, C and E, and also potassium, magnesium, calcium, iron and zinc.

Couscous with roast sweet potato, capsicum and garlic

This wonderful combination of vegetables teams beautifully with the lemony, garlicky couscous. For a non-vegetarian option, you could add grilled skewered cubes of lamb. Preserved lemons are sold in specialist food stores, or substitute grated lemon zest.

2 teaspoons ground cinnamon

2 teaspoons ground cumin

1 tablespoon ground coriander

2 teaspoons dark brown sugar

1 teaspoon chilli flakes

2 teaspoons dried mint

600 g (1 lb 5 oz) orange sweet potato, peeled and cut into 1.5 cm ($^5/_8$ inch) cubes

1 teaspoon olive oil

1 red capsicum (pepper), cut into strips

1 green capsicum (pepper), cut into strips

6 garlic cloves, unpeeled

500 ml (17 fl oz/2 cups) vegetable or chicken stock*

185 g ($6^1/_2$ oz/1 cup) couscous

$^1/_2$ preserved lemon

1 handful coriander (cilantro) leaves

* Use vegetable stock for a vegetarian or vegan meal.

1. Place the cinnamon, cumin, coriander, sugar, chilli flakes and mint in a plastic bag, hold the top closed and shake to combine. Add the sweet potato and shake well to coat it with the spices and herbs.

2. Preheat oven to 180°C (350°F/Gas 4). Heat a shallow baking tin and then pour the oil into it, turning the tin to coat the base. Add the sweet potato mixture, capsicums and garlic cloves and bake for 20–30 minutes until cooked, turning the vegetables once.

3. Heat the stock to boiling point, put the couscous into a bowl and pour the hot stock over it. Cover tightly with foil and leave to stand for about 10 minutes for the couscous to absorb the liquid.

4. Remove and discard the flesh from the preserved lemon and rinse the skin under running water for 1–2 minutes. Chop into small pieces. Squeeze the garlic flesh from the cloves. Use a fork to lightly fold the lemon and garlic through the couscous. Top with the sweet potatoes and capsicums and scatter with coriander.

SERVES 4

PREPARATION TIME: 20 minutes

COOKING TIME: 30 minutes

NUTRITIONAL INFORMATION/SERVING:
8.5 g protein, 3 g fat (0.5 g saturated fat), 54 g carbohydrate, 7.5 g dietary fibre, 175 mg sodium, 1115 kJ (265 Cals)

A source of vitamins A, B1, B3, folate, C and E, and also potassium, magnesium, calcium, iron and zinc.

Rice pie with mushrooms

SERVES 6

PREPARATION TIME: 15 minutes

COOKING TIME: 40–50 minutes

NUTRITIONAL
INFORMATION/SERVING:
16 g protein, 8.5 g fat (2 g
saturated fat), 27 g carbohydrate,
3 g dietary fibre, 145 mg sodium,
1040 kJ (250 Cals)

A source of vitamins A, B1, B2,
B3 and C, and also potassium,
magnesium, calcium, iron and zinc.

A rice pie shell is easy to make and great for those who need a gluten-free alternative to regular pastry.

crust

2 tablespoons sesame seeds

370 g (13 oz/2 cups) cooked brown rice

1 egg, beaten

2 teaspoons dried parsley

filling

2 teaspoons olive oil

1 small onion, finely chopped

1 red capsicum (pepper), thinly sliced

250 g (9 oz) mushrooms, sliced

3 eggs

250 ml (9 fl oz/1 cup) evaporated skim milk

60 g (2¼ oz/½ cup) grated cheddar cheese (7% fat)

1 teaspoon paprika

1. Preheat oven to 180°C (350°F/Gas 4).

2. To make the crust, toast the sesame seeds in a dry frying pan over medium heat until golden brown. Combine the sesame seeds with the rice, egg and parsley and mix well. Press firmly into a greased 20 cm (8 inch) pie dish.

3. To make the filling, heat the oil in a frying pan and cook the onion over low heat for 3–4 minutes. Add the capsicum and mushrooms, cover the pan and cook for 5 minutes, stirring occasionally. Tip the vegetables into the pie shell.

4. Beat the eggs and milk together and pour over the vegetables. Sprinkle with the cheese and paprika and bake for 30–40 minutes, or until the egg has set.

Spicy chickpeas

Tinned chickpeas are a useful convenience product, but cook your own chickpeas from scratch if you prefer.

1 tablespoon olive oil
1 onion, finely chopped
2 teaspoons ground coriander
250 g (9 oz) button mushrooms, sliced
2 x 400 g (14 oz) tins chickpeas, drained and rinsed
185 ml (6 fl oz/¾ cup) dry white wine, vegetable stock or water
2 large tomatoes, skinned (see hint, page 154), or use 400 g (14 oz) tinned tomatoes, no added salt
2 tablespoons chopped coriander (cilantro) leaves or parsley

1. Heat the oil in a large saucepan, add the onion and gently cook for 3–4 minutes until golden brown. Add the ground coriander and freshly ground black pepper and stir to combine.

2. Add the mushrooms, chickpeas, wine and tomatoes. Bring to the boil, then reduce the heat and simmer, uncovered, for 10 minutes. Serve sprinkled with coriander leaves or parsley.

SERVES 4
PREPARATION TIME: 10 minutes
COOKING TIME: 15 minutes

NUTRITIONAL INFORMATION/SERVING:
13 g protein, 8 g fat (1 g saturated fat), 23 g carbohydrate, 10 g dietary fibre, 180 mg sodium, 910 kJ (220 Cals)

A source of vitamins A, B3, C and E, and also potassium, calcium, iron and zinc.

Zucchini frittata

Whip up a quick frittata using eggs and whatever vegetables you have on hand. The frittata is also delicious served cold for lunch with a green salad.

2 teaspoons olive oil
3 zucchini (courgettes), thinly sliced
125 g (4½ oz) button mushrooms, thinly sliced
2 cold, boiled potatoes or sweet potatoes, thinly sliced
2 tablespoons chopped herbs, such as parsley, thyme, oregano or chives
6 eggs

1. Heat the oil in a non-stick frying pan and cook the vegetables over medium heat for 4–5 minutes.

2. Sprinkle the herbs over the vegetables in the pan.

3. Beat the eggs with 3 tablespoons water and pour over the vegetables. Cook over low heat for 8–10 minutes until the egg sets, lifting the edges to allow any uncooked egg mixture to run underneath. Cut into quarters and serve.

SERVES 4
PREPARATION TIME: 15 minutes
COOKING TIME: 15 minutes

NUTRITIONAL INFORMATION/SERVING:
13 g protein, 10 g fat (2.5 g saturated fat), 12 g carbohydrate, 4.5 g dietary fibre, 105 mg sodium, 790 kJ (190 Cals)

A source of vitamins A, B1, B2, B3, B12 and C, and also potassium, iron and zinc.

Lentil burgers

SERVES 4
PREPARATION TIME: 15 minutes
COOKING TIME: 35 minutes

NUTRITIONAL
INFORMATION/SERVING:
27 g protein, 7.5 g fat (1.5 g
saturated fat), 66 g carbohydrate,
15 g dietary fibre, 610 mg sodium,
1830 kJ (435 Cals)

A source of vitamins A, B1, B2,
B3, C and E, and also potassium,
magnesium, calcium, iron and zinc.

These burgers are a great introduction to legumes and are popular with children. The lentil mixture is quite soft, so it may help to refrigerate the mixture for half an hour before shaping it into patties.

200 g (7 oz/1 cup) red lentils
1 onion, chopped
1 teaspoon chopped fresh ginger
45 g (1 1/2 oz/1/2 cup) wheatgerm
3 tablespoons chopped coriander (cilantro) leaves, mint or parsley
1 egg
2 tablespoons sesame seeds
4 flat wholemeal (whole-wheat) hamburger buns
125 g (4 1/2 oz/1/2 cup) natural yoghurt
2 tablespoons mango chutney
shredded lettuce, sliced tomato and beetroot

1. Place the lentils, 500 ml (17 fl oz/1 cup) water, onion and ginger in a saucepan and bring to the boil. Cover and simmer for 20–25 minutes. The lentils should be quite dry after this time, but check frequently to ensure they do not boil dry and burn — you may need to add another 60 ml (2 fl oz/1/4 cup) water. Set aside to cool.

2. Combine the wheatgerm, coriander and egg in a food processor. Blend well, then transfer to a bowl. Add the cooled lentil mixture and stir to combine. Form the mixture into four large patties and press the sesame seeds into the surface.

3. Cook the lentil patties in a non-stick frying pan over medium heat for 4–5 minutes on each side, or until brown.

4. Split and toast the buns. Combine the yoghurt and chutney and spread on the bottom half of the bun. Place a lentil patty on the bun, arrange the lettuce, tomato and beetroot on top, and finish with the remaining bun half.

Polenta with barbecued vegetables

Instant polenta saves time, and using stock instead of water to cook it adds flavour. Barbecue the vegetables for maximum flavour.

SERVES 4
PREPARATION TIME: 15 minutes
COOKING TIME: 30 minutes

NUTRITIONAL
INFORMATION/SERVING:
8.5 g protein, 4 g fat (0.5 g saturated fat), 51 g carbohydrate, 7 g dietary fibre, 60 mg sodium, 1155 kJ (275 Cals)

A source of vitamins A, B1, B3, folate, C and E, and also potassium, magnesium, iron and zinc.

750 ml (26 fl oz/3 cups) chicken or vegetable stock*
150 g (5$^{1}/_{2}$ oz/1 cup) instant polenta
2 teaspoons olive oil
1 onion, sliced
1 red or green capsicum (pepper), sliced
1 eggplant (aubergine), about 300 g (10$^{1}/_{2}$ oz),
    cut into 1 cm ($^{1}/_{2}$ inch) thick slices
2 zucchini (courgettes), sliced lengthways
2 orange sweet potatoes, peeled and sliced
olive oil spray

* Use vegetable stock for a vegetarian or vegan meal.

1. Place the stock into a saucepan and bring to the boil. Add the polenta in a steady stream, stirring constantly. Cook for 3 minutes, then pour into a 20 cm (8 inch) cake tin and leave to cool. Refrigerate until required.

2. Heat the oil in a frying pan and cook the onion over medium heat for 3–4 minutes. Add the capsicum and cook for another 5 minutes, stirring occasionally. Set aside.

3. Spray the eggplant, zucchini and sweet potato with olive oil. Heat a barbecue plate or chargrill pan and cook the vegetables until lightly browned on each side.

4. Turn the polenta out of the tin and cut into triangles. Barbecue the polenta until browned on both sides. Arrange the eggplant, zucchini and sweet potato on the polenta and top with the capsicum mixture.

HINT

There is no need to point out that a meal does not contain meat — and the chances are that when the food is delicious and interesting, the presence or absence of meat is irrelevant.

Vegetables with peanut sauce

This great summery salad has a little more fat than most recipes in this book, but it's good fat. Tamarind is sold as a ready-made purée from Asian food stores or in the Asian section of the supermarket.

peanut sauce
2 tablespoons vegetable stock
1 onion, finely chopped
2 garlic cloves, crushed
1 tablespoon tamarind purée
50 g (1¾ oz/⅓ cup) crushed peanuts
2 teaspoons reduced-salt soy sauce*
2 tablespoons lime or lemon juice
1 tablespoon crunchy peanut butter, no added salt
1 teaspoon chopped fresh ginger
1 teaspoon chopped chilli
125 ml (4 fl oz/½ cup) light coconut milk

2 large potatoes, peeled
2 carrots, cut into julienne strips
120 g (4¼ oz/2 cups) broccoli florets
400 g (14 oz/1 bunch) snake (yard-long) beans, cut into 6 cm (2½ inch) lengths
1 red capsicum (pepper), sliced
90 g (3¼ oz/2 cups) shredded Chinese cabbage (wong bok)
2 Lebanese (short) cucumbers
200 g (7 oz/3 cups) mung bean sprouts
3 hard-boiled eggs, shelled and cut in half

* For gluten-free, use wheat-free tamari.

1. To make the peanut sauce, put the stock in a saucepan, add the onion and garlic and gently cook for 3–4 minutes. Add the remaining sauce ingredients, bring to the boil, cover and simmer for 20 minutes, stirring occasionally, and adding a little water if necessary. While the sauce is cooking, prepare the vegetables.

2. Steam or microwave the potatoes until tender. Cut into thick slices and place in the centre of a large platter.

3. Individually steam the carrots, broccoli and beans until just tender. Immediately place in a colander and run cold water over the vegetables so they remain crisp. Drain and arrange on the platter.

4. Arrange the remaining vegetables and eggs on the platter. Drizzle the peanut sauce over the vegetables.

SERVES 6
PREPARATION TIME: 20 minutes
COOKING TIME: 30 minutes

NUTRITIONAL INFORMATION/SERVING:
14 g protein, 10 g fat (2.5 g saturated fat), 20 g carbohydrate, 9.5 g dietary fibre, 115 mg sodium, 945 kJ (225 Cals)

A source of vitamins A, B1, B2, B3, folate, C and E, and also potassium, magnesium, calcium, iron and zinc.

Falafel

Serve the falafel with salad, or if not cooking gluten-free, serve two to three falafel in a pitta bread with chopped tomato and shredded lettuce, topped with a dollop of tahini mixed with low-fat yoghurt.

300 g (10¹/₂ oz/1¹/₂ cups) dried chickpeas, or 640 g (1 lb 7 oz/4 cups) drained and rinsed tinned chickpeas
1 large onion
1 garlic clove
1 large handful parsley
1 large handful coriander (cilantro) leaves
1 teaspoon ground cumin
2 tablespoons lemon juice
1 egg

1. If using dried chickpeas, place the chickpeas and 1.5 litres (52 fl oz/6 cups) water into a large saucepan. Bring to the boil, then cover and cook for 1 minute. Turn off the heat and leave to stand for 1 hour. (If leaving for a longer period, place in the refrigerator.)

2. Bring the chickpeas back to the boil and then reduce the heat and simmer for about 40 minutes. Drain. Preheat oven to 180°C (350°F/Gas 4).

3. Chop the onion in a food processor. Add the remaining ingredients and chickpeas (if using tinned chickpeas, add them now) and process until well mixed.

4. Form the mixture into about 20 small balls. Place on a greased baking tray and bake for 20 minutes, turning the falafel balls once.

Falafel (front) and Tabouleh (back)

SERVES 6
PREPARATION TIME: 20 minutes
COOKING TIME: 1 hour
(or 20 minutes if using tinned chickpeas) + 1 hour standing time

NUTRITIONAL INFORMATION/SERVING:
12 g protein, 3.5 g fat (0.5 g saturated fat), 27 g carbohydrate, 9 g dietary fibre, 45 mg sodium, 780 kJ (185 Cals)

A source of vitamins A, B1, folate, C and E, and also potassium, magnesium, calcium, iron and zinc.

 HINT

If you are not used to eating pulses start with chickpeas, as their nutty flavour is usually popular.

Tabouleh

Tabouleh is delicious served with barbecued lamb fillets, or make it a complete meal without meat by adding toasted pine nuts.

SERVES 4
PREPARATION TIME: 30 minutes
COOKING TIME: nil

NUTRITIONAL
INFORMATION/SERVING:
7.5 g protein, 6 g fat (1 g
saturated fat), 31 g carbohydrate,
11 g dietary fibre, 35 mg sodium,
890 kJ (210 Cals)

A source of vitamins A, B1, B2, B3,
folate, C and E, and also potassium,
magnesium, calcium, iron and zinc.

175 g (6 oz/1 cup) burghul or bulgur
310 ml (10¾ fl oz/1¼ cups) boiling water
100 g (3½ oz/1 bunch) parsley, chopped
85 g (3 oz/1 bunch) mint, chopped
8 spring onions (scallions), sliced
1 tablespoon olive oil
60 ml (2 fl oz/¼ cup) lemon juice
500 g (1 lb 2 oz) tomatoes, diced

1. Place the burghul in a heatproof bowl, pour the boiling water over, cover and leave for 10 minutes until the water has been absorbed. If any moisture remains, use clean hands to squeeze the burghul.

2. Add the parsley, mint and spring onions and mix gently using a fork.

3. Combine the oil and lemon juice and season with freshly ground black pepper. Pour the dressing over the burghul. Just before serving, add the tomatoes and mix gently with a fork.

Fruity barley pilaf

This dish can be made with brown rice instead of the barley. Serve with a salad or vegetables, or as a side dish with barbecued fish, chicken or meat.

SERVES 4
PREPARATION TIME: 15 minutes
COOKING TIME: 1 hour
(or 35–40 minutes if using
brown rice)

NUTRITIONAL
INFORMATION/SERVING:
9 g protein, 11 g fat (1.5 g
saturated fat), 55 g carbohydrate,
9 g dietary fibre, 60 mg sodium,
1495 kJ (355 Cals)

A source of vitamins B1 and B3,
and also potassium, magnesium,
iron and zinc.

1 tablespoon olive oil
1 onion, chopped
280 g (10 oz/1½ cups) pearl barley
30 g (1 oz/¼ cup) raisins
35 g (1¼ oz/¼ cup) chopped dried apricots
10 cm (4 inch) cinnamon stick
1 teaspoon ground cardamom
810 ml (28 fl oz/3¼ cups) vegetable stock
2 tablespoons slivered almonds

1. Heat the oil in a saucepan and gently cook the onion until golden brown. Add the barley and stir for 3–4 minutes.

2. Add the raisins, apricots, cinnamon stick, cardamom and stock and bring to the boil. Cover and simmer for 1 hour, or until all the liquid has been absorbed and the barley is chewy-tender.

3. Place the almonds in a dry frying pan and toss gently over medium heat until golden brown. Sprinkle on top of the barley pilaf.

Ratatouille

Delicious served hot, or serve the ratatouille cold with crusty sourdough bread if you are not cooking gluten-free.

1 large eggplant (aubergine), sliced
olive oil spray
1 red capsicum (pepper), sliced
500 g (1 lb 2 oz) zucchini (courgettes), sliced
4 large tomatoes, sliced
1 handful basil, torn
2 garlic cloves, crushed

1. Preheat oven to 200°C (400°F/Gas 6).

2. Lightly spray the eggplant with olive oil and cook on a barbecue chargrill plate or chargrill pan until brown.

3. Spray an ovenproof dish with olive oil and place half the eggplant slices on the bottom. Cover with half the sliced capsicum, zucchini and tomato. Sprinkle with basil and dot with garlic. Repeat the layers and spray lightly with olive oil. Cover with foil and bake for 40 minutes, or until the vegetables are tender.

SERVES 4
PREPARATION TIME: 15 minutes
COOKING TIME: 55 minutes

NUTRITIONAL
INFORMATION/SERVING:
6 g protein, 2.5 g fat (0 g saturated fat), 12 g carbohydrate, 9 g dietary fibre, 20 mg sodium, 400 kJ (95 Cals)

A source of vitamins A, B1, B2, B3, folate and C, and also potassium, magnesium, calcium, iron and zinc.

SERVES 4
PREPARATION TIME: 10 minutes
COOKING TIME: 35 minutes

NUTRITIONAL
INFORMATION/SERVING:
13 g protein, 7 g fat (1.5 g
saturated fat), 63 g carbohydrate,
7.5 g dietary fibre, 105 mg sodium,
1525 kJ (365 Cals)

A source of vitamins A, B2, B3
and C, and also potassium, iron
and zinc.

Risotto with mushrooms, peas and sun-dried tomatoes

When making a risotto, use the best quality arborio rice you can find — the meal will still be comparatively inexpensive compared with a meal that contains meat.

4 bay leaves
7–8 saffron threads
1 litre (35 fl oz/4 cups) hot vegetable or chicken stock*
1 tablespoon olive oil
1 onion, finely chopped
250 g (9 oz) mushrooms, sliced
250 g (9 oz/1¼ cups) arborio rice
125 ml (4 fl oz/½ cup) white wine
50 g (1¾ oz/⅓ cup) sun-dried tomatoes, sliced
155 g (5½ oz/1 cup) frozen peas
1 tablespoon grated parmesan cheese

* Use vegetable stock for a vegetarian meal.

1. Put the bay leaves and saffron in a saucepan with the stock and bring to the boil. Cover and leave to simmer over low heat.

2. Heat the oil in a saucepan, add the onion and gently cook without browning for 3–4 minutes. Add the mushrooms and rice and stir for 3–4 minutes.

3. Add the wine to the rice and stir until it evaporates, then add 250 ml (9 fl oz/1 cup) of the stock and stir until the liquid has been absorbed. Continue adding the stock a cup at a time, adding the tomatoes with the third cup of stock and the peas with the final cup. Cook until all the stock has been absorbed.

4. Turn off the heat, stir in the cheese, cover and leave for 1 minute. Remove the bay leaves before serving.

SERVES 4
PREPARATION TIME: 10 minutes
COOKING TIME: 20 minutes

NUTRITIONAL
INFORMATION/SERVING:
7 g protein, 3.5 g fat (0.5 g
saturated fat), 12 g carbohydrate,
8.5 g dietary fibre, 115 mg sodium,
460 kJ (110 Cals)

A source of vitamins A, B1, B2,
folate, C and E, and also potassium,
calcium, iron and zinc.

Spinach and bean curry

Fill the kitchen with the aroma of roasting spices and make this simple, satisfying curry. For the best flavour, buy your spices whole and then grind them as you need them using a mortar and pestle.

2 teaspoons macadamia oil or olive oil
2 medium–large onions, peeled and cut into quarters
1 teaspoon ground cumin
1 teaspoon ground fenugreek
1 tablespoon ground coriander
1 teaspoon chopped fresh ginger
1 teaspoon chopped chilli
4 tomatoes, roughly chopped
400 g (14 oz) green beans, topped and tailed
250 g (9 oz) frozen spinach

1. Heat the oil in a saucepan and gently sauté the onion and spices for 4–5 minutes, stirring several times.

2. Add the tomatoes, beans, spinach and 185 ml (6 fl oz/¾ cup) water and bring to the boil. Cover and simmer for 10–15 minutes, stirring several times as the spinach defrosts. Serve with boiled rice and poppadoms.

Stuffed eggplant

This is a vegetarian dish that works well for anyone who loves eggplant. Serve it with a simple green salad.

2 eggplants (aubergines)
1 small red onion, finely diced
2 slices of wholegrain bread, made into crumbs
125 g (4^1/$_2$ oz/^{1}/$_2$ cup) low-fat ricotta cheese
2 eggs, separated
2 tablespoons grated parmesan cheese
2 teaspoons sesame seeds
2 teaspoons slivered almonds

1. Preheat oven to 180°C (350°F/Gas 4). Place the whole eggplants on the oven shelf, placing a baking tray on the shelf below, and bake for 20 minutes. Remove from the oven and, when cool enough to handle, cut in halves and carefully scoop out the flesh, leaving the shells about 5 mm (1/4 inch) thick. Chop the flesh finely.

2. Combine the eggplant flesh, onion, breadcrumbs, ricotta and egg yolks. Mix well.

3. Beat the egg whites until stiff and then fold into the eggplant mixture. Spoon the mixture into the eggplant shells.

4. Combine the cheese, sesame seeds and almonds and sprinkle over the top of the eggplant halves. Bake for 30 minutes until golden brown.

SERVES 4
PREPARATION TIME: 20 minutes
COOKING TIME: 50 minutes

NUTRITIONAL
INFORMATION/SERVING:
13 g protein, 9 g fat (3.5 g saturated fat), 13 g carbohydrate, 6 g dietary fibre, 240 mg sodium, 785 kJ (185 Cals)

A source of vitamins A, B1, B2, B3, B12 and C, and also potassium, calcium, iron and zinc.

Spinach pie

This spinach pie is delightfully light and perfect for a summer lunch. It is made using frozen spinach but if you prefer to use fresh spinach, use English spinach rather than the stronger tasting silverbeet.

4 sheets filo pastry
olive oil spray
250 g (9 oz) frozen English spinach, thawed
250 g (9 oz/1 cup) low-fat ricotta cheese
2 eggs
pinch of ground nutmeg
4 spring onions (scallions), sliced
3 large handfuls mint, chopped

1. Preheat oven to 180°C (350°F/Gas 4).

2. Place one sheet of filo pastry into a greased 20 cm (8 inch) quiche dish and spray lightly with olive oil. Repeat with the remaining three sheets of filo, rotating each filo sheet about 90 degrees and spraying lightly with oil between each sheet.

3. Combine the spinach, ricotta, eggs, nutmeg, spring onions and mint in a bowl. Spoon the mixture into the pastry shell. Turn the loose edges of the pastry over the spinach to cover it, then spray lightly with olive oil. Bake for 30 minutes, or until the filling is cooked and the pastry is light golden brown.

SERVES 4
PREPARATION TIME: 20 minutes
COOKING TIME: 30 minutes

NUTRITIONAL INFORMATION/SERVING:
13 g protein, 9 g fat (4.5 g saturated fat), 12 g carbohydrate, 3 g dietary fibre, 340 mg sodium, 800 kJ (190 Cals)

A source of vitamins A, B1, B2, folate, C and E, and also potassium, calcium and zinc.

✛ HINT

Filo pastry has very little fat, so is ideal for those following a low-fat diet.

SERVES 4
PREPARATION TIME: 15 minutes
COOKING TIME: 15 minutes

NUTRITIONAL
INFORMATION/SERVING:
23 g protein, 10 g fat (2.5 g
saturated fat), 37 g carbohydrate,
16 g dietary fibre, 200 mg sodium,
1450 kJ (345 Cals)

A source of vitamins A, B1, B2, B3,
folate, C and E, and also potassium,
magnesium, calcium, iron and zinc.

Tacos with spicy beans

Tacos are a popular meal and are easy to prepare, and children love them because they can be eaten with their fingers. However, if serving this for children, you may want to leave out the chilli.

2 teaspoons olive oil
1 large onion, finely chopped
1 garlic clove, crushed
1–2 teaspoons chopped chilli
800 g (1 lb 12 oz) tin tomatoes in tomato juice, no added salt
330 g (11½ oz/2 cups) rinsed and drained tinned red kidneys beans
2 tablespoons red wine vinegar
1 teaspoon dark brown sugar
8 taco shells
shredded lettuce, diced tomato, grated cheddar cheese (7% fat)* and
    natural yoghurt*, to serve

* Omit the cheese and yoghurt for a vegan meal.

1. Heat the oil in a saucepan or large frying pan and gently cook the onion, garlic and chilli for 3–4 minutes.

2. Add the tomatoes, kidney beans, vinegar and brown sugar. Bring to the boil, then reduce the heat and simmer, stirring frequently, for 10 minutes, or until the mixture has thickened.

3. Heat the taco shells in a 180°C (350°F/Gas 4) oven. To prevent them closing up while heating, hang them upside down over the rungs of the oven racks.

4. To serve, place a spoonful of bean mixture into each hot taco shell and top with shredded lettuce, tomato, grated cheese and a dollop of yoghurt.

Sweet potato and rocket frittata

Serve this dish hot or refrigerate to make an easy lunch the next day. It's also suitable to use between two slices of wholegrain bread, or serve with a green salad.

600 g (1 lb 5 oz) orange sweet potatoes, peeled and thinly sliced
2 large onions, thinly sliced
2 teaspoons olive oil
150 g (5½ oz/1 bunch) rocket (arugula), washed and sliced
4 eggs
2 egg whites

1. Steam the sweet potato and onion slices for about 5 minutes, or until just tender.

2. Heat a heavy-based frying pan, add the oil and swirl to coat the bottom of the pan with the oil. Arrange the sweet potato, onion and rocket in layers in the frying pan.

3. Beat the eggs and egg whites together and season with ½ teaspoon freshly ground black pepper. Pour the egg mixture over the vegetables in the pan and cook over low heat for 8–10 minutes, carefully lifting the mixture so any uncooked egg mixture can run underneath. When the eggs are almost set, place under a hot grill (broiler) to brown the top.

SERVES 4
PREPARATION TIME: 15 minutes
COOKING TIME: 15 minutes

NUTRITIONAL
INFORMATION/SERVING:
14 g protein, 7.5 g fat (2 g saturated fat), 27 g carbohydrate, 5.5 g dietary fibre, 150 mg sodium, 960 kJ (230 Cals)

A source of vitamins A, B1, B2, B3, B12, C and E, and also potassium, magnesium, calcium, iron and zinc.

Stir-fried tofu and vegetables

SERVES 4

PREPARATION TIME: 15 minutes

COOKING TIME: 10 minutes

NUTRITIONAL
INFORMATION/SERVING:
15 g protein, 9.5 g fat (1 g
saturated fat), 9 g carbohydrate,
6.5 g dietary fibre, 200 mg sodium,
755 kJ (180 Cals)

A source of vitamins A, B1,
B2, folate, C and E, and also
potassium, calcium, iron and zinc.

Tofu tends to be bland on its own but when teamed with flavoursome ingredients it's delicious and usually popular with small children because it's so easy to eat. Tofu is made from soya beans and is rich in protein.

2 tablespoons unsalted peanuts
2 teaspoons sesame oil
1 onion, cut into 8 wedges
2 garlic cloves, crushed
2 teaspoons chopped fresh ginger
400 g (14 oz/1 bunch) snake (yard-long) beans, cut into 6 cm (2½ inch) lengths
1 red capsicum (pepper), sliced
200 g (7 oz) button mushrooms, sliced
1 tablespoon oyster sauce*
125 ml (4 fl oz/½ cup) water or vegetable stock
300 g (10½ oz) firm tofu, cut into 2 cm (¾ inch) cubes
juice of 1 lime
coriander (cilantro) leaves, to serve

* Omit the oyster sauce for a gluten-free, vegetarian or vegan meal.

1. Heat a wok over medium heat, add the peanuts and toss them until they are beginning to brown. Tip the peanuts onto a plate and roughly chop.

2. Add the oil, onion, garlic and ginger to the wok and stir-fry for 2 minutes, then add the beans, capsicum and mushrooms and continue stir-frying for another 4–5 minutes.

3. Stir in the oyster sauce (if using), water or stock and tofu cubes and cook for 1–2 minutes. Remove from the heat and add the lime juice. Serve over steamed rice, sprinkled with the toasted peanuts and coriander.

Pumpkin and chive soufflés

Serve this easy soufflé with a tossed green salad and a good sourdough bread for a simple lunch.

SERVES 4
PREPARATION TIME: 15 minutes
COOKING TIME: 20–25 minutes

NUTRITIONAL
INFORMATION/SERVING:
9 g protein, 3 g fat (1 g
saturated fat), 15 g carbohydrate,
1.5 g dietary fibre, 145 mg sodium,
510 kJ (120 Cals)

A source of vitamins A, B1 and B12,
and also potassium and calcium.

3 tablespoons plain (all-purpose) flour
250 ml (9 fl oz/1 cup) skim milk
2 egg yolks
250 g (9 oz/1 cup) mashed butternut pumpkin (squash)
1 tablespoon dijon mustard
1 tablespoon snipped chives
3 egg whites

1. Preheat oven to 190°C (375°F/Gas 5).

2. Put the flour and a little of the milk in a saucepan and stir to make a paste. Gradually add the remaining milk. Cook over low heat until the mixture has thickened, stirring constantly.

3. Add the egg yolks to the milk mixture, one at a time, beating well after each addition. Stir in the pumpkin, mustard and chives.

4. Beat the egg whites until stiff. Fold a quarter of the egg whites into the pumpkin mixture, then gently fold in the remaining egg whites. Pour the mixture into four 250 ml (9 fl oz/1 cup) greased soufflé dishes and bake for 15–20 minutes, or until the soufflés are well risen and golden brown.

Beetroot risotto

This risotto is vibrantly coloured and flavoured by beetroot. Risottos are a great weeknight dish for when you haven't planned ahead, as you'll find you have most of the ingredients already in your pantry.

1 tablespoon olive oil
1 onion, finely chopped
250 g (9 oz/1¼ cups) arborio rice
1 tablespoon finely chopped rosemary
2 beetroot (beets), peeled and finely grated
125 ml (4 fl oz/½ cup) white wine
1 litre (35 fl oz/4 cups) hot vegetable or chicken stock*
1 tablespoon grated parmesan cheese
1 tablespoon slivered almonds, toasted

* Use vegetable stock for a vegetarian meal.

1. Heat the oil in a large saucepan over low heat and cook the onion, without browning, for 3–4 minutes. Add the rice and rosemary and stir for 1–2 minutes.

2. Add the beetroot and wine and stir until the wine evaporates. Pour about 250 ml (9 fl oz/1 cup) of the hot stock into the rice and stir until it is absorbed. Continue adding the stock a cup at a time, stirring after each addition, until the stock is all used.

3. Stir the parmesan into the risotto, turn off the heat, cover and leave to stand for 1 minute. Serve topped with almonds.

SERVES 4
PREPARATION TIME: 15 minutes
COOKING TIME: 35 minutes

NUTRITIONAL INFORMATION/SERVING:
8.5 g protein, 8.5 g fat (1.5 g saturated fat), 59 g carbohydrate, 4.5 g dietary fibre, 130 mg sodium, 1465 kJ (350 Cals)

A source of vitamins B3, folate and C, and also potassium, magnesium, iron and zinc.

SALADS AND VEGETABLES

The healthiest diets have lots of fresh and delicious vegetables. Once you get used to enjoying the great variety of vegetables available, you'll find you feel deprived if you have a day without them.

SERVES 4
PREPARATION TIME: 5 minutes
COOKING TIME: 10 minutes

NUTRITIONAL
INFORMATION/SERVING:
3.5 g protein, 5 g fat (0.5 g
saturated fat), 4.5 g carbohydrate,
4 g dietary fibre, 25 mg sodium,
320 kJ (75 Cals)

A source of vitamins A, B2, B3,
folate, C and E, and also potassium,
magnesium, iron and zinc.

Beans with spices and walnuts

Serve these luscious green beans hot or refrigerate any leftovers for lunch the following day.

1 tablespoon walnut pieces
500 g (1 lb 2 oz) green beans, topped and tailed
2 teaspoons walnut oil or olive oil
1 small onion, finely chopped
1 teaspoon hot mustard*
2 teaspoons paprika
2 tablespoons white wine vinegar

* Use mustard powder or check the mustard is gluten-free.

1. Toast the walnuts in a dry frying pan over medium heat until golden brown. Tip onto a plate and set aside.

2. Steam the beans for 3–4 minutes until just tender.

3. While the beans are cooking, heat the oil in a frying pan and cook the onion over low heat for 3–4 minutes. Add the mustard, paprika, vinegar and drained beans. Season with freshly ground black pepper. Toss gently and serve topped with the toasted walnuts.

Beetroot, sesame and horseradish salad

*Serve this salad with hummus and a gluten-free bread, or if you aren't cooking
a vegetarian meal, this is delicious with duck, kangaroo, lamb or beef. Use a food
processor to grate the beetroot.*

SERVES 4
PREPARATION TIME: 15 minutes
COOKING TIME: 10 minutes

NUTRITIONAL
INFORMATION/SERVING:
3 g protein, 3.5 g fat (0.5 g
saturated fat), 10 g carbohydrate,
4 g dietary fibre, 110 mg sodium,
345 kJ (80 Cals)

A source of vitamins folate and C,
and also potassium and iron.

1 teaspoon cumin seeds
2 teaspoons sesame seeds
2 teaspoons olive oil
1 small onion, finely chopped
1 garlic clove, crushed
3 beetroot (beets), peeled and grated
125 ml (4 fl oz/1/2 cup) red wine
2 teaspoons horseradish sauce*

* Check the horseradish sauce is gluten-free.

1. Heat a frying pan over medium heat and fry the cumin and sesame seeds for
   1–2 minutes, stirring constantly, until the sesame seeds are golden brown. Tip
   onto a plate and set aside.

2. Add the olive oil to the hot frying pan and cook the onion and garlic for about
   3 minutes over low heat, taking care that the onion does not brown. Add the
   beetroot and continue cooking, stirring constantly, for 3–4 minutes. Add the wine
   and simmer for 3 minutes, stirring occasionally. Stir in the horseradish and
   toasted seeds. Serve hot or cold.

 HINT

If you can't buy fresh
vegetables, frozen ones
are the next best thing.
Tinned vegetables also
retain many of their
vitamins, and nutrients
such as the antioxidant
lycopene are more easily
absorbed by the body from
tinned tomatoes than
fresh tomatoes.

SERVES 4
PREPARATION TIME: 20 minutes
COOKING TIME: 4 minutes

NUTRITIONAL
INFORMATION/SERVING:
10 g protein, 5.5 g fat (1 g
saturated fat), 11 g carbohydrate,
10 g dietary fibre, 15 mg sodium,
570 kJ (135 Cals)

A source of vitamins A, B1, B2, B3,
folate and C, and also potassium,
magnesium, calcium, iron and zinc.

Bean salad

Served with some crisp lettuce and sun-ripened tomatoes, this salad makes a perfect lunch or summer meal. If not preparing a gluten-free meal, you may like to serve with a chunk of wholemeal bread.

400 g (14 oz) green beans, topped and tailed, halved
200 g (7 oz/1/2 bunch) snake (yard-long) beans, cut into 6 cm (2 1/2 inch) lengths
160 g (5 1/2 oz/1 cup) rinsed and drained tinned red kidney beans
100 g (3 1/2 oz) button mushrooms, sliced
1 red capsicum (pepper), sliced
1 green capsicum (pepper), sliced
70 g (2 1/2 oz/1 cup) mung bean sprouts
2 large handfuls parsley, chopped

dressing
1 garlic clove, crushed
1 teaspoon crumbled dried rosemary
2 tablespoons lemon juice
1 tablespoon olive oil

1. Steam the green beans and snake beans for 3–4 minutes, or until just tender. Rinse immediately under cold water and drain.

2. Combine the beans with the remaining salad ingredients.

3. Combine all the dressing ingredients, season with freshly ground black pepper and pour over the salad. Leave to stand for at least 10 minutes before serving.

HINT

There is always some loss of vitamins when vegetables are cooked. Steaming is the best method, followed closely by microwaving, as long as the vegetables are cooked with minimum or no water and are not overcooked. If you must boil vegetables, use as little water as possible.

Carrot and hazelnut salad

Prepare this salad just before you are ready to serve it so the carrot stays fresh.

2 tablespoons chopped hazelnuts
500 g (1 lb 2 oz) carrots, peeled
4 spring onions (scallions), sliced
90 g (3¼ oz/1 cup) sunflower sprouts
1 tablespoon sunflower seeds
juice of 1 orange
1 tablespoon extra virgin olive oil

1. Toast the hazelnuts in a dry frying pan over medium heat until golden brown, taking care they do not burn. Remove from the pan and set aside.

2. Finely grate the carrots, preferably using a food processor. Toss lightly with the spring onions, sunflower sprouts, sunflower seeds and half the toasted hazelnuts.

3. Process the remaining hazelnuts, the orange juice and olive oil in a small blender. Pour over the salad and season with freshly ground black pepper.

SERVES 4
PREPARATION TIME: 15 minutes
COOKING TIME: 3 minutes

NUTRITIONAL INFORMATION/SERVING:
3.5 g protein, 10 g fat (1 g saturated fat), 10 g carbohydrate, 5.5 g dietary fibre, 60 mg sodium, 590 kJ (140 Cals)

A source of vitamins A, B1, B3, folate, C and E, and also potassium and iron.

Caramelized onions

The natural sugars in onions will caramelize with slow cooking. Cooked this way, onions make a delicious topping for baked potatoes. A food processor is useful to slice the onions thinly.

1 tablespoon olive oil
2 large onions, thinly sliced
1 teaspoon soft brown sugar
2 tablespoons balsamic vinegar

1. Heat the oil in a saucepan, add the onions and sugar, cover and leave to cook over low heat for 30 minutes, stirring occasionally. Add the balsamic vinegar and increase the heat, stirring constantly for 15 minutes, or until the onions are a rich brown colour.

SERVES 4
PREPARATION TIME: 10 minutes
COOKING TIME: 45 minutes

NUTRITIONAL INFORMATION/SERVING:
1.5 g protein, 5 g fat (0.5 g saturated fat), 5.5 g carbohydrate, 1.5 g dietary fibre, 10 mg sodium, 300 kJ (70 Cals)

A source of vitamin C.

Cabbage with chilli

This is a fresh accompaniment to steamed rice and barbecued fish or chicken. Cabbage is a highly nutritious vegetable and also contains some valuable anti-cancer compounds.

1 teaspoon olive oil
1 garlic clove, crushed
2 teaspoons thinly sliced lemon grass, white part only
1 teaspoon chopped fresh ginger
1 small chilli, seeded and thinly sliced
2 tablespoons vegetable or chicken stock*
400 g (14 oz/5⅓ cups) shredded cabbage
1 red capsicum (pepper), sliced
100 g (3½ oz) mushrooms, sliced
180 g (6 oz/2 cups) snow pea (mangetout) sprouts
1 tablespoon chopped mint

* Use vegetable stock for a vegetarian or vegan meal.

1. Heat the oil in a wok or large frying pan over low heat and cook the garlic, lemon grass, ginger and chilli for 2–3 minutes. Add the stock and bring to the boil.

2. Add the cabbage, capsicum and mushrooms to the pan and stir over medium heat for 4–5 minutes until hot.

3. Add the sprouts and mint and toss to combine. Serve at once.

SERVES 4
PREPARATION TIME: 5 minutes
COOKING TIME: 10 minutes

NUTRITIONAL INFORMATION/SERVING:
5 g protein, 1.5 g fat (0 g saturated fat), 6 g carbohydrate, 6.5 g dietary fibre, 30 mg sodium, 245 kJ (60 Cals)

A source of vitamins A, B2, B3, folate and C, and also potassium and iron.

 HINT

Prepare vegetables as close to mealtime as possible because oxygen in the air destroys some of the vitamins in the vegetables.

Greek-style vegetables

Consumption of vegetables in Greece is high, probably because the vegetables are cooked and served in flavoursome juices, which are mopped up with quality bread. Serve this dish hot or cold.

125 ml (4 fl oz/^{1}/2 cup) white wine
1 tablespoon extra virgin olive oil
2 garlic cloves, crushed
2 bay leaves
1 teaspoon dried thyme or 1 tablespoon chopped fresh thyme
2 rosemary sprigs
12 baby onions, peeled but left whole
6 baby eggplants (aubergines), halved lengthways
^{1}/2 fennel bulb, sliced
1 red capsicum (pepper), sliced
12 small zucchini (courgettes), larger ones halved lengthways
400 g (14 oz) green beans
200 g (7 oz) small mushrooms, left whole
2 tablespoons lemon juice

1. Place 125 ml (4 fl oz/^{1}/2 cup) water, the wine, oil, garlic, bay leaves, thyme and rosemary sprigs in a large frying pan or wok. Bring to the boil, then add the onions, cover and simmer for 10–15 minutes.

2. Add the remaining vegetables, cover and simmer for a further 10 minutes, or until the vegetables are tender. Remove the bay leaves and rosemary. Just before serving, sprinkle with the lemon juice. Serve hot or cold with crusty bread or a suitable bread if cooking gluten-free.

SERVES 4
PREPARATION TIME: 15 minutes
COOKING TIME: 20–25 minutes

NUTRITIONAL INFORMATION/SERVING:
10 g protein, 6.5 g fat (0.5 g saturated fat), 17 g carbohydrate, 13 g dietary fibre, 40 mg sodium, 690 kJ (165 Cals)

A source of vitamins A, B1, B2, B3, folate, C and E, and also potassium, magnesium, calcium, iron and zinc.

HINT

Lemon juice will make green vegetables lose their colour, so add it just before serving or at the table.

Mushroom salad with crunchy topping

SERVES 4

PREPARATION TIME: 15 minutes
+ 15 minutes refrigeration time

COOKING TIME: 10 minutes

NUTRITIONAL
INFORMATION/SERVING:
6 g protein, 5.5 g fat (1 g
saturated fat), 11 g carbohydrate,
4.5 g dietary fibre, 95 mg sodium,
505 kJ (120 Cals)

A source of vitamins A, B1, B2,
B3 and C, and also potassium.

Serve this salad for lunch or with barbecued meat. Mushrooms are a good source of many B group vitamins, so they complement other vegetables that provide betacarotene and vitamin C.

3 slices of wholemeal (whole-wheat) bread, crusts removed
1 tablespoon extra virgin olive oil
1 garlic clove, crushed
1 tablespoon chopped basil
1 tablespoon chopped parsley
60 ml (2 fl oz/¼ cup) lemon juice
1 teaspoon caster (superfine) sugar
1 teaspoon dijon mustard
400 g (14 oz) button mushrooms, sliced
1 red capsicum (pepper), thinly sliced

1. Preheat oven to 200°C (400°F/Gas 6). Cut the bread into 1 cm (½ inch) cubes and place on a baking tray. Bake for 5–10 minutes, or until the bread is crisp and golden. Allow to cool.

2. Mix together the oil, garlic, herbs, lemon juice, sugar and mustard in a bowl. Season with freshly ground black pepper. Add the mushrooms and toss gently. Refrigerate for at least 15 minutes.

3. When ready to serve, toss the mushroom mixture with the capsicum and sprinkle the bread cubes on top. Serve at once.

Broccolini with almonds

Broccolini is a cross between broccoli and Chinese broccoli (gai larn) and is similar in flavour to broccoli, although a little sweeter. The whole of the vegetable is eaten, including its long, slender stems.

400 g (14 oz/2 bunches) broccolini
125 ml (4 fl oz/$^1/_2$ cup) vegetable or chicken stock*
30 g (1 oz/$^1/_4$ cup) slivered almonds
1 garlic clove
2 teaspoons finely grated lemon zest

* Use vegetable stock for a vegetarian or vegan meal.

1. Steam the broccolini for 2–3 minutes until tender.

2. While the broccolini is cooking, heat the stock in a microwave or in a saucepan over low heat. Transfer to a small blender and process with the almonds, garlic and lemon zest. Season with freshly ground black pepper. Toss through the broccolini and serve at once.

SERVES 4
PREPARATION TIME: 5 minutes
COOKING TIME: 7 minutes

NUTRITIONAL
INFORMATION/SERVING:
5.5 g protein, 4.5 g fat (0.5 g saturated fat), 8 g carbohydrate, 2 g dietary fibre, 35 mg sodium, 380 kJ (90 Cals)

A source of vitamins A, B2, B3, folate, C and E, and also potassium, magnesium and iron.

 HINT

Instead of draining off the water used to cook your vegetables, keep the water (it contains vitamins) in the freezer to use later in stocks or soups.

SERVES 4
PREPARATION TIME: 15 minutes
COOKING TIME: 30 minutes

NUTRITIONAL
INFORMATION/SERVING:
6 g protein, 7.5 g fat (1 g
saturated fat), 11 g carbohydrate,
5.5 g dietary fibre, 25 mg sodium,
565 kJ (135 Cals)

A source of vitamins A, B1, B2, B3,
folate, C and E, and also potassium,
magnesium, iron and zinc.

Roasted red capsicum and tomato salad

This is a great salad to make when red capsicums and tomatoes are cheap, plentiful and full-flavoured. Serve this salad on its own as a first course, or with grilled fish, steak or chicken.

4 red capsicums (peppers)
1 tablespoon pine nuts
60 g (2¼ oz/2 cups) picked watercress
100 g (3½ oz/2 cups) baby English spinach
4 very ripe tomatoes, sliced
1 tablespoon extra virgin olive oil
1 tablespoon balsamic vinegar
1 tablespoon sliced basil

1. Preheat oven to 250°C (500°F/Gas 9). Place the capsicums on the oven shelf and put a baking tray on the shelf below to catch any juices. Bake for 30 minutes, or until the skin has blistered and blackened. Alternatively, hold the capsicums on a fork over a gas flame, turning so that the skin blisters and blackens.

2. Place the capsicums into a bowl, cover and leave until cool enough to handle. Peel off the capsicum skins, discard the skins and remove the seeds. (Do not wash the capsicum as this dilutes the flavour.) Slice into strips.

3. Toast the pine nuts in a dry frying pan over low–medium heat until golden brown. Remove from the pan and set aside.

4. Divide the watercress and spinach among individual serving dishes. Arrange the tomatoes and capsicum strips on top.

5. Combine the oil and vinegar and drizzle a little over each salad. Top with the basil and toasted pine nuts.

Broccoli sesame salad (back) and
Roasted red capsicum and tomato salad (front)

SERVES 4
PREPARATION TIME: 15 minutes
COOKING TIME: 10 minutes

NUTRITIONAL
INFORMATION/SERVING:
10 g protein, 7 g fat (0.5 g
saturated fat), 7 g carbohydrate,
10 g dietary fibre, 105 mg sodium,
470 kJ (110 Cals)

A source of vitamins A, B1, B2, B3,
folate, C and E, and also potassium,
magnesium, iron and zinc.

Broccoli sesame salad

This is an ideal salad to serve with grilled chicken, beef, lamb or fish. If desired, make the salad an hour or so before it is required and then drizzle over the dressing just before serving.

1 tablespoon sesame seeds
500 g (1 lb 2 oz) broccoli florets
100 g (3¹/₂ oz) snow peas (mangetout), trimmed
300 g (10¹/₂ oz) baby corn, halved lengthways
4 spring onions (scallions), sliced
2 teaspoons sesame oil
2 tablespoons lemon juice
1 teaspoon honey
2 teaspoons reduced-salt soy sauce*

* For gluten-free, use wheat-free tamari.

1. Toast the sesame seeds in a dry frying pan over medium heat, taking care that the seeds do not burn. Remove from the pan and set aside.

2. Steam the broccoli for 3–4 minutes. Rinse immediately under cold water and drain well. Steam the snow peas for 1–2 minutes. Rinse under cold water and drain.

3. Place the broccoli, snow peas, baby corn and spring onions in a serving dish and toss together.

4. Combine the sesame oil, lemon juice, honey and soy sauce. Drizzle over the salad and sprinkle with the toasted sesame seeds.

HINT

Broccoli is a potent source
of sulphoraphane, one
of the first anti-cancer
compounds isolated
from vegetables.

Mushrooms with lemon

Mushrooms are a great accompaniment to barbecued or grilled fish, chicken or lamb. This makes a great picnic dish — cook it at home and carry in an airtight container.

2 teaspoons olive oil
1 red onion, thinly sliced
1 garlic clove, crushed
1 teaspoon chopped chilli
2 tablespoons lemon juice
2 teaspoons finely grated lemon zest
125 ml (4 fl oz/$\frac{1}{2}$ cup) vegetable or chicken stock*
500 g (1 lb 2 oz) baby mushrooms
1 tablespoon snipped chives

* Use vegetable stock for a vegetarian or vegan meal.

1. Heat the oil in a frying pan and cook the onion, garlic and chilli over low heat for 3–4 minutes.

2. Add the lemon juice, zest, stock and mushrooms. Cover and simmer for 5 minutes, or until the mushrooms are tender. Sprinkle with chives and serve hot or cold.

SERVES 4
PREPARATION TIME: 5 minutes
COOKING TIME: 10 minutes

NUTRITIONAL INFORMATION/SERVING:
5.5 g protein, 3 g fat (0.5 g saturated fat), 4.5 g carbohydrate, 4 g dietary fibre, 20 mg sodium, 275 kJ (65 Cals)

A source of vitamins A, B2, B3 and C, and also potassium.

 HINT

Never use bicarbonate of soda (baking soda) to make vegetables look brightly coloured. It destroys their vitamins and imparts an unpleasant flavour.

Snow peas and mushrooms with ginger

This is a simple way to enhance the flavour of vegetables. The garlic is not crushed but only lightly smashed with the side of a knife so as not to be too overwhelming. Serve with steamed rice.

1 garlic clove
185 ml (6 fl oz/¾ cup) vegetable or chicken stock*
2 teaspoons thinly sliced fresh ginger
300 g (10½ oz) snow peas (mangetout), trimmed
150 g (5½ oz) mushrooms, sliced
6 spring onions (scallions), sliced
2 tablespoons dry sherry
2 teaspoons reduced-salt soy sauce**

* Use vegetable stock for a vegetarian or vegan meal.
** For gluten-free, use wheat-free tamari.

1. Lightly smash the garlic using the flat side of a knife. Put the stock and smashed garlic clove in a saucepan. Bring to the boil and cook until the liquid has reduced to 60 ml (2 fl oz/¼ cup). Remove the garlic clove.

2. Place the reduced stock, ginger, vegetables and sherry in a wok or large frying pan. Stir-fry for 3–4 minutes, tossing frequently, then add the soy sauce. Serve with steamed rice.

SERVES 4
PREPARATION TIME: 5 minutes
COOKING TIME: 10 minutes

NUTRITIONAL
INFORMATION/SERVING:
6.5 g protein, 0.5 g fat (0 g saturated fat), 8.5 g carbohydrate, 6 g dietary fibre, 90 mg sodium, 315 kJ (75 Cals)

A source of vitamins A, B1, B2, B3 and C, and also potassium and iron.

Stir-fried brussels sprouts with almonds

When handled and cooked correctly, brussels sprouts are a wonderful vegetable, far from the overcooked, sulphurous-smelling specimens of childhood memories. When buying sprouts, choose smaller green sprouts as these tend to be sweetest, and avoid any with signs of yellowing — these will have a less than pleasant taste.

SERVES 4
PREPARATION TIME: 5 minutes
COOKING TIME: 10 minutes

NUTRITIONAL INFORMATION/SERVING:
6 g protein, 4.5 g fat (0.5 g saturated fat), 4.5 g carbohydrate, 5.5 g dietary fibre, 40 mg sodium, 350 kJ (85 Cals)

A source of vitamins B1, B2, B3, folate, C and E, and also potassium and iron.

1 tablespoon flaked almonds
1 teaspoon olive oil
1 teaspoon sesame oil
1 garlic clove
1 small onion, sliced
500 g (1 lb 2 oz) brussels sprouts, trimmed and sliced lengthways into 4 or 5 pieces
2 tablespoons orange juice

1. Toast the almonds in a dry frying pan over medium heat, taking care not to burn them. Tip them onto a plate to cool.

2. Add the olive and sesame oils to the pan, then add the garlic and onion and cook for 2–3 minutes.

3. Add the brussels sprouts and orange juice and stir-fry for 3–4 minutes, or until just tender. Sprinkle with the almonds and serve at once.

Potatoes Anna

This recipe traditionally uses cream and butter and is very high in fat, but this low-fat version also tastes good. Use a food processor to slice the potatoes and onions.

SERVES 4
PREPARATION TIME: 20 minutes
COOKING TIME: 45 minutes

NUTRITIONAL INFORMATION/SERVING:
11 g protein, 1 g fat (0 g saturated fat), 32 g carbohydrate, 4 g dietary fibre, 100 mg sodium, 780 kJ (185 Cals)

A source of vitamins B1, B2, B3 and C, and also potassium, magnesium, calcium, iron and zinc.

1 large garlic clove, cut in half
olive oil spray
4 potatoes, peeled and very thinly sliced
2 onions, thinly sliced
1 tablespoon finely grated orange zest
310 ml (10¾ fl oz/1¼ cups) evaporated skim milk
ground nutmeg

1. Preheat oven to 180°C (350°F/Gas 4). Rub the inside of a casserole dish with the cut garlic. Discard the garlic and lightly spray inside the dish with olive oil.

2. Layer the potatoes and onions into the dish, sprinkling each layer with a little of the orange zest and plenty of freshly ground black pepper.

3. Pour the milk over the potato and onions and bake for 45 minutes, or until the potatoes are tender. Sprinkle with nutmeg and serve hot.

Potato and pumpkin bake

This dish is traditionally made with butter, but this low-fat version tastes good too.

125 ml (4 fl oz/1/2 cup) white wine or stock*
400 g (14 oz) butternut pumpkin (squash), peeled and cut into chunks
400 g (14 oz) potatoes, peeled and cut into chunks
2 green apples, peeled, cored and sliced
125 g (41/2 oz/1/2 cup) non-fat natural yoghurt
pinch of ground nutmeg
2 egg whites
1 tablespoon chopped mint

* Use vegetable stock for a vegetarian meal.

1. Place the wine, pumpkin, potatoes and apples into a saucepan, cover and cook over medium heat for 15 minutes, or until the vegetables and apples are tender.

2. Preheat oven to 180°C (350°F/Gas 4).

3. Mash the vegetables and apple, adding the yoghurt and nutmeg and seasoning with freshly ground black pepper.

4. Beat the egg whites until stiff, then gently fold the egg whites into the vegetables along with the mint. Pour into a greased ovenproof dish and bake for 15 minutes.

SERVES 4
PREPARATION TIME: 10 minutes
COOKING TIME: 30 minutes

NUTRITIONAL
INFORMATION/SERVING:
9 g protein, 1 g fat (0.5 g saturated fat), 35 g carbohydrate, 5 g dietary fibre, 65 mg sodium, 770 kJ (185 Cals)

A source of vitamins A, B1, B2, B3 and C, and also potassium, magnesium, calcium and iron.

Coleslaw with herbed honey dressing

SERVES 4
PREPARATION TIME: 15 minutes
COOKING TIME: nil

NUTRITIONAL
INFORMATION/SERVING:
2.5 g protein, 7 g fat (1 g
saturated fat), 12 g carbohydrate,
5.5 g dietary fibre, 50 mg sodium,
505 kJ (120 Cals)

A source of vitamins B3, folate,
C and E, and also potassium.

This is not the typical coleslaw we are most familiar with, heavily laden with thick dressing, but a lighter, less fattening version. Many ready-made coleslaw dressings are also high in salt, but this one tastes great without any salt.

dressing
1 orange
2 teaspoons honey
1 tablespoon macadamia oil or extra virgin olive oil
1 tablespoon thyme leaves

salad
450 g (1 lb/6 cups) finely shredded savoy cabbage
1 apple, thinly sliced
125 g (4½ oz/1 cup) thinly sliced celery
1 tablespoon chopped pecans

1. To make the dressing, finely grate the zest from the orange and then squeeze its juice. Combine the zest and juice with the honey, oil and thyme.

2. Combine the cabbage, apple, celery and dressing and toss well. Just before serving, add the pecans.

HINT

Raw vegetables are an excellent substitute for cooked vegetables as they have higher levels of many vitamins. There is no reason why children should not have plain raw vegetables on their plates at the table.

Red cabbage with apple

This dish is delicious served hot or cold and goes especially well with pork dishes.

SERVES 4

PREPARATION TIME: 10 minutes

COOKING TIME: 20 minutes

NUTRITIONAL INFORMATION/SERVING:
4 g protein, 4 g fat (0.5 g saturated fat), 13 g carbohydrate, 7 g dietary fibre, 30 mg sodium, 420 kJ (100 Cals)

A source of vitamins B1, B2, B3, folate, C and E, and also potassium and iron.

2 teaspoons olive oil
1 small onion
1/2 small red cabbage, shredded
1 apple, peeled, cored and sliced
125 ml (4 fl oz/1/2 cup) apple juice
1/2 teaspoon caraway seeds
2 teaspoons sesame seeds, toasted

1. Heat the oil in a frying pan or wok, add the onion and cook over low heat for 2–3 minutes, without browning.

2. Add the cabbage, apple, apple juice and caraway seeds, then cover and cook for 15 minutes. Remove the lid and continue cooking until the liquid has evaporated. Serve hot or refrigerate until needed. Just before serving, sprinkle the sesame seeds on top.

Pineapple, carrot and raisin salad

This is an easy salad that is usually popular with children. Use a food processor to grate the carrot finely.

SERVES 4

PREPARATION TIME: 15 minutes

COOKING TIME: nil

NUTRITIONAL INFORMATION/SERVING:
3.5 g protein, 3 g fat (0.5 g saturated fat), 43 g carbohydrate, 7.5 g dietary fibre, 80 mg sodium, 880 kJ (210 Cals)

A source of vitamins A, B1, B3 and C, and also potassium, magnesium, calcium, iron and zinc.

125 g (41/2 oz/1 cup) raisins
450 g (1 lb) tin pineapple pieces in juice, drained
4 carrots, peeled and finely grated
2 tablespoons sunflower seeds
1 tablespoon honey
2 tablespoons lemon juice
2 tablespoons chopped mint

1. Combine the raisins, pineapple, carrot and sunflower seeds. Mix well.

2. Combine the honey, lemon juice and mint to make a dressing. Add to the salad and toss lightly. Serve at once.

Spaghetti squash

This amazing vegetable is just like crunchy spaghetti. Use it in place of spaghetti or as a vegetable.

1 spaghetti squash (about 1 kg/2 lb 4 oz)
1 tablespoon flaked almonds
2 teaspoons olive oil
1 onion, sliced
1 red capsicum (pepper), thinly sliced
1 garlic clove
1 large handful basil

1. Steam the whole squash for about 25 minutes, or until tender when pierced with a skewer. Allow to cool for 5–10 minutes.

2. While the squash is cooking, toast the almonds in a dry frying pan over low heat, tossing to prevent them burning. Tip onto a plate to cool.

3. Heat the oil in a frying pan and cook the onion, capsicum and garlic over low heat for about 5 minutes.

4. Cut the cooled squash in half lengthways and remove the seeds. Using a fork, pull the 'spaghetti' strands of the squash from the sides and add to the frying pan. Add the basil and season with freshly ground black pepper and toss gently. Serve at once.

SERVES 4
PREPARATION TIME: 5 minutes
COOKING TIME: 30 minutes

NUTRITIONAL INFORMATION/SERVING:
3 g protein, 5 g fat (0.5 g saturated fat), 11 g carbohydrate, 7.5 g dietary fibre, 35 mg sodium, 430 kJ (105 Cals)

A source of vitamins A, B1, B3 and C, and also potassium and iron.

Tomato and bread salad

This salad is similar to the panzanella served in Italy. You need to use bread such as an Italian-style wood-fired bread or sourdough for this recipe.

800 g (1 lb 12 oz) ripe tomatoes
2 Lebanese (short) cucumbers
200 g (7 oz) Italian-style bread, cut into 2.5 cm (1 inch) cubes
2 tablespoons finely snipped chives
1 large handful basil, torn

dressing
1 garlic clove, cut in half
1 tablespoon extra virgin olive oil
2 tablespoons balsamic vinegar
2 tablespoons orange juice

1. Quarter the tomatoes and squeeze out the seeds (it doesn't matter if a few remain). Dice the tomatoes.

2. Cut the cucumbers in half lengthways and scoop out the seeds. Dice the cucumber flesh into small pieces and combine with the tomato, bread cubes, chives and basil.

3. To make the dressing, combine all the ingredients in a screw-top jar and shake well. Remove the garlic and then pour the dressing over the tomato mixture. Toss well and set aside for 5 minutes before serving, so that the bread soaks up the dressing.

SERVES 4
PREPARATION TIME: 20 minutes + 5 minutes standing time
COOKING TIME: nil

NUTRITIONAL INFORMATION/SERVING:
7 g protein, 6.5 g fat (1 g saturated fat), 30 g carbohydrate, 5 g dietary fibre, 250 mg sodium, 870 kJ (210 Cals)

A source of vitamins A, B1, B2, B3, folate, C and E, and also potassium, magnesium, calcium, iron and zinc.

SERVES 4
PREPARATION TIME: 15 minutes
COOKING TIME: 15 minutes

NUTRITIONAL
INFORMATION/SERVING:
6.5 g protein, 0.5 g fat (0 g
saturated fat), 24 g carbohydrate,
3.5 g dietary fibre, 110 mg sodium,
635 kJ (150 Cals)

A source of vitamins B1, B2, B3 and
C, and also potassium, magnesium,
calcium and iron.

HINT

Vegetables are ideal for
those watching their
weight as they are
nutrient-dense but have
few kilojoules.

Potato salad

*Potato salad is often drowned in unhealthy mayonnaise. This one is lighter in fat,
thanks to the low-fat yoghurt, but is still high in flavour.*

500 g (1 lb 2 oz) small new potatoes, unpeeled
125 ml (4 fl oz/½ cup) white wine
250 g (9 oz/1 cup) low-fat natural yoghurt
2 teaspoons dijon mustard*
2 tablespoons lemon juice
1 tablespoon snipped chives
1 tablespoon chopped mint
1 tablespoon chopped parsley
paprika, to serve

* Check the mustard is gluten-free.

1. Steam the potatoes for 15 minutes, or until just cooked. While the potatoes are
   hot, cut in half, place into a bowl and pour the wine over them. Cover and leave
   until cool.

2. Combine the yoghurt, mustard and lemon juice. Add to the potatoes, along with
   the chives, mint and parsley. Toss well and sprinkle with paprika.

Oven-baked spicy potato wedges

Baking potato wedges in the oven is a much healthier alternative to deep-frying them in oil.

1 teaspoon sumac
1 tablespoon paprika
2 teaspoons ground cumin
2 tablespoons dried parsley
750 g (1 lb 10 oz) potatoes, preferably king edward or pontiac, peeled and cut into wedges
olive oil spray

1. Preheat oven to 220°C (425°F/Gas 7). Spread a sheet of baking paper on a flat baking tray.

2. Place the sumac, paprika, cumin, parsley and 1/4 teaspoon freshly ground black pepper into a plastic bag. Add the potato wedges, hold the neck of the bag tight and shake to coat the potatoes with the spices.

3. Arrange the potatoes in a single layer on the baking paper. Spray lightly with olive oil and bake for 25 minutes, or until the potato wedges are golden brown.

SERVES 4
PREPARATION TIME: 10 minutes
COOKING TIME: 25 minutes

NUTRITIONAL INFORMATION/SERVING:
4 g protein, 1.5 g fat (0 g saturated fat), 32 g carbohydrate, 5.5 g dietary fibre, 15 mg sodium, 630 kJ (150 Cals)

A source of vitamins A, B1, B3 and C, and also potassium, magnesium and iron.

Zucchini in tomato

Smaller zucchini are sweeter and more flavoursome than the larger ones. Choose small bulb spring onions too, if possible.

185 ml (6 fl oz/3/4 cup) white wine or stock*
400 g (14 oz) tin chopped tomatoes in tomato juice, no added salt
1 tablespoon finely grated lemon zest
1 teaspoon coriander seeds
40 g (1 1/2 oz/1/3 cup) raisins
250 g (9 oz) bulb spring onions (scallions), trimmed but left whole
600 g (1 lb 5 oz) small zucchini (courgettes)

* Use vegetable stock for a vegetarian or vegan meal.

1. Combine the wine, tomatoes, lemon zest and coriander seeds in a frying pan or wok. Bring to the boil, then reduce the heat, cover and simmer for 5 minutes.

2 Add the raisins, bulb spring onions and zucchini, cover and simmer gently for 10 minutes.

SERVES 4
PREPARATION TIME: 5 minutes
COOKING TIME: 20 minutes

NUTRITIONAL INFORMATION/SERVING:
3.5 g protein, 1 g fat (0 g saturated fat), 17 g carbohydrate, 5.5 g dietary fibre, 30 mg sodium, 380 kJ (90 Cals)

A source of vitamins A, B2, B3 and C, and also potassium, magnesium and iron.

Pumpkin salad with seeds

You get the best flavour from the pumpkin if you barbecue the pumpkin slices, but a large frying pan or chargrill pan can be used instead.

SERVES 4
PREPARATION TIME: 15 minutes
COOKING TIME: 10 minutes

NUTRITIONAL
INFORMATION/SERVING:
7 g protein, 10 g fat (2 g
saturated fat), 16 g carbohydrate,
5 g dietary fibre, 15 mg sodium,
760 kJ (180 Cals)

A source of vitamins A, B1, B2,
B3, C and E, and also potassium,
magnesium, calcium, iron and zinc.

750 g (1 lb 10 oz) butternut pumpkin (squash), peeled, seeded and
    cut into thin slices
olive oil spray
200 g (7 oz/4 cups) baby English spinach

dressing
2 tablespoons sesame seeds
1 tablespoon sunflower seeds
1 tablespoon olive oil
2 tablespoons cider vinegar
1 teaspoon honey

1. Spray the pumpkin slices with olive oil and then barbecue on the grill plate for 4–5 minutes, turning once.

2. Place some of the English spinach on a platter. Overlap the cooked pumpkin slices on top of the spinach, then scatter with the remaining spinach.

3. To make the dressing, toast the sesame and sunflower seeds in a dry frying pan over low heat until golden brown, taking care they do not burn. Remove from the pan.

4. Combine the oil, vinegar and honey and stir until well blended. Add the toasted sesame and sunflower seeds, stir well and drizzle over the pumpkin.

Braised leeks

SERVES 4

PREPARATION TIME: 5 minutes

COOKING TIME: 15 minutes

NUTRITIONAL
INFORMATION/SERVING:
2.5 g protein, 5.5 g fat (1 g
saturated fat), 5.5 g carbohydrate,
3 g dietary fibre, 30 mg sodium,
325 kJ (80 Cals)

A source of vitamins A, B3 and C,
and also potassium.

These leeks are wonderful served hot or cold. Try to find small leeks, as they will be more tender and sweeter than the larger ones.

250 ml (9 fl oz/1 cup) vegetable or chicken stock*
4 small leeks, washed thoroughly
2 bay leaves
a few thyme sprigs
1 tablespoon extra virgin olive oil
1 tablespoon white wine vinegar
1 teaspoon soft brown sugar
1 tablespoon chopped parsley

* Use vegetable stock for a vegetarian or vegan meal.

1. Put the stock in a large frying pan and bring to the boil. Continue to boil, uncovered, until reduced by half.

2. Put the leeks in the pan, arranging them in a single layer. Add the remaining ingredients, except the parsley. Bring to the boil, cover tightly, then reduce the heat to low and simmer for 10 minutes. Remove the bay leaves and thyme sprigs. Sprinkle with parsley and serve hot or cold.

Italian-style fennel

SERVES 4

PREPARATION TIME: 5 minutes

COOKING TIME: 20 minutes

NUTRITIONAL
INFORMATION/SERVING:
3.5 g protein, 2.5 g fat (0.5 g
saturated fat), 11 g carbohydrate,
7 g dietary fibre, 80 mg sodium,
355 kJ (85 Cals)

A source of vitamins A, B3 and C,
and also potassium and iron.

Fennel is a great accompaniment to grilled or barbecued fish, beef or chicken. If preferred, substitute whole baby zucchini or baby eggplant for the fennel.

2 teaspoons olive oil
1 onion, finely chopped
1 garlic clove, crushed
400 g (14 oz) tin tomatoes in tomato juice, no added salt
2 large fennel bulbs, cut lengthways into quarters
1 teaspoon dried basil
2 bay leaves
2 tablespoons chopped parsley

1. Heat the oil in a frying pan and cook the onion and garlic over low heat for 2–3 minutes until the onion has softened.

2. Add the tomatoes, fennel, basil and bay leaves, cover and simmer for 15 minutes. Remove the bay leaves and sprinkle with parsley. Serve hot or cold.

Celeriac with honey dressing

Although it bears little physical resemblance to its celery relative, this knobby winter vegetable has a wonderfully subtle celery-like flavour. Once the root has been peeled and cut, it will quickly turn brown, so toss the celeriac with lemon juice to prevent this happening.

1 celeriac bulb (about 450 g/1 lb)
2 tablespoons lemon juice
300 g (10½ oz) mixed lettuce leaves
250 g (9 oz) cherry tomatoes

dressing
2 tablespoons orange juice
2 teaspoons honey
1 teaspoon dijon mustard*
1 teaspoon finely grated orange zest
1 tablespoon tarragon vinegar
1 tablespoon olive oil

* Check the mustard is gluten-free.

1. Peel the celeriac and cut into fine strips. Toss the celeriac with lemon juice to prevent it going brown.

2. Combine all the dressing ingredients and pour over the celeriac.

3. Line a shallow bowl with lettuce leaves, pile the celeriac in the centre and decorate with cherry tomatoes.

SERVES 4
PREPARATION TIME: 15 minutes
COOKING TIME: nil

NUTRITIONAL
INFORMATION/SERVING:
3 g protein, 5.5 g fat (0.5 g saturated fat), 12 g carbohydrate, 7.5 g dietary fibre, 60 mg sodium, 455 kJ (110 Cals)

A source of vitamins A, B1, B2, B3 and C, and also potassium, magnesium, iron and zinc.

Green papaya salad

We usually think of papaya as an orange fruit, but the unripe form is delicious to use as a vegetable. Green papaya is available from Asian greengrocers and some supermarkets. Use a food processor blade for easy grating.

2 tablespoons unsalted peanuts
1 small green papaya, peeled and grated
1 small red onion, thinly sliced
1 carrot, grated
100 g (3½ oz) snow peas (mangetout), trimmed
1 red capsicum (pepper), thinly sliced
1 handful mint
1 handful coriander (cilantro) sprigs
1 handful purple Thai basil (or use green basil)

dressing
1 teaspoon grated palm sugar (jaggery) or soft brown sugar
finely grated zest and juice of 2 limes
1 teaspoon fish sauce*
1 teaspoon chopped chilli

* Omit the fish sauce if vegetarian.

1. Toast the peanuts in a dry frying pan over medium heat until golden brown. Remove from the pan and set aside. When cool, roughly chop the peanuts.

2. Combine the papaya, onion, carrot, snow peas, capsicum and herbs in a serving bowl. Gently toss together.

3. Combine all the ingredients for the dressing and pour over the salad. Toss well and serve topped with the toasted peanuts.

SERVES 4
PREPARATION TIME: 15 minutes
COOKING TIME: 2 minutes

NUTRITIONAL INFORMATION/SERVING:
5 g protein, 3.5 g fat (0.5 g saturated fat), 15 g carbohydrate, 6.5 g dietary fibre, 120 mg sodium, 460 kJ (110 Cals)

A source of vitamins A, B1, B2, B3 and C, and also potassium, magnesium, calcium, iron and zinc.

PASTA AND NOODLES

Pasta is part of life for most busy people. It's versatile and popular — and healthy, providing it's not drowned in a rich sauce or piled with an excess of cheese. For gluten-free recipes in this chapter, substitute gluten-free pasta.

Creamy pasta with fennel and spinach

SERVES 4
PREPARATION TIME: 10 minutes
COOKING TIME: 20 minutes

NUTRITIONAL
INFORMATION/SERVING:
20 g protein, 8 g fat (4 g
saturated fat), 72 g carbohydrate,
8.5 g dietary fibre, 190 mg sodium,
1880 kJ (450 Cals)

A source of vitamins A, B1, B2,
B3 and C, and also potassium,
magnesium, calcium, iron and zinc.

This is an easy and fresh-flavoured vegetarian meal to whip up quickly.

375 g (13 oz) pasta, such as spiralli or penne
2 teaspoons olive oil
2 garlic cloves, crushed
1 small fennel bulb, thinly sliced
250 g (9 oz) frozen spinach
250 g (9 oz/1 cup) low-fat ricotta cheese
finely grated zest of 1 lemon

1. Cook the pasta in a large saucepan of boiling water until just tender.

2. While the pasta is cooking, heat the oil in a frying pan and stir-fry the garlic
   and fennel over medium heat for 4–5 minutes. Add the spinach and stir until
   the spinach has defrosted and is hot. Remove from the heat and stir in the ricotta
   and lemon zest.

3. When the pasta is cooked, drain quickly so that it retains some of the cooking
   water, and return to the saucepan. Stir in the spinach mixture and toss gently
   to combine.

HINT

For a quick and easy pasta
meal, add broccoli or
cauliflower florets to the
pasta for the last few
minutes of cooking. Drain
and toss with freshly
ground black pepper and
parmesan cheese.

Pasta vegetable bake

This vegetable bake combines a great variety of vegetables. When buying tinned tomatoes, look for tomatoes with no added salt. Serve this delicious bake with a tossed green salad for a casual weekend lunch.

375 g (13 oz) penne pasta
2 teaspoons olive oil
1 onion, finely chopped
1 teaspoon dried oregano
1 small eggplant (aubergine), peeled and cut into 2 cm (3/4 inch) dice
2 zucchini (courgettes), grated
1 red capsicum (pepper), sliced
400 g (14 oz) tin chopped tomatoes
2 eggs, beaten
olive oil spray
50 g (1 3/4 oz/1/2 cup) dry breadcrumbs
25 g (1 oz/1/4 cup) grated parmesan cheese
1 tablespoon wholegrain mustard

1. Cook the pasta in a large saucepan of boiling water until just tender, then drain.

2. Heat the oil in a frying pan and cook the onion and oregano over medium heat for 2 minutes. Add the eggplant, zucchini, capsicum and tomatoes, bring to the boil and cook for 10 minutes, or until the eggplant is soft.

3. Combine the pasta, vegetable mixture and eggs in a large bowl.

4. Preheat oven to 180°C (350°F/Gas 4). Spray a 20 cm (8 inch) round cake tin with olive oil and sprinkle half the breadcrumbs over the base of the tin. Spoon the pasta mixture into the tin and press down well. Bake for 30–35 minutes. Allow to stand for 5 minutes, then turn out onto an ovenproof plate.

5. Combine the remaining breadcrumbs, cheese and mustard and spread over the top of the pasta bake. Place under a hot grill (broiler) for 1 minute, or until the top is golden brown.

SERVES 6
PREPARATION TIME: 20 minutes
COOKING TIME: 50 minutes
+ 5 minutes standing time

NUTRITIONAL
INFORMATION/SERVING:
14 g protein, 6 g fat (2 g saturated fat), 55 g carbohydrate, 6 g dietary fibre, 225 mg sodium (or 185 mg if using no added salt tomatoes), 1405 kJ (335 Cals)

A source of vitamins A, B1, B2, B3 and C, and also potassium, calcium, iron and zinc.

Creamy salmon pasta

Salmon is a rich source of omega 3 fatty acids and these are still present in tinned salmon. This is a great low-fat way to get a creamy sauce without using cream.

SERVES 4

PREPARATION TIME: 15 minutes

COOKING TIME: 15 minutes

NUTRITIONAL
INFORMATION/SERVING:
30 g protein, 6 g fat (1.5 g
saturated fat), 77 g carbohydrate,
7.5 g dietary fibre, 350 mg sodium,
2040 kJ (485 Cals)

A source of vitamins A, B2, B3,
B12 and C, and also potassium,
magnesium, calcium, iron, zinc
and iodine.

375 g (13 oz) pasta, such as spirals, shells or fettucine
125 ml (4 fl oz/$\frac{1}{2}$ cup) chicken stock
6 spring onions (scallions), sliced
250 g (9 oz) mushrooms, sliced
1 red capsicum (pepper), sliced
1 large handful basil, chopped
210 g (7$\frac{1}{2}$ oz) tin salmon, drained
250 ml (9 fl oz/1 cup) low-fat evaporated milk
1 tablespoon grated parmesan cheese

1. Cook the pasta in a large saucepan of boiling water until just tender. Drain.

2. While the pasta is cooking, heat the stock in a saucepan and add the spring onions, mushrooms and capsicum. Cook for 2 minutes, tossing gently.

3. Add the basil, salmon, evaporated milk and cheese and season with freshly ground black pepper.

4. Add the mushroom sauce to the drained pasta and toss to combine. Serve at once, with a tossed green salad.

HINT

Instead of cream in a pasta sauce, use low-fat evaporated milk. It's not quite as good as the real thing, but it's a reasonable second best and saves 35 grams of fat for every 100 ml.

Pasta with tomato and mushroom sauce

SERVES 4

PREPARATION TIME: 10 minutes

COOKING TIME: 30 minutes

NUTRITIONAL
INFORMATION/SERVING:
19 g protein, 5.5 g fat (1.5 g
saturated fat), 75 g carbohydrate,
11 g dietary fibre, 150 mg sodium
(or 105 mg if using no added salt
tomato paste), 1800 kJ (430 Cals)

A source of vitamins A, B1, B2, B3,
B6, C and E, and also potassium,
magnesium, calcium, iron and zinc.

This sauce freezes well, so you might like to make double quantities and freeze half for another time.

> 375 g (13 oz) spaghetti
> 2 teaspoons olive oil
> 1 large onion, thinly sliced
> 2 garlic cloves, crushed
> 1 kg (2 lb 4 oz) very ripe tomatoes, peeled
> 250 ml (9 fl oz/1 cup) red wine
> 2 tablespoons tomato paste (concentrated purée)*
> 1 teaspoon dried oregano
> 1 teaspoon dried basil
> 300 g (10½ oz) mushrooms, sliced
> 2 tablespoons finely grated parmesan cheese
> torn basil leaves

> ** If watching your salt intake, use tomato paste with no added salt.*

1. Cook the spaghetti in a large saucepan of boiling water until tender.

2. While the pasta is cooking, heat the oil in a saucepan and cook the onion and garlic over medium heat for 5 minutes, without browning.

3. Add the tomatoes, wine, tomato paste and dried herbs. Bring to the boil, cover and simmer for 10 minutes.

4. Add the mushrooms, stir well and cook for a further 5 minutes.

5. Drain the pasta. Serve the sauce over the hot pasta and sprinkle with parmesan cheese and basil.

HINT

To peel tomatoes, remove the core and cut a small cross in the end of each tomato. Place in a heatproof bowl, cover with boiling water, leave for 1 minute and drain. Transfer to a bowl of cold water, then peel off the skins.

Pasta with chicken and spring vegetables

A pasta such as penne is best for this dish as its hollow tubular shape will pick up and hold the sauce. A spiral pasta such as fusilli or pasta shells would also work well. If cooking a vegetarian meal, simply omit the chicken.

250 g (9 oz) penne or spiral pasta
2 teaspoons olive oil
6 spring onions (scallions), sliced
1 small chilli, thinly sliced (optional)
400 g (14 oz/2 bunches) asparagus, cut into 4 cm (1½ inch) pieces
150 g (5½ oz) snow peas (mangetout), trimmed
150 g (5½ oz) shredded cooked chicken
185 ml (6 fl oz/¾ cup) white wine or vegetable stock
250 g (9 oz/1 cup) low-fat ricotta cheese
2 teaspoons dijon mustard
2 tablespoons lemon juice
2 tablespoons finely chopped parsley

1. Cook the pasta in a large saucepan of boiling water until just tender. Drain.

2. While the pasta is cooking, heat the oil in a saucepan and cook the spring onions, chilli (if using) and asparagus over medium heat for 2 minutes. Add the snow peas, chicken and wine, bring to the boil, then reduce the heat and simmer for 2 minutes.

3. Remove from the heat and stir in the ricotta, mustard and lemon juice. Return to the heat and stir until the sauce is hot, but do not let it boil. Serve over the hot pasta and sprinkle with parsley.

SERVES 4
PREPARATION TIME: 10 minutes
COOKING TIME: 20 minutes

NUTRITIONAL INFORMATION/SERVING:
30 g protein, 10 g fat (4.5 g saturated fat), 52 g carbohydrate, 7.5 g dietary fibre, 200 mg sodium, 1790 kJ (430 Cals)

A source of vitamins A, B1, B2, B3, B12, C and E, and also potassium, magnesium, calcium, iron and zinc.

 HINT

Cook pasta only until it is *al dente* (literally 'to the tooth') so that it creates a lower glycaemic load within the body. This means it will be digested slowly and will provide energy over a longer period compared with pasta that is cooked until it is soggy.

Start testing pasta by tasting a piece 2 minutes before the stated cooking time. Cooking times for different types and brands of pasta can vary, so follow the cooking times given on the packet.

Prawn and citrus pasta

Fresh citrus flavours make this a great summer dish for either lunch or dinner, and the vegetables give an added bonus of lots of vitamins and antioxidants.

375 g (13 oz) pasta
400 g (14 oz/1 bunch) snake (yard-long) beans, cut into 3–4 cm (1¼–1½ inch)
    lengths, or 300 g (10½ oz) green beans, topped and tailed
2 teaspoons olive oil
500 g (1 lb 2 oz) raw prawns (shrimp), peeled and deveined
200 g (7 oz/1 bunch) asparagus, cut into 3–4 cm (1¼–1½ inch) lengths
1 red capsicum (pepper), sliced
250 ml (9 fl oz/1 cup) orange juice
2 tablespoons lemon juice
2 oranges, peeled and divided into segments
1 tablespoon lemon thyme or chopped parsley

1. Cook the pasta in a large saucepan of boiling water until just tender.

2. While the pasta is cooking, steam the beans for 3–4 minutes.

3. Heat the oil in a wok or frying pan and gently stir-fry the prawns for 2 minutes, or until the prawns start to turn pink. Add the beans, asparagus, capsicum and orange and lemon juice and bring to the boil. Simmer, uncovered, for 2 minutes. Add the orange segments and lemon thyme.

4. Drain the pasta, add the sauce and toss lightly. Serve at once.

SERVES 4
PREPARATION TIME: 20 minutes
COOKING TIME: 20 minutes

NUTRITIONAL INFORMATION/SERVING:
28 g protein, 4 g fat (0.5 g saturated fat), 80 g carbohydrate, 9.5 g dietary fibre, 220 mg sodium, 2000 kJ (480 Cals)

A source of vitamins A, B1, B2, B3, B12 and C, and also potassium, magnesium, calcium, iron, zinc and iodine.

 HINT

When draining pasta, leave a little water clinging to the hot pasta, as this helps the sauce cling to the pasta.

Pasta with pesto and sun-dried tomatoes

SERVES 4
PREPARATION TIME: 10 minutes
COOKING TIME: 15 minutes

NUTRITIONAL
INFORMATION/SERVING:
17 g protein, 17 g fat (3 g
saturated fat), 79 g carbohydrate,
9.5 g dietary fibre, 95 mg sodium,
2270 kJ (540 Cals)

A source of vitamins A, B1, B2,
B3 and C, and also potassium,
magnesium, calcium, iron and zinc.

Although this dish has more fat than most recipes in this book, it's 'good' fat and there is much less of it than in more traditional pestos. The parmesan is sprinkled on at the end, rather than being blended in with the rest of the pesto ingredients, where the flavour can get a bit lost.

375 g (13 oz) pasta
100 g (3¹/₂ oz/²/₃ cup) sun-dried tomatoes, sliced
120 g (4¹/₄ oz/1 bunch) basil, leaves picked to give 60 g (2¹/₄ oz)
2 garlic cloves
2 tablespoons lemon juice
2 tablespoons olive oil
2 tablespoons pine nuts
2 tablespoons grated parmesan cheese

1. Cook the pasta in a large saucepan of boiling water. When the pasta is almost cooked, add the sun-dried tomatoes.

2. While the pasta is cooking, place the basil, garlic, lemon juice, olive oil and pine nuts in a food processor or blender and blend well.

3. When the pasta is cooked, drain quickly so that it retains some of the cooking water, and return to the saucepan. Stir in the pesto mixture and serve in heated bowls. Top with grated parmesan.

HINT

Buy dried tomatoes from the vegetable section of the supermarket rather than those bottled in oil. To reconstitute dried tomatoes, place them in a small bowl, cover with boiling water and leave for 15 minutes. Drain and reserve the liquid to use in soups or sauces.

Tuna lasagne

This lasagne takes much less time to prepare than most lasagnes — great for when time is limited. If desired, assemble the lasagne, then cover and refrigerate for up to 24 hours before baking.

10 spring onions (scallions), sliced
1 garlic clove, crushed
800 g (1 lb 12 oz) tin chopped tomatoes in tomato juice
1 tablespoon tomato paste (concentrated purée), no added salt
2 tablespoons chopped parsley
425 g (15 oz) tin tuna in spring water
2 tablespoons plain (all-purpose) flour
500 ml (17 fl oz/2 cups) skim milk
2 eggs, beaten
pinch of ground nutmeg
12 instant lasagne sheets
1 tablespoon grated parmesan cheese
60 g (2¼ oz/½ cup) grated low-fat cheese
1 teaspoon paprika

1. Combine the spring onions, garlic, tomatoes, tomato paste and parsley in a bowl and season with freshly ground black pepper. Gently mix in the tuna.

2. Blend the flour with a little of the milk in a saucepan to make a paste, then add the remaining milk. Stir over low heat for 3–4 minutes until thick. Add the beaten eggs and nutmeg.

3. Preheat oven to 180°C (350°F/Gas 4). Grease a shallow 40 x 20 cm (16 x 8 inch) rectangular casserole or ovenproof dish.

4. Dip the lasagne sheets in hot water for 1 minute, then spread four sheets over the base of the dish. Top with half the tuna mixture. Repeat these layers (dipping the lasagne sheets in hot water for each layer) and top with the remaining lasagne. Pour the sauce over the top. Sprinkle with the combined cheeses and paprika and bake for 30–40 minutes, or until the lasagne is golden brown and cooked through.

SERVES 6
PREPARATION TIME: 20 minutes
COOKING TIME: 35–45 minutes

NUTRITIONAL
INFORMATION/SERVING:
29 g protein, 4 g fat (1.5 g saturated fat), 37 g carbohydrate, 4.5 g dietary fibre, 270 mg sodium, 1290 kJ (310 Cals)

A source of vitamins A, B1, B2, B3, B12 and C, and also potassium, magnesium, calcium, iron, zinc and iodine.

Spinach lasagne

SERVES 6
PREPARATION TIME: 15 minutes
COOKING TIME: 45 minutes

NUTRITIONAL
INFORMATION/SERVING:
18 g protein, 9.5 g fat (5.5 g
saturated fat), 23 g carbohydrate,
5.5 g dietary fibre, 275 mg sodium,
1050 kJ (250 Cals)

A source of vitamins A, B1, B2,
B3, C and E, and also potassium,
magnesium, calcium, iron and zinc.

This lasagne doesn't take long to assemble and is a wonderful option if cooking a vegetarian meal. Frozen vegetables, such as spinach or peas, still retain all their nutritional value, so are a great standby when your fresh vegetable stores are running low or you have little time.

2 teaspoons olive oil
1 large onion, thinly sliced
2 garlic cloves, crushed
250 g (9 oz) mushrooms, sliced
2 x 250 g (9 oz) packets frozen spinach (or use 800 g/1 lb 12 oz fresh
    English spinach)
7½ instant lasagne sheets
500 g (1 lb 2 oz/2 cups) low-fat ricotta cheese
2 tablespoons grated parmesan cheese

1. Heat the oil in a frying pan and gently cook the onion and garlic for 3–4 minutes, without browning. Add the mushrooms and continue cooking for 3–4 minutes. Stir in the spinach and cook until the spinach has thawed and is hot.

2. Preheat oven to 180°C (350°F/Gas 4). Grease a shallow 24 x 18 cm (9½ x 7 inch) ovenproof dish.

3. Dip two and a half lasagne sheets in hot water for 1 minute, then place on the bottom of the dish. Cover with half the spinach mixture and dot one-third of the ricotta on top. Repeat, then top with the remaining two and a half lasagne sheets, finishing with a layer of ricotta. Sprinkle with parmesan and bake for 30 minutes.

HINT

Frozen vegetables can
be stored for up to
six months.

Rice noodles with tofu, chilli and cashews

SERVES 4
PREPARATION TIME: 10 minutes
COOKING TIME: 15 minutes

NUTRITIONAL
INFORMATION/SERVING:
11 g protein, 8.5 g fat (1 g
saturated fat), 40 g carbohydrate,
6 g dietary fibre, 80 mg sodium,
1150 kJ (275 Cals)

A source of vitamins A, B1, B3 and
C, and also potassium, magnesium
and iron.

Fresh rice noodles are available in most supermarkets and are delivered daily to Asian supermarkets. You can buy them precut into thin or thick widths or as a slab, which you will need to slice yourself. This recipe is a good way to introduce the family to tofu.

2 tablespoons cashew nuts
400 g (14 oz) fresh rice noodles
2 teaspoons sesame oil
1 onion, thinly sliced
1 garlic clove, crushed
1 teaspoon finely chopped red chilli
200 g (7 oz) snow peas (mangetout), trimmed
100 g (3½ oz/2 cups) baby English spinach
300 g (10½ oz) firm tofu, cut into 2 cm (¾ inch) cubes
finely grated zest and juice of 1 lime
1 handful coriander (cilantro) leaves

1. Put the cashews in a dry frying pan and toss gently over medium heat until they brown slightly. Tip onto a plate to cool.

2. Put the rice noodles in a bowl and cover with boiling water. Leave to soak for 3 minutes, or follow the directions on the packet, then drain.

3. Heat the sesame oil in a wok over medium heat and stir-fry the onion, garlic and chilli for 3–4 minutes. Add the snow peas and spinach and continue stir-frying for another 3 minutes. Add the tofu and toss until heated through.

4. Drain the noodles and add to the wok, along with the lime zest and juice. Toss the noodles to coat with the sauce. Serve at once, topped with the coriander and toasted cashews.

Thai-style noodles

If cooking gluten-free, make sure you choose rice noodles. This recipe works equally well with hokkien (egg) noodles, but these contain wheat. Check different brands of light coconut milk as their fat content varies a lot. Choose one with less than 6 grams of fat per 100 grams.

300 g (10½ oz) fresh rice noodles
2 teaspoons sesame oil
1–2 tablespoons Thai curry paste*
1 onion, thinly sliced
300 g (10½ oz) boneless, skinless chicken breasts, sliced into strips
1 carrot, cut into thin strips
250 ml (9 fl oz/1 cup) stock or water
180 g (6 oz/4 cups) shredded Chinese cabbage (wong bok)
juice of 1 lime
125 ml (4 fl oz/½ cup) light coconut milk
200 g (7 oz/3 cups) mung bean sprouts
1 handful coriander (cilantro) leaves

* Check the curry paste is gluten-free.

1. Put the rice noodles in a bowl and cover with boiling water. Leave to soak for 3 minutes, or follow the directions on the packet, then drain.

2. Meanwhile, heat the oil in a wok over medium heat and stir-fry the curry paste, onion and chicken for 5 minutes. Add the carrot and stock and cook for a further 3–4 minutes.

3. Add the noodles to the wok, along with the cabbage, lime juice and coconut milk. Bring to the boil and cook for 1 minute.

4. Divide the bean sprouts among four bowls and top with the noodle mixture and coriander. Serve at once.

SERVES 4
PREPARATION TIME: 15 minutes
COOKING TIME: 10 minutes

NUTRITIONAL INFORMATION/SERVING:
23 g protein, 8.5 g fat (2 g saturated fat), 29 g carbohydrate, 4.5 g dietary fibre, 220 mg sodium, 1165 kJ (280 Cals)

A source of vitamins A, B1, B2, B3 and C, and also potassium, magnesium and iron.

Rice noodles with veal

This is a useful gluten-free recipe for weeknight dinners. Vary it by using different vegetables or substituting chicken, fish or prawns for the veal.

250 g (9 oz) fresh rice noodles
2 teaspoons sesame oil
1 tablespoon thinly sliced lemon grass, white part only
1 large onion, sliced
1 teaspoon finely chopped chilli
1 garlic clove, crushed
2 teaspoons thinly sliced fresh ginger
400 g (14 oz) lean veal steak, cut into strips
250 ml (9 fl oz/1 cup) white wine or stock*
1 red capsicum (pepper), sliced
300 g (10½ oz) broccoli, cut into florets
250 g (9 oz) green beans, sliced
3 baby bok choy (pak choy), sliced
2 teaspoons pure cornflour (cornstarch)**
2 tablespoons water
1 handful coriander (cilantro) leaves

* Check the stock is gluten-free or use wine.
** Check the cornflour is gluten-free.

1. Put the rice noodles in a bowl and cover with boiling water. Leave to soak for 3 minutes, or follow the directions on the packet, then drain.

2. Heat the oil in a large wok or frying pan, add the lemon grass, onion, chilli, garlic and ginger and stir-fry for 2–3 minutes over low heat.

3. Increase the heat to medium, add the veal and stir-fry for 3–4 minutes.

4. Add the wine and stir well to dislodge any bits from the base of the wok. Add the capsicum, broccoli, beans and bok choy, cover and simmer for 3–4 minutes.

5. Add the noodles and toss well to heat through. Combine the cornflour with the water and stir until smooth. Add the cornflour paste to the wok and cook for 1 minute. Remove from the wok and serve sprinkled with coriander.

SERVES 4
PREPARATION TIME: 15 minutes
COOKING TIME: 15 minutes

NUTRITIONAL INFORMATION/SERVING:
31 g protein, 6 g fat (1 g saturated fat), 27 g carbohydrate, 7.5 g dietary fibre, 160 mg sodium, 1185 kJ (285 Cals)

A source of vitamins A, B1, B2, B3, B12 and C, and also potassium, magnesium, calcium, iron and zinc.

Pasta with rocket, rosemary and lemon

This is a simple weeknight meal, ideal in summer.

SERVES 4
PREPARATION TIME: 10 minutes
COOKING TIME: 20 minutes

NUTRITIONAL
INFORMATION/SERVING:
14 g protein, 11 g fat (1.5 g
saturated fat), 70 g carbohydrate,
7.5 g dietary fibre, 90 mg sodium,
1835 kJ (440 Cals)

A source of vitamins A, B3, C
and E, and also potassium,
magnesium, calcium and iron.

375 g (13 oz) pasta
2 teaspoons olive oil
2 garlic cloves
2 tablespoons finely chopped rosemary
125 ml (4 fl oz/1/2 cup) vegetable stock or white wine
300 g (101/2 oz) rocket (arugula) leaves
grated zest and juice of 1 lemon

1. Cook the pasta in a large saucepan of boiling water.

2. When the pasta is almost cooked, heat the oil in a small saucepan over medium heat and stir-fry the garlic and rosemary for 2 minutes. Add the stock and bring to the boil.

3. Just before draining the pasta, add the rocket to the water and boil for 30 seconds. Drain the pasta and rocket and stir in the lemon zest, lemon juice, rosemary mixture and some freshly ground black pepper. Serve at once.

HINT

Don't add oil to the
water when cooking pasta
or the sauce won't stick
to the pasta.

Spaghetti bolognese

This is a great way to get some vegetables into those reluctant to eat them. The red wine adds flavour to the sauce and its alcohol will evaporate, so this dish is fine for children. If preferred, use stock or water.

400 g (14 oz) lean minced (ground) beef
1 onion, chopped
1 tablespoon paprika
2 teaspoons dried oregano
250 ml (9 fl oz/1 cup) red wine
400 g (14 oz) tin tomatoes in tomato juice
1 large carrot, grated
2 zucchini (courgettes), grated
1 small eggplant (aubergine), peeled and cut into 1.5 cm ($^5/_8$ inch) dice
375 g (13 oz) spaghetti
2 tablespoons finely grated parmesan cheese

1. Cook the beef and onion in a large wok or frying pan for 15 minutes, or until the meat browns.

2. Add the paprika and oregano and cook for a further 2–3 minutes, stirring well.

3. Add the wine, tomatoes, carrot, zucchini and eggplant. Bring to the boil, then cover and simmer for 40 minutes, stirring occasionally.

4. Cook the spaghetti in a large saucepan of boiling water until tender. Drain and serve topped with the bolognese sauce and grated parmesan.

SERVES 4
PREPARATION TIME: 15 minutes
COOKING TIME: 1 hour

NUTRITIONAL INFORMATION/SERVING:
37 g protein, 7.5 g fat (3 g saturated fat), 77 g carbohydrate, 11 g dietary fibre, 220 mg sodium, 2200 kJ (525 Cals)

A source of vitamins A, B1, B2, B3, B12 and C, and also potassium, magnesium, calcium, iron and zinc.

SEAFOOD DISHES

Seafood is a valuable source of omega 3 fats — the very best of the best. The world's seafood stocks are running low and there are no nutritional advantages to eating excessive amounts of seafood. We can get all the health benefits by including seafood in just two meals a week.

Carpaccio of salmon

Ask your fishmonger for a thick piece of salmon suitable to serve raw, and use your sharpest knife when slicing it.

SERVES 4

PREPARATION TIME: 10 minutes
+ 30 minutes freezing time

COOKING TIME: nil

NUTRITIONAL
INFORMATION/SERVING:
16 g protein, 4.5 g fat (1 g
saturated fat), 1 g carbohydrate,
1.5 g dietary fibre, 60 mg sodium,
465 kJ (110 Cals)

A source of vitamins A, B1,
B2, B3, B12 and C, and also
potassium and iodine.

300 g (10½ oz) piece of fresh salmon, skin removed
200 g (7 oz) mesclun salad mix
2 teaspoons olive oil
1 teaspoon finely grated lemon zest
2 tablespoons lemon juice
½ teaspoon wasabi paste (optional)
1 tablespoon thinly sliced basil leaves

1. Use tweezers to remove any bones from the salmon. Cover the salmon and place in the freezer for 30 minutes. Remove and slice the salmon as thinly as possible.

2. Arrange the mesclun leaves on serving plates. Top with the salmon slices and sprinkle with plenty of coarsely ground black pepper.

3. Combine the oil, lemon zest, lemon juice and wasabi (if using) and drizzle over the salmon. Sprinkle with the basil.

HINT

Before cooking or eating salmon fillets, you need to check if there are any bones. Run your fingers over each fillet to locate the bones, then remove them with either your fingers or using a pair of tweezers.

Barbecued octopus

Octopus is easy to cook but to prevent it becoming tough, make sure the octopus is fresh and do not overcook it. When barbecuing octopus or shellfish, the barbecue plate must be very hot. If you are cooking a lot of seafood, cook it in batches so the hotplate isn't too crowded and the temperature remains high.

600 g (1 lb 5 oz) baby octopus
1 tablespoon olive oil
125 ml (4 fl oz/¹/₂ cup) red wine
2 garlic cloves, crushed
1 teaspoon honey
2 teaspoons dried oregano

1. Remove the heads from the octopus and cut out the small 'beak' in the centre of the tentacles. Cut each octopus in half.

2. Combine the remaining ingredients in a shallow dish. Add the octopus, turn to coat in the marinade, then cover and refrigerate for at least 30 minutes.

3. Heat the barbecue hotplate to very hot. Remove the octopus from the marinade and cook for 6–8 minutes, brushing with the marinade several times. The octopus will turn red and curl up slightly. Serve with salad and plenty of crusty bread or a suitable gluten-free bread.

SERVES 4

PREPARATION TIME: 15 minutes
+ 30 minutes marinating time

COOKING TIME: 8 minutes

NUTRITIONAL
INFORMATION/SERVING:
22 g protein, 5.5 g fat (1 g
saturated fat), 1.5 g carbohydrate,
0 g dietary fibre, 450 mg sodium,
625 kJ (150 Cals)

A source of vitamins B1, B2 and B3,
and also potassium, magnesium,
iron and iodine.

SERVES 4

PREPARATION TIME: 15 minutes
+ 15 minutes marinating time

COOKING TIME: 5–10 minutes

NUTRITIONAL
INFORMATION/SERVING:
31 g protein, 7 g fat (1 g
saturated fat), 2.5 g carbohydrate,
1.5 g dietary fibre, 300 mg sodium,
815 kJ (195 Cals)

A source of vitamins A, B1, B3, B12,
C and E, and also potassium,
magnesium, calcium, iron, zinc
and iodine.

Barbecued sesame seafood

Served with a tossed green salad and a loaf of gluten-free bread, this is entertaining at its easiest. Serve with sourdough bread if you aren't cooking gluten-free.

2 teaspoons sesame oil
2 tablespoons lime juice
2 garlic cloves, crushed
2 teaspoons chopped fresh ginger
1 small chilli, seeded and sliced (optional)
2 tablespoons sesame seeds
4 small boneless fish fillets
12 king prawns (shrimp), peeled and deveined, tails left intact
8 scallops
olive oil spray
2 tablespoons chopped parsley
1 lemon, cut into wedges

1. Combine the sesame oil, lime juice, garlic, ginger, chilli (if using) and sesame seeds in a shallow dish. Add the fish, prawns and scallops and turn to coat in the marinade. Cover and leave to marinate in the refrigerator for 15 minutes.

2. Spray the barbecue hotplate lightly with olive oil and heat. Remove the seafood from the marinade and place on the barbecue plate, turning once. Fish fillets usually cook in 5–10 minutes, depending on their thickness, while prawns and scallops cook in 4–6 minutes. Brush the seafood with the marinade while cooking.

3. When cooked, place the seafood on a serving platter and garnish with parsley and lemon wedges.

HINT

To prevent fish becoming dry, make sure you don't overcook it. Test to see if it is done by inserting a fork into the flesh. If it flakes easily, it is cooked. Fillets or cutlets usually take only 5–10 minutes to cook. Whole fish take longer, depending on the size.

SERVES 4
PREPARATION TIME: 20 minutes
COOKING TIME: 20 minutes

NUTRITIONAL
INFORMATION/SERVING:
19 g protein, 10 g fat (3.5 g
saturated fat), 12 g carbohydrate,
3.5 g dietary fibre, 410 mg sodium,
885 kJ (210 Cals)

A source of vitamins A, B1, B2,
B3 and C, and also potassium,
magnesium, calcium, iron and zinc.

Spinach and salmon roulade

This delicious special-occasion dish can be served warm or cold. Use two bunches (about 800 g/1 lb 12 oz) of fresh English spinach if desired. Silverbeet (Swiss chard) is not suitable in this recipe, as the flavour is too strong.

2 x 250 g (9 oz) packets frozen spinach, thawed
30 g (1 oz/¼ cup) pure cornflour (cornstarch)*
2 tablespoons skim milk powder
4 spring onions (scallions), thinly sliced
3 eggs, separated
2 teaspoons olive oil
100 g (3½ oz) button mushrooms, sliced
250 g (9 oz/1 cup) low-fat ricotta cheese
220 g (7¾ oz) tin red salmon, drained
1 tablespoon chopped lemon thyme
2 teaspoons finely grated lemon zest

* Check the cornflour is gluten-free.

1. Line a Swiss roll tin (jelly roll tin) with baking paper and preheat oven to 180°C (350°F/Gas 4).

2. Purée the spinach, cornflour, milk powder, spring onions and egg yolks in a blender or food processor.

3. Beat the egg whites until stiff, then gently fold through the spinach mixture. Spoon into the prepared tin and bake for 20 minutes.

4. While the roulade is baking, heat the oil in a small frying pan and cook the mushrooms over low heat for 5 minutes.

5. Combine the mushrooms, ricotta, salmon, lemon thyme and lemon zest and season with freshly ground black pepper.

6. Turn the roulade onto another piece of baking paper and gently spread the salmon mixture over the roulade. Roll up, using the paper to help. Place the roulade, seam side down, on the work surface and leave to stand for 5 minutes if serving warm, or refrigerate and serve cold.

Barbecued fish with tomato salsa

Use different varieties of fish, according to the season — your fishmonger will be able to advise you.

1 teaspoon olive oil

2 teaspoons finely grated lime zest

2 tablespoons lime juice

2 tablespoons torn basil

4 fish cutlets (about 700 g/1 lb 9 oz), such as kingfish, blue eye, ocean perch or gemfish

olive oil spray

salsa

500 g (1 lb 2 oz) ripe tomatoes

1 small red onion, finely chopped

1 large handful basil, finely chopped

1 tablespoon lime juice

1. Combine the oil, lime zest, lime juice and basil in a shallow dish. Add the fish and turn to coat with the mixture. Cover and refrigerate for 15 minutes, or longer if desired.

2. To make the salsa, first skin the tomatoes by removing the core and cutting a small cross in the end of each tomato. Place in a heatproof bowl, cover with boiling water, leave for 1 minute and drain. Transfer to a bowl of cold water, then peel off the skins. Cut the tomatoes into quarters and squeeze out the seeds, then cut into small dice. Combine with the onion, basil and lime juice.

3. Spray a barbecue hotplate lightly with olive oil and heat to hot. Cook the fish for 5–10 minutes, turning once and brushing with any remaining marinade. Serve with the salsa, and with steamed potatoes and a green vegetable such as broccoli, beans or asparagus.

SERVES 4

PREPARATION TIME: 15 minutes + 15 minutes marinating time

COOKING TIME: 5–10 minutes

NUTRITIONAL INFORMATION/SERVING:
45 g protein, 3.5 g fat (0 g saturated fat), 5 g carbohydrate, 2.5 g dietary fibre, 165 mg sodium, 965 kJ (230 Cals)

A source of vitamins A, B1, B2, B3, B12 and C, and also potassium, magnesium, calcium, iron, zinc and iodine.

Thai-style fish

Any white-fleshed fish is suitable for this quick and easy recipe. The cooking time of the fish will depend on the thickness of the fillet, so watch carefully so you don't overcook it. Serve with steamed rice and steamed snake (yard-long) beans.

1 teaspoon sesame oil
4 spring onions (scallions), sliced
1 garlic clove, crushed
1 teaspoon chopped chilli
1 tablespoon chopped mint
3 lemon grass stems, white part only, thinly sliced
4 makrut (kaffir lime) leaves, thinly sliced
4 fish steaks or fillets
2 tablespoons lime juice
1 teaspoon grated palm sugar (jaggery) or soft brown sugar
2 teaspoons fish sauce
2 ripe tomatoes, cut into eighths
2 large handfuls coriander (cilantro) leaves

1. Heat the oil in a wok or heavy-based frying pan and cook the onions, garlic, chilli, mint, lemon grass and lime leaves over low heat for 2–3 minutes.

2. Add the fish and cook for 5–7 minutes, turning once. Remove the fish and set aside, covered, to keep warm.

3. Add the lime juice, palm sugar, fish sauce and tomatoes to the wok or pan and cook for 3–4 minutes, until the tomatoes are heated through but are not mushy. Spoon over the fish and sprinkle with coriander.

SERVES 4
PREPARATION TIME: 15 minutes
COOKING TIME: 15 minutes

NUTRITIONAL INFORMATION/SERVING:
44 g protein, 3 g fat (0 g saturated fat), 4.5 g carbohydrate, 1 g dietary fibre, 350 mg sodium, 955 kJ (230 Cals)

A source of vitamins A, B1, B2, B3, B12 and C, and also potassium, calcium, magnesium, zinc and iodine.

Barbecued fish

SERVES 4

PREPARATION TIME: 5 minutes
+ 15 minutes marinating time

COOKING TIME: 5–10 minutes

NUTRITIONAL
INFORMATION/SERVING:
43 g protein, 2 g fat (0.5 g
saturated fat), 0.5 g carbohydrate,
0 g dietary fibre, 155 mg sodium,
820 kJ (195 Cals)

A source of vitamins B2, B3, B12
and C, and also potassium,
magnesium, zinc and iodine.

A barbecue is ideal for this recipe, but you could use a grill tray lined with foil or cook the fish in a heavy-based non-stick frying pan. This recipe is suitable for fish such as blue eye, kingfish, salmon or ocean trout.

125 ml (4 fl oz/½ cup) white wine
2 tablespoons lemon juice
1 teaspoon coarsely cracked black pepper
2 tablespoons chopped herbs, such as thyme, parsley, rosemary, oregano
   or a mixture of herbs
4 fish steaks (about 700 g/1 lb 9 oz)

1. Combine the wine, lemon juice, pepper and herbs in a shallow dish. Place the fish in the marinade, turn each steak over and leave for 15 minutes. Alternatively, cover and leave to marinate in the refrigerator until you are ready to cook.

2. Remove the fish from the marinade, reserving the marinade, and place them on a hot barbecue plate or under a hot grill (broiler). Cook the fish for no more than 5–10 minutes, turning once. The fish is cooked when it flakes easily when tested with a fork. Do not overcook the fish. Remove to a serving plate.

3. While the fish is cooking, boil the reserved marinade in a small saucepan for 1 minute, then pour over the cooked fish.

Fish and rice balls

Try this recipe for a delicious first course or serve it as a meal with stir-fried vegetables. You need a steamer for this recipe — use a bamboo or a stainless steel one, or sit the rice balls on a metal rack in a deep frying pan with a lid.

200 g (7 oz/1 cup) long-grain white rice
400 g (14 oz) boneless white fish fillets
170 g (6 oz) tinned water chestnuts, drained and chopped
4 spring onions (scallions), sliced
1 large handful coriander (cilantro) leaves, chopped
1 teaspoon chopped fresh ginger
2 teaspoons fish sauce
2 egg whites
4 makrut (kaffir lime) leaves

1. Soak the rice in 500 ml (17 fl oz/2 cups) water for at least 2 hours. Drain and tip the rice into a shallow bowl.

2. Place the fish, water chestnuts, spring onions, coriander, ginger, fish sauce and egg whites in a food processor and process until well mixed.

3. Using wet hands, take a tablespoon of the fish mixture and roll it in the rice. Continue in this way to make about 16 balls.

4. Place the fish balls on a lightly oiled sheet of baking paper in a steamer. Put some water and the lime leaves in a saucepan, sit the steamer on top of the pan, then cover and steam the fish balls for 15 minutes, or until cooked through.

SERVES 4

PREPARATION TIME: 30 minutes + 2 hours soaking for rice

COOKING TIME: 15 minutes

NUTRITIONAL INFORMATION/SERVING:
31 g protein, 1 g fat (0 g saturated fat), 44 g carbohydrate, 2.5 g dietary fibre, 310 mg sodium, 1330 kJ (320 Cals)

A source of vitamins A, B2, B3 and B12, and also potassium, magnesium, iron, zinc and iodine.

 HINT

Whole fish can be baked on the barbecue wrapped in foil, shiny side in. Cover with the barbecue hood if you have one. Cooking the fish this way retains both moisture and flavour, and cooking outside eliminates any 'fishy' smells in the kitchen — and there's less washing up too.

Ocean trout with dill sauce

If desired, use salmon, coral trout or any white-fleshed fish instead of ocean trout.

SERVES 4
PREPARATION TIME: 15 minutes
COOKING TIME: 10 minutes

NUTRITIONAL
INFORMATION/SERVING:
39 g protein, 5 g fat (1.5 g
saturated fat), 3.5 g carbohydrate,
0.5 g dietary fibre, 150 mg sodium,
910 kJ (220 Cals)

A source of vitamins B1, B2, B3
and B12, and also potassium,
magnesium, calcium, zinc
and iodine.

sauce
125 ml (4 fl oz/$1/2$ cup) white wine
2 tablespoons lemon juice
1 tablespoon snipped chives
200 g (7 oz) low-fat natural yoghurt
2 teaspoons dijon mustard*
1 tablespoon chopped dill

olive oil spray
4 ocean trout steaks, each about 175 g (6 oz)
2 tablespoons chopped dill, extra

* Check the mustard is gluten-free.

1. To make the sauce, heat the wine, lemon juice and chives in a saucepan and simmer until the liquid has reduced by two-thirds. Strain, reserving the liquid, and discard the chives. Stir the liquid into the yoghurt, along with the mustard and dill.

2. Heat a heavy-based frying pan or barbecue hotplate and spray lightly with olive oil. Cook the fish for 3–4 minutes on each side, being careful not to overcook it, and serve with the sauce and extra dill.

HINT

Fresh whole fish should have bright eyes that have not become sunken. Fresh fish fillets should look firm. Reject any that are discoloured or have water oozing out of them.

Prawns with honey and balsamic vinegar

This is a simple healthy recipe that is ideal for entertaining.

2 garlic cloves, crushed
1 small onion, finely chopped
2 tablespoons balsamic vinegar
2 tablespoons lemon juice
1 tablespoon honey
1 tablespoon wholegrain mustard*
800 g (1 lb 12 oz) raw prawns (shrimp), peeled and deveined, tails left intact
1 green or yellow capsicum (pepper), cut into 3 cm (1¼ inch) squares
1 red capsicum (pepper), cut into 3 cm (1¼ inch) squares

* Check the mustard is gluten-free.

1. Soak some bamboo skewers in cold water for 15 minutes (so they won't burn on the barbecue), or use metal skewers.

2. Combine the garlic, onion, vinegar, lemon juice, honey and mustard in a shallow dish and add the prawns. Cover and refrigerate for 15 minutes, or longer if desired.

3. Heat the barbecue hotplate. Remove the prawns from the marinade, reserving the marinade. Thread the prawns and capsicums onto the skewers and barbecue until cooked, brushing with a little of the marinade.

4. Boil any remaining marinade in a small saucepan for 1 minute and serve over the cooked prawns. Serve with steamed rice and a green salad.

HINT

Before barbecuing prawns (shrimp), split them along the back with small sharp scissors and hook out the dark vein that runs the length of the prawn.

Barbecued whole salmon with lemon salsa

This is a great dish for Christmas lunch or for a party. Any leftover salmon is excellent cold on sandwiches or in a salad the next day. If you don't have a hooded barbecue, cook the fish in a moderate oven.

40 g (1½ oz/2 bunches) lemon thyme
1 whole salmon, about 3–4 kg (7–9 lb), scaled and cleaned
1 lemon, halved

lemon salsa
finely grated zest and juice of 2 lemons
2 teaspoons palm sugar (jaggery) or soft brown sugar
1 red onion, very finely chopped
1 large handful coriander (cilantro) sprigs
4 Lebanese (short) cucumbers, finely diced

1. Oil the shiny side of a large piece of heavy foil and place a third of the lemon thyme on the oiled foil. Top with the salmon. Place the lemon halves and another third of the thyme inside the fish and scatter the remaining thyme on top of the fish. Fold the foil to enclose the salmon completely.

2. Heat the barbecue hotplate and cook the salmon for 15–20 minutes (close the hood if you have a hooded barbecue), then turn the fish over and cook for another 15–20 minutes. Unwrap the foil and transfer the salmon to a serving platter.

3. While the salmon is cooking, combine all the ingredients for the lemon salsa. Serve in a bowl alongside the salmon.

SERVES 16–20
PREPARATION TIME: 15 minutes
COOKING TIME: 30–40 minutes

NUTRITIONAL INFORMATION/SERVING:
38 g protein, 5 g fat (1.5 g saturated fat), 1.5 g carbohydrate, 1 g dietary fibre, 95 mg sodium, 865 kJ (205 Cals)

A source of vitamins A, B1, B2, B3 and B12, and also potassium, magnesium, zinc and iodine.

Seeded prawns

This makes great party food or serve as a main course with steamed rice and zucchini (courgettes) that have been halved lengthways and barbecued. Toast the sesame seeds in a dry frying pan, watching them carefully because they burn easily.

1 tablespoon honey

2 tablespoons lime juice

1 tablespoon hoisin sauce*

1 teaspoon reduced-salt soy sauce*

1 kg (2 lb 4 oz) raw prawns (shrimp), peeled and deveined, tails left intact

2 tablespoons sesame seeds, toasted

1 tablespoon fennel seeds

1 tablespoon sunflower seeds, crushed slightly

2 teaspoons ground coriander

1 teaspoon ground cumin

1 teaspoon paprika

* For gluten-free, omit the hoisin sauce and use wheat-free tamari in place of soy sauce.

1. Soak some small bamboo skewers in cold water for 15 minutes (so they won't burn on the barbecue), or use metal skewers.

2. Combine the honey, lime juice, hoisin sauce and soy sauce in a shallow dish. Add the prawns, cover and refrigerate for at least 15 minutes.

3. Remove the prawns from the marinade and thread onto the skewers. Combine the seeds and spices and roll the prawns in the mixture. Heat the barbecue hotplate or a chargrill pan over high heat and cook the prawns for 3–4 minutes, or until they turn pink.

SERVES 4

PREPARATION TIME: 20 minutes + 15 minutes marinating time

COOKING TIME: 5 minutes

NUTRITIONAL INFORMATION/SERVING: 30 g protein, 7 g fat (1 g saturated fat), 10 g carbohydrate, 3 g dietary fibre, 650 mg sodium, 910 kJ (220 Cals)

A source of vitamins B1, B2, B3, B12 and E, and also potassium, magnesium, calcium, iron, zinc and iodine.

Marinara sauce with pasta

SERVES 4

PREPARATION TIME: 10 minutes

COOKING TIME: 15 minutes

NUTRITIONAL
INFORMATION/SERVING:
36 g protein, 5 g fat (1 g
saturated fat), 73 g carbohydrate,
7 g dietary fibre, 250 mg sodium,
2040 kJ (485 Cals)

A source of vitamins A, B1, B2, B3,
B12 and C, and also potassium,
magnesium, calcium, iron, zinc
and iodine.

If marinara mix is not available, combine raw seafood of your choice, including fish, octopus, scallops, prawns and mussels.

375 g (13 oz) pasta*
2 teaspoons olive oil
1 onion, sliced
1 garlic clove, crushed
2 tablespoons tomato paste (concentrated purée), no added salt
400 g (14 oz) tin chopped tomatoes in juice, no added salt
125 ml (4 fl oz/½ cup) white wine
500 g (1 lb 2 oz) seafood marinara mix
2 tablespoons lemon juice
2 tablespoons chopped parsley

* For gluten-free, use gluten-free pasta.

1. Cook the pasta in a large saucepan of boiling water until just tender.

2. While the pasta is cooking, heat the oil in a large frying pan or wok and cook the onion and garlic over medium heat for 3–4 minutes. Add the tomato paste, tomatoes and wine and bring to the boil.

3. Add the seafood and cook for 3–4 minutes, or until the fish flakes easily when tested with a fork.

4. Drain the pasta and return to the saucepan. Stir in the lemon juice and hot seafood mixture. Serve in deep bowls sprinkled with parsley.

Middle-Eastern spicy fish

Tahini is a thick paste made from crushed white sesame seeds. It adds flavour and also thickens the yoghurt sauce for the fish. If preferred, you can cook the fish on the barbecue.

300 g (10½ oz/1¼ cups) low-fat natural yoghurt
1 teaspoon chopped chilli
1 teaspoon turmeric
1 teaspoon ground cumin
2 teaspoons ground coriander
2 large handfuls parsley, finely chopped
4 boneless fish fillets (about 700 g/1 lb 9 oz), such as blue eye, salmon or ling
1 teaspoon finely grated lemon zest
2 tablespoons lemon juice
2 teaspoons tahini

1. Combine 125 g (4½ oz/½ cup) of the yoghurt with the chilli, turmeric, cumin, coriander, parsley and ½ teaspoon freshly ground black pepper in a shallow dish. Add the fish and turn to coat with the spice mixture. Place the fish on a baking tray lined with foil or baking paper. Cover and refrigerate for 15 minutes.

2. Preheat oven to 180°C (350°F/Gas 4). Bake the fish for 10–15 minutes, or until the flesh flakes easily when tested with a fork.

3. While the fish is cooking, combine the remaining yoghurt with the lemon zest, lemon juice and tahini and stir well. Serve with the cooked fish.

SERVES 4

PREPARATION TIME: 15 minutes + 15 minutes refrigeration time

COOKING TIME: 10–15 minutes

NUTRITIONAL INFORMATION/SERVING:
48 g protein, 3.5 g fat (0.5 g saturated fat), 6 g carbohydrate, 1.5 g dietary fibre, 210 mg sodium, 1085 kJ (260 Cals)

A source of vitamins A, B1, B2, B3, B12 and C, and also potassium, magnesium, calcium, iron, zinc and iodine.

Seafood pizza

SERVES 4
PREPARATION TIME: 30 minutes
+ 1 hour standing time
COOKING TIME: 20 minutes

NUTRITIONAL
INFORMATION/SERVING:
23 g protein, 4.5 g fat (0.5 g
saturated fat), 41 g carbohydrate,
7.5 g dietary fibre, 280 mg sodium,
1240 kJ (295 Cals)

A source of vitamins A, B1, B2, B3
and C, and also potassium,
magnesium, iron and zinc.

It takes time to make the pizza dough, but it's fun and worth the effort. If you're rushed for time, start with a good-quality bought pizza base. Extra gluten is added to the flour to produce a crispier pizza crust, and it can be bought in most large supermarkets.

base

7 g (¼ oz) sachet dried yeast
2 tablespoons lukewarm water
1 teaspoon sugar
110 g (3¾ oz/¾ cup) wholemeal (whole-wheat) flour
90 g (3¼ oz/¾ cup) plain (all-purpose) flour
1 tablespoon gluten
125 ml (4 fl oz/½ cup) lukewarm water, extra
1 teaspoon dried Italian herbs
2 teaspoons olive oil

topping

60 g (2¼ oz/¼ cup) tomato paste (concentrated purée), no added salt
2 teaspoons dried oregano
1 large onion, sliced
1 red capsicum (pepper), cut into thin strips
2 zucchini (courgettes), thinly sliced
250 g (9 oz) seafood marinara mix
12 black olives
2 tablespoons chopped parsley

1. To make the base, combine the yeast, lukewarm water and sugar and leave for 10–15 minutes until bubbles appear.

2. Sift the flours and gluten into a large bowl, tipping the bits left in the sieve back into the bowl. Add the extra lukewarm water, dried herbs, oil and yeast mixture and mix well. Knead well for 10 minutes, or until smooth and shiny, adding a little more flour if necessary. Place the dough in a greased bowl, then place the bowl in a large plastic bag and leave in a warm place for about 1 hour, or until the dough has doubled in bulk.

3. Preheat oven to 200°C (400°F/Gas 6).

4. Punch the dough down, knead well and then roll out to a 30 cm (12 inch) circle. Place on a greased pizza tray.

5. Spread the tomato paste over the pizza dough. Sprinkle with oregano, onion, capsicum, zucchini and the marinara mix and arrange the olives on top. Bake for 20 minutes, or until cooked. Sprinkle with parsley and serve at once.

MAINS WITH MEAT AND CHICKEN

Meat and chicken are excellent foods with plenty of protein, vitamins and minerals. Skip this chapter if you are vegetarian — enjoy the dishes if you're not! The portions of meat or chicken recommended fit with a healthy diet — but always serve with vegetables or a salad.

Chicken with raspberry vinegar

SERVES 4
PREPARATION TIME: 10 minutes
COOKING TIME: 15 minutes

NUTRITIONAL
INFORMATION/SERVING:
25 g protein, 6.5 g fat (1.5 g
saturated fat), 1 g carbohydrate,
0 g dietary fibre, 210 mg sodium,
720 kJ (170 Cals)

A source of vitamins B2, B3
and B12, and also potassium,
iron and zinc.

Make this delicious dish when you're in a hurry. Raspberry vinegars can vary in thickness and sweetness, so you may need to adjust the lemon juice quantities to suit — let your taste buds guide you.

1 teaspoon olive oil
500 g (1 lb 2 oz) boneless, skinless chicken thighs, trimmed of excess fat
1 tablespoon dijon mustard*
2 tablespoons raspberry vinegar
1–2 tablespoons lemon juice, to taste
1 tablespoon finely chopped parsley

* Check the mustard is gluten-free.

1. Heat a heavy-based frying pan and add the oil. Cook the chicken over medium heat, covered, for about 5 minutes on each side.

2. Move the chicken to one side of the pan. Add the mustard, vinegar, lemon juice and 2 tablespoons water to the pan and bring to the boil.

3. Remove the chicken and sauce to a plate and serve sprinkled with parsley. Serve with steamed new potatoes and a green salad.

Veal steaks with lemon

Veal and lemon are a classic combination, and here the veal steaks are baked with a tangy lemon paste. To make the paste the lemons are blended, skin and all, to give the paste a strong lemon flavour and more texture. The lemon mixture is also good with chicken thighs or pork steaks.

1 lemon
2 garlic cloves
2 tablespoons chopped parsley
1 tablespoon reduced-salt soy sauce*
1 teaspoon soft brown sugar
4 veal steaks, about 170 g (6 oz) each

* For gluten-free, use wheat-free tamari.

1. Slice the lemon and remove the seeds, but do not peel. Place the lemon slices, garlic, parsley, soy sauce and brown sugar into a blender and process until well chopped, adding a little water if necessary to make a chunky paste.

2. Place the veal in a shallow ovenproof dish, spoon the lemon paste over, cover and refrigerate for at least 30 minutes. Preheat oven to 180°C (350°F/Gas 4).

3. Bake the veal for 20–30 minutes, or until the veal is cooked, taking care not to overcook it. Serve with steamed vegetables.

SERVES 4

PREPARATION TIME: 15 minutes + 30 minutes marinating time

COOKING TIME: 30 minutes

NUTRITIONAL INFORMATION/SERVING:
40 g protein, 3 g fat (1 g saturated fat), 2.5 g carbohydrate, 1 g dietary fibre, 295 mg sodium, 850 kJ (205 Cals)

A source of vitamins B1, B2, B3, B12 and C, and also potassium, iron and zinc.

Roast chicken with herbs and lemon

There are few dishes as universally appealing as roast chicken. Add a slight twist with lemon and herb flavourings, and enjoy this chicken either hot or cold.

SERVES 4

PREPARATION TIME: 5 minutes

COOKING TIME: 1–1¼ hours

NUTRITIONAL INFORMATION/SERVING (WITHOUT SKIN): 27 g protein, 7.5 g fat (2.5 g saturated fat), 0.5 g carbohydrate, 0.5 g dietary fibre, 75 mg sodium, 745 kJ (180 Cals)

NUTRITIONAL INFORMATION/SERVING (WITH SKIN): 26 g protein, 14 g fat (4.5 g saturated fat), 0.5 g carbohydrate, 0.5 g dietary fibre, 75 mg sodium, 970 kJ (230 Cals)

A source of vitamins B2, B3 and B12, and also iron and zinc.

35 g (1¼ oz/1 small bunch) rosemary, or 20 g (¾ oz/1 bunch) lemon thyme
2 lemons
1 organic or free-range chicken, about 1.5 kg (3 lb 5 oz), trimmed of fat

1. Preheat oven to 180°C (350°F/Gas 4).

2. Place half the rosemary or thyme and half a lemon inside the chicken. Place the chicken in a roasting tin with the breast uppermost. Tuck the remaining herbs under the wings and into the thighs. Slice the remaining lemons, remove the seeds and place the lemon slices over the chicken.

3. Roast the chicken for 1 hour and then pierce the thigh with a skewer to check if the chicken is cooked. If the juices are pink, cook for a further 15 minutes. The chicken is cooked when the juices are clear.

4. Remove from the oven, cover with foil and set aside to rest for 5 minutes (this increases the tenderness). Serve the chicken with chunks of baked sweet potato, baked onion halves and a green vegetable.

HINT

Free range and organic chickens are not fed antibiotics as growth promotants. The flesh from these chickens is usually firmer and less flabby and has more flavour than regular chicken.

Beef, beans and beer

SERVES 4

PREPARATION TIME: 20 minutes

COOKING TIME: 2 hours

NUTRITIONAL
INFORMATION/SERVING:
33 g protein, 7 g fat (2 g
saturated fat), 15 g carbohydrate,
8 g dietary fibre, 200 mg sodium,
1085 kJ (260 Cals)

A source of vitamins B1, B2, B3,
B12 and C, and also potassium,
magnesium, iron and zinc.

The alcohol from the beer evaporates during cooking but leaves a great flavour. Rinsing the kidney beans removes some of the salt.

500 g (1 lb 2 oz) lean round steak, cut into 2 cm (3/4 inch) cubes
1 teaspoon olive oil
1 large onion, sliced
1 eggplant (aubergine), diced
1 teaspoon mustard powder
1 teaspoon dried basil
370 ml (13 fl oz) can low alcohol beer
425 g (15 oz) tin red kidney beans, rinsed

1. Preheat oven to 160°C (315°F/Gas 2–3).

2. Brown the meat in a non-stick frying pan. Place in a casserole dish.

3. Add the oil to the same frying pan and cook the onion over medium heat for 2–3 minutes. Place on top of the meat.

4. Add the eggplant, mustard powder, basil, beer, beans and 125 ml (4 fl oz/1/2 cup) water to the casserole dish. Bake for 2 hours, or until the beef is tender.

HINT

Feed-lot cattle often have a hormone implant inserted in the ear. If you prefer to avoid meat from these animals, ask your butcher for grass-fed beef or buy organic beef.

Chicken with lime and mango

This is a quick meal that is popular with all ages.

125 ml (4 fl oz/½ cup) lime juice
2 tablespoons brandy or orange juice
1 large mango, peeled and diced
4 boneless, skinless chicken breasts, about 600 g (1 lb 5 oz)

1. Combine the lime juice, brandy and mango in a shallow dish. Add the chicken breasts and turn several times to coat with the marinade. Cover and refrigerate for 15 minutes, or overnight.

2. Remove the chicken from the marinade and place on a heated barbecue hotplate or in a hot non-stick frying pan. Cook for 10–15 minutes, turning several times and brushing with the marinade. Serve with potatoes, which have been steamed and mashed, or with steamed new potatoes and salad or vegetables.

SERVES 4

PREPARATION TIME: 10 minutes
+ 15 minutes marinating time

COOKING TIME: 15 minutes

NUTRITIONAL
INFORMATION/SERVING:
35 g protein, 3.5 g fat (1 g saturated fat), 11 g carbohydrate, 1 g dietary fibre, 85 mg sodium, 900 kJ (215 Cals)

A source of vitamins A, B1, B2, B3, B12 and C, and also potassium, magnesium, iron and zinc.

 HINT

Chicken breasts do not dry out as they once did because the flesh is left on the bone for 24 hours, giving an effect similar to the ageing of steak.

Lamb shanks with lemon and lentils

Lamb shanks with lentils makes a hearty and nutritious winter meal. The flavours are even better if this dish is made a day or two ahead and then reheated. Remove any fat that settles on top before you heat it.

4 lamb shanks, trimmed of all fat
1 large onion, diced
1 eggplant (aubergine), diced
800 g (1 lb 12 oz) tin tomatoes, no added salt
500 ml (17 fl oz/2 cups) red or white wine, or water
3–4 rosemary sprigs
1 lemon, sliced
185 g (6 1/2 oz/1 cup) green lentils
250 g (9 oz) mushrooms, sliced
juice and finely grated zest of 1 lemon
2 tablespoons chopped mint

1. Preheat oven to 180°C (350°F/Gas 4).

2. Place the shanks into a large casserole dish with the onion, eggplant, tomatoes and wine. Top with the rosemary and lemon slices, then cover and bake for 1 1/2 hours.

3. Add the lentils, mushrooms and 375 ml (13 fl oz/1 1/2 cups) water and bake for a further 45 minutes, or until the lentils are soft. Sprinkle with lemon juice and serve topped with lemon zest and mint. Serve with steamed vegetables.

SERVES 4
PREPARATION TIME: 15 minutes
COOKING TIME: 2 1/4 hours

NUTRITIONAL
INFORMATION/SERVING:
48 g protein, 4 g fat (1.5 g saturated fat), 30 g carbohydrate, 14 g dietary fibre, 165 mg sodium, 1485 kJ (355 Cals)

A source of vitamins A, B1, B2, B3, B12 and E, and also potassium, magnesium, calcium, iron and zinc.

Moroccan-style lamb with chickpeas

SERVES 6
PREPARATION TIME: 15 minutes
COOKING TIME: 1 hour

NUTRITIONAL
INFORMATION/SERVING:
30 g protein, 8 g fat (2 g
saturated fat), 35 g carbohydrate,
8.5 g dietary fibre, 200 mg sodium,
1400 kJ (335 Cals)

A source of vitamins B1, B2, B3,
B12 and E, and also potassium,
magnesium, calcium, iron and zinc.

We all need to include more legumes in our diet. Chickpeas have a mild, nutty flavour and are the perfect foil for the spicy, fruity flavours of this Moroccan lamb. This dish is suitable for freezing.

1 teaspoon olive oil
600 g (1 lb 5 oz) lean lamb, cut into cubes
1 large onion, cut into eighths
1 garlic clove, crushed
2 teaspoons ground coriander
1 teaspoon ground allspice
¼ teaspoon freshly ground black pepper
500 ml (17 fl oz/2 cups) chicken stock
70 g (2½ oz/½ cup) dried apricots
110 g (3¾ oz/½ cup) pitted prunes
60 g (2¼ oz/½ cup) raisins
2 x 400 g (14 oz) tins chickpeas, drained and rinsed
1 tablespoon slivered almonds, toasted

1. Preheat oven to 180°C (350°F/Gas 4).

2. Heat a heavy-based frying pan, add the oil and cook the lamb and onion over medium heat until brown. Add the garlic and spices and cook for 2 minutes.

3. Add the stock and dried fruit. Transfer to an ovenproof dish, cover and bake for 45 minutes.

4. Add the chickpeas, stir well and bake, uncovered, for a further 10 minutes. Sprinkle almonds on top just before serving.

HINT

Always rinse tinned legumes such as red kidney beans and chickpeas to remove some of the salt.

Chicken and rice cake

Make this easy recipe in summer and serve with a big green salad. It's also an ideal dish to pack for picnics.

600 g (1 lb 5 oz) boneless, skinless chicken thighs, cut into 2.5 cm (1 inch) squares
625 g (1 lb 6 oz/2¹/₂ cups) low-fat natural yoghurt
1 teaspoon ground cinnamon
¹/₂ teaspoon coarsely ground black pepper
2 teaspoons paprika
1 teaspoon turmeric
500 g rice (1 lb 2 oz/2¹/₂ cups), preferably Doongara or basmati rice
2 egg yolks

1. Combine the chicken, 500 g (1 lb 2 oz/2 cups) of the yoghurt and the spices in a large bowl. Cover and refrigerate for at least 1 hour, or leave to marinate in the refrigerator overnight. Remove half a cup of the yoghurt marinade from the chicken and reserve.

2. Put the rice and 1.5 litres (52 fl oz/6 cups) water in a saucepan, bring to the boil and cook for 5 minutes (the rice will not be fully cooked). Drain.

3. Preheat oven to 180°C (350°F/Gas 4). Grease a 20 cm (8 inch) round ovenproof dish or cake tin.

4. Combine 280 g (10 oz/1¹/₂ cups) of the partially cooked rice with the egg yolks and the reserved half a cup of yoghurt marinade. Press the rice mixture over the base of the dish.

5. Spoon half the chicken and yoghurt mixture on top of the rice, then half the remaining rice, the rest of the chicken and finish with the remaining rice. Spoon the remaining yoghurt over the top and bake for 1¹/₄ hours (cover with foil if it starts to brown too quickly). Set aside for 5 minutes, then invert onto a serving platter. Cut into wedges to serve.

SERVES 6
PREPARATION TIME: 30 minutes
+ 1 hour standing time
COOKING TIME: 1¹/₄ hours

NUTRITIONAL
INFORMATION/SERVING:
34 g protein, 6.5 g fat (2 g saturated fat), 72 g carbohydrate, 2 g dietary fibre, 150 mg sodium, 2085 kJ (500 Cals)

A source of vitamins B1, B2, B3 and B12, and also potassium, magnesium, calcium, iron and zinc.

Stir-fried beef with water chestnuts

SERVES 4
PREPARATION TIME: 15 minutes
COOKING TIME: 10 minutes

NUTRITIONAL
INFORMATION/SERVING:
31 g protein, 6 g fat (1.5 g
saturated fat), 14 g carbohydrate,
8.5 g dietary fibre, 260 mg sodium,
965 kJ (230 Cals)

A source of vitamins A, B1, B2, B3,
B12 and C, and also potassium,
magnesium, iron and zinc.

The secret to a good stir-fry is to work fast and to keep the wok very hot. Have all your ingredients sliced and measured out — that way, once you start stir-frying, there's no need to stop. If preferred, substitute boneless, skinless chicken breasts for the beef.

2 teaspoons sesame oil
1 onion, cut into wedges
1 garlic clove, crushed
400 g (14 oz) lean rump steak, cut into thin strips
2 teaspoons chopped fresh ginger
1/2 Chinese cabbage (wong bok), about 320 g (11¼ oz), shredded
225 g (8 oz) tin water chestnuts, drained and sliced
250 g (9 oz) mixed mushrooms, such as button, enoki and Swiss brown, sliced
125 g (4½ oz) snow peas (mangetout)
1 tablespoon oyster sauce*
200 g (7 oz/3 cups) mung bean sprouts

* For gluten-free, omit the oyster sauce.

1. Heat a wok or large non-stick frying pan, add the oil and stir-fry the onion, garlic and beef over medium heat for 3–4 minutes. Do not overcook.

2. Add the ginger, Chinese cabbage, water chestnuts, mushrooms and snow peas and continue stir-frying for 2–3 minutes.

3. Combine the oyster sauce with 125 ml (4 fl oz/½ cup) water and add to the wok. Add the bean sprouts and toss to combine, but do not cook for too long or they will lose their crisp texture. Serve at once with rice or noodles.

HINT

For stir-fried dishes, freeze meat or chicken breasts for 30 minutes or so before slicing. Using a sharp knife, it is then easy to thinly slice the flesh. This helps the meat to cook quickly and stay tender.

Chicken with prunes and nuts

SERVES 4
PREPARATION TIME: 10 minutes
COOKING TIME: 25 minutes

NUTRITIONAL
INFORMATION/SERVING:
32 g protein, 9.5 g fat (1.5 g
saturated fat), 17 g carbohydrate,
5 g dietary fibre, 130 mg sodium,
1200 kJ (285 Cals)

A source of vitamins B1, B2, B3,
B12 and C, and also potassium,
magnesium, iron and zinc.

This easy dish is always popular and is delicious served either with steamed rice or rice noodles. If you are not concerned about gluten-free, you may like to serve with burghul wheat.

110 g (3¾ oz/½ cup) pitted prunes
2 tablespoons blanched almonds
125 ml (4 fl oz/½ cup) dry sherry
60 ml (2 fl oz/¼ cup) orange juice
1 teaspoon finely grated orange zest
1 teaspoon ground cinnamon
600 g (1 lb 5 oz) boneless, skinless chicken thighs
1 tablespoon chopped coriander (cilantro) leaves or parsley

1. Place the prunes, almonds, sherry, orange juice, orange zest and cinnamon into a saucepan and bring to the boil. Simmer for 2 minutes.

2. Cut each chicken thigh in half and add to the saucepan. Cover and simmer for 20 minutes. Just before serving, sprinkle with freshly ground black pepper and coriander or parsley.

Lamb burgers with minted yoghurt

Buy lean lamb and ask the butcher to mince it for you if lean mince is not available.

130 g (4½ oz/¾ cup) burghul or bulgur
250 ml (9 fl oz/1 cup) boiling water
350 g (12 oz) lean lamb, minced (ground)
4 spring onions (scallions), sliced
1 egg, lightly beaten
3 handfuls mint, chopped
1 large handful coriander (cilantro) leaves
1 teaspoon finely grated lemon zest
1 tablespoon lemon juice
oil, to grease
200 g (7 oz) low-fat natural yoghurt
1 large tomato, diced

1. Place the burghul in a heatproof bowl, pour the boiling water over, cover and leave for 10 minutes until the water has been absorbed. If any moisture remains, use clean hands to squeeze the burghul.

2. Combine the burghul, lamb, spring onions, egg, half the mint, half the coriander, lemon zest and lemon juice. Form the mixture into four patties and flatten slightly. Heat the barbecue hot plate and lightly oil. Cook the patties on each side for 7–8 minutes, or until brown.

3. Combine the yoghurt, tomato and remaining mint and coriander.

4. Serve the lamb burgers topped with the yoghurt mixture. Serve at once.

SERVES 4
PREPARATION TIME: 20 minutes
COOKING TIME: 20 minutes

NUTRITIONAL
INFORMATION/SERVING:
28 g protein, 5 g fat (2 g saturated fat), 30 g carbohydrate, 4.5 g dietary fibre, 130 mg sodium, 1185 kJ (285 Cals)

A source of vitamins A, B1, B2, B3, B12 and C, and also potassium, magnesium, calcium, iron and zinc.

 HINT

When meat and chicken are barbecued, small quantities of cancer-causing compounds, called heterocyclic amines, form. By marinating meat or chicken for as little as 5 minutes in a mixture that includes some kind of sugar, these harmful chemicals do not form.

Lamb kibbeh

This is a great way to combine lean meat and wholegrains. Burghul is a nutritious grain with a soft, chewy texture and is made from wheat kernels that have been steamed or parboiled, then dried and crushed. It is often confused with cracked wheat, which is similar, but has not been parboiled.

175 g (6 oz/1 cup) burghul or bulgur, or use cracked wheat
250 ml (9 fl oz/1 cup) boiling water
50 g (1³/₄ oz/¹/₃ cup) pine nuts
400 g (14 oz) lean lamb, minced (ground)
1 onion, finely chopped
2 teaspoons sumac
1 teaspoon cracked black pepper
olive oil

1. Preheat oven to 180°C (350°F/Gas 4).

2. Place the burghul in a heatproof bowl, pour the boiling water over, cover and leave for 10 minutes until the water has been absorbed. If any moisture remains, use clean hands to squeeze the burghul.

3. Toast the pine nuts in a dry frying pan over medium heat until golden brown. Set aside.

4. Combine the lamb, onion, sumac, pepper and burghul, adding 60 ml (2 fl oz/¹/₄ cup) iced water if needed. (A food processor makes this easy.)

5. Spoon half the kibbeh mixture into a greased 18 cm (7 inch) square baking dish or non-stick cake tin. Sprinkle with two-thirds of the pine nuts, then press the remaining meat mixture on top. Press firmly and mark the top of the kibbeh with diamond shapes.

6. Brush with a little olive oil and press a pine nut or two into each diamond. Bake for 40 minutes. Serve with tabouleh (page 100) and a green salad.

SERVES 4
PREPARATION TIME: 20 minutes
COOKING TIME: 40 minutes

NUTRITIONAL INFORMATION/SERVING:
28 g protein, 14 g fat (2.5 g saturated fat), 36 g carbohydrate, 5 g dietary fibre, 85 mg sodium, 1570 kJ (375 Cals)

A source of vitamins B1, B2, B3 and B12, and also potassium, magnesium, iron and zinc.

 HINT

If your butcher or supermarket can't assure you that minced (ground) meat is lean, buy lean lamb, beef or pork and ask to have it minced for you.

SERVES 4

PREPARATION TIME: 10 minutes

COOKING TIME: 20 minutes

NUTRITIONAL
INFORMATION/SERVING:
32 g protein, 5.5 g fat (1.5 g
saturated fat), 5 g carbohydrate,
2.5 g dietary fibre, 80 mg sodium,
840 kJ (200 Cals)

A source of vitamins A, B1, B2, B3,
B12 and C, and also potassium,
magnesium, iron and zinc.

Chicken breast with flaming sauce

This pretty dish is simple and easy to make. The sauce is also delicious served with steamed potatoes, green beans or asparagus.

4 boneless, skinless chicken breasts
whole chives, for garnish

sauce
3 ripe tomatoes
2 teaspoons olive oil
1 small onion, roughly chopped
1 garlic clove, crushed
1 tablespoon paprika
1/2 teaspoon dried thyme
1 large red capsicum (pepper), sliced

1. To make the sauce, first skin the tomatoes by removing the cores and cutting a small cross in the end of each tomato. Place in a heatproof bowl, cover with boiling water, leave for 1 minute and drain. Transfer to a bowl of cold water, then peel off the skins. Cut into quarters and squeeze out the seeds, then roughly dice the tomato flesh.

2. Heat the oil in a saucepan or frying pan and cook the onion, covered, over medium heat for 2–3 minutes. Add the garlic, paprika and thyme and cook for a further 1 minute. Add the capsicum and tomatoes and cook for 10 minutes, or until soft. Purée the mixture in a food processor until smooth.

3. While the sauce is cooking, grill (broil) or barbecue the chicken for 6–8 minutes, turning once, being careful not to overcook the chicken. Serve the chicken on top of the sauce and garnish with whole chives.

Steamed chicken with style

Steamed chicken can be dry but this easy method produces moist, succulent chicken every time. Use the chicken in sandwiches, wraps, tacos or salads.

1 organic or free-range chicken, about 1.5 kg (3 lb 5 oz)
1.5 litres (52 fl oz/6 cups) boiling water
2 teaspoons chopped fresh ginger
2 spring onions (scallions), thinly sliced
1 tablespoon lemon juice
1 tablespoon reduced-salt soy sauce*
2 teaspoons sesame oil
2 tablespoons dry sherry

* For gluten-free, use wheat-free tamari.

1. Remove and discard the fat from inside and around the tail area of the chicken. Place the chicken into a large saucepan and pour the boiling water over, to cover the chicken. Leave for 1 minute, then drain off the water and pat the chicken dry using paper towels.

2. Combine the ginger, spring onions, lemon juice, soy sauce, sesame oil and sherry and brush over the inside and outside of the chicken.

3. Place the chicken in a bamboo or metal steamer. Place the steamer over a saucepan or wok of boiling water, cover and steam the chicken for 1 hour. Before serving, remove and discard the skin.

SERVES 4
PREPARATION TIME: 15 minutes
COOKING TIME: 1 hour

NUTRITIONAL INFORMATION/SERVING:
37 g protein, 10 g fat (2.5 g saturated fat), 1 g carbohydrate, 0 g dietary fibre, 275 mg sodium, 1050 kJ (250 Cals)

A source of vitamins B2, B3 and B12, and also potassium, magnesium, iron and zinc.

Pork with pears and juniper berries

SERVES 4
PREPARATION TIME: 20 minutes
+ 15 minutes marinating time
COOKING TIME: 15 minutes

NUTRITIONAL
INFORMATION/SERVING:
35 g protein, 5 g fat (1 g
saturated fat), 19 g carbohydrate,
2 g dietary fibre, 245 mg sodium,
1070 kJ (255 Cals)

A source of vitamins B1, B2, B3
and C, and also potassium, iron
and zinc.

Juniper berries are hard, dark-purple berries often used in northern European cooking in pork and game dishes, and their citrusy pine scent is used to flavour gin. The berries need to be lightly crushed before use to release their flavour and aroma. To do this, place the berries in a plastic bag and hit with a bottle to crush.

1 tablespoon honey
1 tablespoon reduced-salt soy sauce*
2 tablespoons gin or orange juice
600 g (1 lb 5 oz) lean pork fillets
1½ tablespoons juniper berries, crushed
2 teaspoons olive oil
2 pears, peeled, cored and cut in halves
¼ teaspoon ground cinnamon

* For gluten-free, use wheat-free tamari.

1. Mix together the honey, soy sauce and gin or orange juice in a shallow dish. Dip the pork fillets into the mixture and then into the crushed juniper berries, pressing the berries onto the pork. Set aside to marinate for 15 minutes.

2. Heat a large heavy-based frying pan over medium heat, add the oil and cook the pork for 8–10 minutes, turning once.

3. While the pork is cooking, slice each pear half lengthways, without cutting right through, so the slices can fan out. Push the pork to one side of the pan. Add the pears to the pan and sprinkle with cinnamon. Cook for a further 2–3 minutes until the pears are hot but still firm. Remove the pork and pears from the pan and leave the pork to rest for 5 minutes. Serve with steamed vegetables and new potatoes.

HINT

If you need to flatten pork, veal or chicken fillets, place them between sheets of baking paper and hit them with the flat side of a meat mallet or a glass bottle.

SERVES 6
PREPARATION TIME: 15 minutes
COOKING TIME: 45 minutes

NUTRITIONAL
INFORMATION/SERVING:
25 g protein, 6.5 g fat (1.5 g
saturated fat), 18 g carbohydrate,
3.5 g dietary fibre, 90 mg sodium,
965 kJ (230 Cals)

A source of vitamins A, B1, B2, B3,
B12 and C, and also potassium,
magnesium, iron and zinc.

Chicken loaf with apricot sauce

This loaf is delicious cold with a salad and also makes an excellent filling for sandwiches. Make sure you check that uncontaminated (by wheat grains) oats are available and suitable for those on a gluten-free diet. Make the loaf with minced veal if you prefer.

chicken loaf
2 tablespoons sesame seeds, toasted
500 g (1 lb 2 oz) minced (ground) chicken
100 g (3¹⁄₂ oz/1 cup) rolled (porridge) oats*
60 ml (2 fl oz/¹⁄₄ cup) evaporated skim milk
1 egg
1 large carrot, grated
90 g (3¹⁄₄ oz/1 cup) chopped mushrooms
3 spring onions (scallions), sliced
1 teaspoon dried thyme
1 large handful mint, chopped

apricot sauce
125 ml (4 fl oz/¹⁄₂ cup) orange juice
125 ml (4 fl oz/¹⁄₂ cup) chicken stock
35 g (1¹⁄₄ oz/¹⁄₄ cup) dried apricots

* Check the oats are gluten-free.

1. Preheat oven to 180°C (350°F/Gas 4). Grease a 21 x 11 cm (8¹⁄₄ x 4¹⁄₄ inch) loaf (bar) tin and sprinkle with 1 tablespoon of the sesame seeds.

2. Combine all the remaining ingredients for the chicken loaf, except for the sesame seeds, and press the mixture into the tin. Sprinkle with the remaining sesame seeds, then bake for 45 minutes. Allow to stand for 5 minutes before turning out. If serving cold, allow to cool in the tin.

3. While the loaf is cooking, make the apricot sauce. Combine all the ingredients in a small saucepan, bring to the boil, then cover and simmer for 15 minutes. Purée in a food processor until smooth. Spoon the sauce over the chicken loaf to serve.

Chicken with almond sauce

This recipe is based on a traditional Spanish dish, which is served in the north-eastern region.

olive oil spray
4 boneless, skinless chicken breasts
50 g (1¾ oz/⅓ cup) blanched almonds, toasted
2 slices of stale wholemeal (whole-wheat) bread, crusts removed
1 tablespoon soft brown sugar
1 teaspoon ground cinnamon
125 ml (4 fl oz/½ cup) white wine vinegar
185 ml (6 fl oz/¾ cup) chicken stock

1. Lightly spray a heavy-based non-stick frying pan with olive oil and place over medium heat. Cook the chicken for 10 minutes, turning once.

2. While the chicken is cooking, place the almonds, bread, sugar, cinnamon and some freshly ground black pepper into a food processor. Gradually pour in the vinegar and stock and process to a thick sauce.

3. Pour the sauce over the chicken and simmer, covered, for 15 minutes, stirring occasionally. Serve with steamed vegetables.

SERVES 4
PREPARATION TIME: 10 minutes
COOKING TIME: 25 minutes

NUTRITIONAL INFORMATION/SERVING:
34 g protein, 10 g fat (1.5 g saturated fat), 11 g carbohydrate, 2 g dietary fibre, 155 mg sodium, 1155 kJ (275 Cals)

A source of vitamins B1, B2, B3 and B12, and also potassium, magnesium, iron and zinc.

Veal osso bucco

This dish needs long, slow cooking and is ideal to cook a day or two ahead to allow the flavours to develop. The eggplant will partially disintegrate into the sauce and will help to thicken it.

750 g (1 lb 10 oz) osso bucco pieces
1 teaspoon olive oil
1 large onion, sliced
1 garlic clove, crushed
1 tablespoon paprika
800 g (1 lb 12 oz) tin tomatoes, no added salt
1 eggplant (aubergine), peeled and diced
125 g (4½ oz/1 cup) sliced celery
1 teaspoon dried basil
4 bay leaves
250 ml (9 fl oz/1 cup) red wine
250 ml (9 fl oz/1 cup) stock or water
1 tablespoon finely grated lemon zest
300 g (10½ oz) button mushrooms
2 tablespoons chopped parsley

1. Preheat oven to 160°C (315°F/Gas 2–3). Brown the veal on all sides in a heavy-based frying pan and then place into a large, flameproof casserole dish.

2. Add the olive oil, onion and garlic to the frying pan and stir over medium heat for 3–4 minutes, or until the onion softens.

3. Add the paprika, tomatoes, eggplant, celery, basil, bay leaves, red wine, stock or water and half the lemon zest to the pan. Bring to the boil, then remove from the heat and pour over the veal. Place the lid on the casserole dish and bake for 1½ hours. If desired, cool at this stage and refrigerate until required.

4. Add the mushrooms to the dish and return to the oven and cook for a further 15 minutes (or if reheating the dish the next day, you can add the mushrooms to the casserole dish and cook on the stovetop).

5. Just before serving, sprinkle with parsley and the remaining lemon zest. Serve with steamed green beans.

SERVES 4
PREPARATION TIME: 15 minutes
COOKING TIME: 2 hours

NUTRITIONAL INFORMATION/SERVING:
28 g protein, 2.5 g fat (0.5 g saturated fat), 14 g carbohydrate, 8 g dietary fibre, 165 mg sodium, 810 kJ (195 Cals)

A source of vitamins A, B1, B2, B3, B12 and C, and also potassium, magnesium, calcium, iron and zinc.

Lamb steaks in pomegranate molasses

SERVES 4
PREPARATION TIME: 10 minutes
COOKING TIME: 30 minutes

NUTRITIONAL
INFORMATION/SERVING:
33 g protein, 5.5 g fat (2.5 g
saturated fat), 6 g carbohydrate,
0 g dietary fibre, 260 mg sodium,
880 kJ (210 Cals)

A source of vitamins B1, B2, B3
and B12, and also potassium,
iron and zinc.

Pomegranate molasses is available from Middle Eastern food shops and some delicatessens. If you can't find it, substitute dark brown sugar.

2 tablespoons pomegranate molasses
1 tablespoon reduced-salt soy sauce*
2 tablespoons lemon juice
4 lean lamb steaks, about 600 g (1 lb 5 oz)

* For gluten-free, use wheat-free tamari.

1. Combine the molasses, soy sauce and lemon juice in a shallow ovenproof dish. Add the lamb steaks and turn to coat each side with the marinade. Refrigerate for at least 15 minutes.

2. Preheat oven to 180°C (350°F/Gas 4). Bake the lamb in its marinade for 30 minutes, turning the lamb once. Serve with rice, noodles or potatoes, and vegetables or a green salad.

HINT

Add flavour to lean meats, seafood and skinless chicken by using marinades based on red wine, flavoured vinegars or citrus juices with a little brown sugar or honey and herbs for extra flavour.

Lamb with sumac and dried fruit

The slight lemony tang of sumac gives this dish an intriguing flavour and marries beautifully with the sweetness of the dried fruit. Sumac is a dark-red spice made from the dried and crushed seeds of berries and is often used in Turkish, Lebanese and North African cooking.

2 teaspoons sumac
4 lean lamb steaks, about 600 g (1 lb 5 oz)
1 teaspoon olive oil
8 dried apricot halves
60 g (2¼ oz/½ cup) raisins
185 ml (6 fl oz/¾ cup) orange juice
1 teaspoon wholegrain mustard*

* Check the mustard is gluten-free.

1. Rub the sumac into both sides of the lamb steaks.

2. Heat a large heavy-based frying pan over medium heat, add the oil and cook the lamb for 10 minutes, turning once.

3. Add the apricots, raisins and orange juice and cook for a further 5 minutes. Stir in the mustard. Serve with steamed potatoes or rice and a green vegetable.

SERVES 4
PREPARATION TIME: 10 minutes
COOKING TIME: 15 minutes

NUTRITIONAL INFORMATION/SERVING:
34 g protein, 7 g fat (2.5 g saturated fat), 20 g carbohydrate, 2 g dietary fibre, 150 mg sodium, 1170 kJ (280 Cals)

A source of vitamins B1, B2, B3, B12 and C, and also potassium, magnesium, iron and zinc.

DESSERTS AND SWEET TREATS

Dessert is most people's favourite part of the meal. Some desserts are a nutritionist's nightmare — but some fit perfectly into a healthy diet.

Steamed apricot pudding with orange sauce

Steamed puddings are the ultimate winter comfort food, and this one has the added bonus of being low in fat. Use an aluminium pudding basin if you have one, as these come with their own clip-on lids, or use a heatproof basin and cover with foil. Make a pleat in the foil, as this enables the foil to expand as the pudding cooks.

SERVES 4

PREPARATION TIME: 15 minutes
+ 20 minutes standing

COOKING TIME: 1 hour

NUTRITIONAL
INFORMATION/SERVING:
9.5 g protein, 4 g fat (1 g saturated fat), 38 g carbohydrate, 3.5 g dietary fibre, 210 mg sodium, 945 kJ (225 Cals)

A source of vitamins A, B1, B2, B3 and C, and also potassium, magnesium, calcium, iron and zinc.

olive oil spray
4 slices of wholemeal (whole-wheat) bread, without crusts
70 g (2^{1}/$_{2}$ oz/^{1}/$_{2}$ cup) chopped dried apricots
250 ml (9 fl oz/1 cup) skim milk
1 tablespoon honey
2 eggs
1 teaspoon finely grated orange zest
^{1}/$_{2}$ teaspoon vanilla essence

sauce
250 ml (9 fl oz/1 cup) orange juice
1 tablespoon cornflour (cornstarch)
1 tablespoon orange juice, extra
1 tablespoon brandy

1. Spray a 1.25 litre (44 fl oz/5 cup) pudding basin with olive oil.

2. Cut each slice of bread into cubes (do not cut through all the slices at once, or the bread will be doughy). Combine the bread cubes with the apricots.

3. Beat together the milk, honey, eggs, orange zest and vanilla. Pour over the bread and leave for 20 minutes.

4. Pour the pudding mixture into the oiled basin and attach the lid, or cover with buttered foil (make a pleat in the foil) and secure with string. Place the pudding basin in a large saucepan and pour in enough water to come halfway up the side of the basin. Steam the pudding over low heat for 1 hour.

5. While the pudding is steaming, make the sauce. Heat the orange juice in a small saucepan until almost boiling. Blend the cornflour with the extra juice and brandy to make a smooth paste. Stir the cornflour mixture into the hot juice and cook for 2–3 minutes, or until thickened.

6. When the pudding is cooked, turn out onto a platter and serve with the sauce.

Brandied oranges

These oranges are a perfect foil for a rich dinner — and they can be prepared ahead. Because the oranges are served whole, it is a good idea to set the table with a small knife and fork, as well as a spoon to scoop up the delicious syrup.

4 oranges
2 tablespoons honey
2 tablespoons brandy

1. Using a potato peeler or a very sharp knife, cut the peel from two of the oranges. Slice the peel into thin strips.

2. Put the orange peel in a small saucepan, cover with water and bring to the boil. Reduce the heat and simmer gently for 10 minutes. Drain and rinse well.

3. Combine 250 ml (9 fl oz/1 cup) water and honey in a large saucepan and bring to the boil. Add the drained peel and simmer for 5 minutes, or until the peel looks clear. Using a slotted spoon, remove the peel and reserve both the peel and syrup.

4. Peel and remove the pith from the remaining oranges, leaving them whole. Add the four whole oranges to the syrup and simmer for 2 minutes, then add the brandy. Cool, then chill well. Serve each orange in a glass dish with some of the syrup, topped with the orange peel shreds.

SERVES 4

PREPARATION TIME: 15 minutes + chilling time

COOKING TIME: 20 minutes

NUTRITIONAL INFORMATION/SERVING:
2 g protein, 0 g fat (0 g saturated fat), 25 g carbohydrate, 4 g dietary fibre, 5 mg sodium, 545 kJ (130 Cals)

A source of vitamins B1, B3 and C.

Mangoes in champagne

SERVES 4
PREPARATION TIME: 10 minutes
COOKING TIME: nil

NUTRITIONAL
INFORMATION/SERVING:
2 g protein, 0.5 g fat (0 g
saturated fat), 21 g carbohydrate,
2.5 g dietary fibre, 10 mg sodium,
545 kJ (130 Cals)

A source of vitamins A, B3 and C,
and also potassium.

This quick and easy dessert is also ideal for children — but use orange juice instead of champagne. If preferred, substitute peaches for the mangoes.

4 mangoes
finely grated zest and juice of 1 orange
250 ml (9 fl oz/1 cup) champagne
mint sprigs, to serve

1. Peel the mangoes and cut slices from each.

2. Combine the orange zest, juice and champagne. Pour over the mango slices and leave for 10 minutes. Decorate with a sprig of mint and serve with almond bread.

Balsamic berries

SERVES 4
PREPARATION TIME: 10 minutes
+ 15 minutes standing time
COOKING TIME: nil

NUTRITIONAL
INFORMATION/SERVING:
2 g protein, 0 g fat (0 g
saturated fat), 7.5 g carbohydrate,
3 g dietary fibre, 10 mg sodium,
170 kJ (40 Cals)

A source of vitamin C and B3.

Strawberries with balsamic vinegar are delicious. If you can't find palm sugar, use soft brown sugar and microwave for 15 seconds to dissolve the sugar.

1 tablespoon grated palm sugar (jaggery)
2 tablespoons balsamic vinegar
500 g (1 lb 2 oz) fresh strawberries, hulled and halved

1. Combine the palm sugar and vinegar, stirring well to dissolve the sugar.

2. Pour over the strawberries and leave for 15 minutes, or up to 1 hour in the refrigerator if preferred. Serve with low-fat yoghurt or ice cream, if desired.

Mangoes in champagne (back) and Balsamic berries (front)

Mango sorbet

SERVES 4

PREPARATION TIME: 10 minutes
+ 2 hours freezing time

COOKING TIME: nil

NUTRITIONAL
INFORMATION/SERVING:
3 g protein, 0 g fat (0 g
saturated fat), 43 g carbohydrate,
1.5 g dietary fibre, 30 mg sodium,
750 kJ (180 Cals)

A source of vitamins A, B2,
B3 and C.

If mangoes are out of season, substitute papaya or melon. Sorbet, as with all ice creams, is best served when it has softened a little, to appreciate its full flavour.

> 3 mangoes, skin and stones removed
> 2 egg whites
> 115 g (4 oz/½ cup) caster (superfine) sugar

1. Purée the mango flesh in a blender.

2. Beat the egg whites in a clean, dry bowl until soft peaks form, gradually adding the sugar.

3. Gently fold the mango purée into the egg white mixture. Spoon into an ice cream machine and churn, following the manufacturer's instructions. Alternatively, pour into a shallow dish and freeze until the edges turn solid, then remove from the freezer and beat in an electric mixer. Refreeze until solid. Soften the sorbet in the refrigerator for 30 minutes before serving.

Coffee cream pots

SERVES 4

PREPARATION TIME: 10 minutes
+ at least 1 hour refrigeration

COOKING TIME: nil

NUTRITIONAL
INFORMATION/SERVING:
16 g protein, 5 g fat (3.5 g
saturated fat), 19 g carbohydrate,
0 g dietary fibre, 125 mg sodium,
800 kJ (190 Cals)

A source of vitamins A, B2 and B3,
and also calcium and zinc.

Here's a great recipe for those who like a rich-tasting creamy dessert, which is made without any cream. Use small individual straight-sided dishes for serving.

> 500 g (1 lb 2 oz/2 cups) low-fat ricotta cheese
> 2 tablespoons strong coffee (use decaffeinated if desired)
> 55 g (2 oz/¼ cup) caster (superfine) sugar
> pinch of ground cinnamon
> 1 tablespoon brandy

1. Put all the ingredients in the bowl of an electric mixer and beat until very smooth. Spoon into four small dishes and refrigerate for at least 1 hour.

Poached peaches

Use white or yellow peaches for this dessert, or substitute nectarines.

4 peaches
250 ml (9 fl oz/1 cup) white wine
1 tablespoon honey
1 piece of cinnamon stick
2 teaspoons finely grated orange zest

1. Skin the peaches by pouring boiling water over them. Leave for 1 minute, then drain. The skins will peel off easily.

2. Place the whole peeled peaches in a saucepan and add the honey, cinnamon stick and orange zest. Bring to the boil, cover and simmer for 5 minutes. Turn off the heat and leave until cold. Remove the cinnamon stick and chill the peaches until ready to serve.

SERVES 4
PREPARATION TIME: 10 minutes
COOKING TIME: 5 minutes

NUTRITIONAL INFORMATION/SERVING:
1 g protein, 0 g fat (0 g saturated fat), 13 g carbohydrate, 1.5 g dietary fibre, 5 mg sodium, 235 kJ (55 Cals)

A source of vitamins B3 and C.

Banana whip

No dessert is as simple as this recipe, which I first made over 35 years ago. Serve it in crisp ice cream cones for children.

6 bananas, peeled

1. Place the bananas in a freezer bag and freeze for at least 2 hours, or until frozen (they will never be rock hard).

2. Break the frozen bananas into chunks and process in a food processor until the chunks break up and turn into a thick creamy soft-serve. Serve at once in small bowls or place in a freezer tray for up to 24 hours.

SERVES 6
PREPARATION TIME: 5 minutes + 2 hours freezing time
COOKING TIME: nil

NUTRITIONAL INFORMATION/SERVING:
2 g protein, 0 g fat (0 g saturated fat), 24 g carbohydrate, 2.5 g dietary fibre, 5 mg sodium, 430 kJ (105 Cals)

A source of vitamins B2, B3, B6 and C, and also potassium.

Raspberry ice cream

Berries are not only delicious but they contain lots of healthy antioxidants that help us fight disease. Fresh berries should be used soon after they are bought, as they don't store for long. Frozen berries will work just as well if fresh are unavailable, but let them thaw first.

500 ml (17 fl oz/2 cups) skim milk
125 ml (4 fl oz/½ cup) evaporated skim milk
50 g (1¾ oz/½ cup) skim milk powder
1 tablespoon pure cornflour (cornstarch)*
1 teaspoon vanilla essence
3 tablespoons honey
300 g (10½ oz) fresh or frozen raspberries, thawed

* Check cornflour is gluten-free.

1. Combine all the ingredients, except the raspberries, in a blender or food processor.

2. Pour the mixture into a saucepan and heat gently, stirring continuously until the mixture boils and thickens. Cool slightly.

3. Add the raspberries to the mixture, then spoon into an ice cream machine and churn, following the manufacturer's instructions. Alternatively, pour into a shallow dish and freeze until the edges turn solid, then remove from the freezer and beat in an electric mixer. Refreeze until solid. Leave to soften a little in the refrigerator before serving.

SERVES 6

PREPARATION TIME: 15 minutes + 1–4 hours freezing time

COOKING TIME: 5 minutes

NUTRITIONAL INFORMATION/SERVING:
10 g protein, 0.5 g fat (0 g saturated fat), 28 g carbohydrate, 2 g dietary fibre, 115 mg sodium, 635 kJ (150 Cals)

A source of vitamins B1, B2, B3 and C, and also potassium, calcium and zinc.

 HINT

In summer, freeze fruits for a refreshing snack or even dessert. Seedless grapes, chunks of peeled melon, peach or apricot halves, peeled bananas and orange quarters all freeze well.

Lemon heart with berries

You'll need a heart-shaped baking tin for this dessert, although you could use a round one or set them in individual moulds. This luscious but light dessert would be ideal for a Valentine's Day dinner party.

SERVES 6

PREPARATION TIME: 20 minutes
+ 3 hours setting time

COOKING TIME: nil

NUTRITIONAL
INFORMATION/SERVING:
11 g protein, 3.5 g fat (2 g
saturated fat), 13 g carbohydrate,
3.5 g dietary fibre, 135 mg sodium,
560 kJ (135 Cals)

A source of vitamins B2, B3 and C,
and also calcium and zinc.

2 teaspoons powdered gelatine
2 tablespoons lemon juice
250 g (9 oz/1 cup) low-fat ricotta cheese
250 g (9 oz/1 cup) low-fat natural yoghurt
2 egg whites
2 tablespoons caster (superfine) sugar

fruit topping
250 g (9 oz) strawberries
300 g (10½ oz) frozen raspberries, thawed
1 tablespoon rum (optional)

1. Soften the gelatine in 1 tablespoon cold water in a saucepan. Add the lemon juice and heat gently until the gelatine dissolves.

2. Beat together the ricotta, yoghurt and gelatine mixture.

3. Beat the egg whites until firm peaks form, gradually adding the sugar. Gently fold into the ricotta mixture.

4. Rinse a heart-shaped baking tin with cold water. Pour the ricotta mixture into the tin and refrigerate for 2–3 hours.

5. Meanwhile, make the fruit topping. Hull the strawberries and slice them. Combine with the raspberries and rum (if using) and leave to stand, covered, for at least 30 minutes. Turn the lemon heart out of the tin and top with the berries.

HINT

If using frozen berries in baked goods, thaw the berries first. Either sit them on a paper towel, which will soak up the water, or gently pat them dry after they have thawed. Too much water will only dilute their flavour.

Baked stuffed apples

Baked apples are a healthy dessert that is easy to make. Choose green apples, such as granny smiths, as these hold their shape well when cooked. Or you can try other apples such as golden delicious, braeburn, jonagold or pink lady.

    4 green apples, cored
    12 pitted prunes
    12 pecans
    250 ml (9 fl oz/1 cup) apple juice

1. Preheat oven to 180°C (350°F/Gas 4). Using a sharp knife, make a tiny slit around the centre of each apple so the skin will not burst while cooking.

2. Stuff each apple with three prunes and three pecans.

3. Place the apples in an ovenproof dish, just large enough to hold them. Pour the apple juice over the apples and bake for 25 minutes. Serve hot.

SERVES 4

PREPARATION TIME: 10 minutes

COOKING TIME: 25 minutes

NUTRITIONAL INFORMATION/SERVING:
1.5 g protein, 3 g fat (0 g saturated fat), 31 g carbohydrate, 5.5 g dietary fibre, 5 mg sodium, 645 kJ (155 Cals)

A source of vitamins B3 and C, and also potassium.

 HINT

Baked apples can also be prepared in a hurry in the microwave. One apple needs 2$\frac{1}{2}$ minutes and two apples need 4 minutes in the microwave. To prevent the apples bursting when being baked or microwaved, make a thin sharp cut around the middle of the apple skin.

Peach crumble

Vary this healthy crumble by using different fruits — peaches, apricots, apples or plums are delicious. Pie pack peaches are tinned peaches with no added liquid or other ingredients, and may also be labelled 'baker's peaches'.

SERVES 6
PREPARATION TIME: 15 minutes
COOKING TIME: 25 minutes

NUTRITIONAL
INFORMATION/SERVING:
5.5 g protein, 9 g fat (2.5 g saturated fat), 25 g carbohydrate, 5 g dietary fibre, 25 mg sodium, 845 kJ (200 Cals)

A source of vitamins A, B1, B2, B3, C and E, and also potassium, magnesium, iron and zinc.

2 x 400 g (14 oz) tins pie pack peaches
1 teaspoon ground cinnamon
100 g (3 1/2 oz/1 cup) rolled (porridge) oats
45 g (1 1/2 oz/1/2 cup) wheatgerm
15 g (1/2 oz/1/4 cup) flaked coconut
2 tablespoons dark brown sugar
2 tablespoons sunflower seeds
2 tablespoons chopped hazelnuts
2 tablespoons reduced-fat dairy blend

1. Preheat oven to 180°C (350°F/Gas 4). Place the peaches in an 18 cm (7 inch) square ovenproof dish or divide the mixture among individual ramekins.

2. Place the remaining dry ingredients into a bowl and rub in the dairy blend with your fingertips, mixing until well combined. Spoon over the peaches and press down slightly. If using the larger dish, bake for 25 minutes, or until the crumble is golden. If using the ramekins, bake for 15–20 minutes.

SERVES 6

PREPARATION TIME: 30 minutes
+ overnight standing time

COOKING TIME: 5 minutes

NUTRITIONAL
INFORMATION/SERVING:
8 g protein, 2 g fat (0.5 g
saturated fat), 38 g carbohydrate,
11 g dietary fibre, 220 mg sodium,
850 kJ (205 Cals)

A source of vitamins B1, B2, B3
and C, and also potassium,
magnesium, iron and zinc.

Summer berry pudding

Serve this at Christmas time instead of a heavy pudding, flaming it with brandy for a dramatic effect. Use frozen berries if desired.

8–10 slices of bread, crusts removed
60 ml (2 fl oz/¼ cup) blackcurrant juice
2 tablespoons sugar
1.5 kg (3 lb 5 oz) mixed berries

1. Line the base and side of a 1 litre (35 fl oz/4 cup) pudding basin with the bread, cutting the slices to fit. Avoid leaving any gaps, but do not overlap the bread. Reserve the leftover bread.

2. Heat the blackcurrant juice in a saucepan and add the sugar, stirring until the sugar dissolves. Add the berries and squash slightly to release the juices.

3. Tip the berries and the juice into the bread-lined pudding basin, reserving about 125 ml (4 fl oz/½ cup) of the juices. Top with the remaining bread and pour the reserved juices over the bread.

4. Cover with plastic wrap and fit a flat plate into the top of the basin. Place a heavy tin or other weight on top and refrigerate for at least 12 hours. Turn the pudding out onto a plate to serve. Serve with thick low-fat natural yoghurt or cream.

Apricot soufflé

Soufflés are easier to make than they seem, and their puffed golden domes straight from the oven are an impressive finale to any meal.

140 g (5 oz/1 cup) dried apricots
125 ml (4 fl oz/½ cup) orange juice
light olive oil spray
3 egg whites
2 tablespoons caster (superfine) sugar

1. Place the apricots and orange juice in a saucepan, bring to the boil, then cover and cook over low heat for 10 minutes. Cool for 10 minutes, then purée in a blender.

2. Preheat oven to 160°C (315°F/Gas 2–3). Lightly spray four 250 ml (9 fl oz/1 cup) soufflé dishes with olive oil.

3. Beat the egg whites until soft peaks form, add the sugar and continue beating until the sugar has dissolved.

4. Fold the apricot purée into the egg whites and spoon into the soufflé dishes. Bake for 15–20 minutes, or until the soufflés are well risen. Serve at once.

SERVES 4
PREPARATION TIME: 20 minutes
COOKING TIME: 20 minutes

NUTRITIONAL INFORMATION/SERVING:
4.5 g protein, 0 g fat (0 g saturated fat), 25 g carbohydrate, 3.5 g dietary fibre, 55 mg sodium, 490 kJ (115 Cals)

A source of vitamins A, B3 and C, and also potassium and iron.

HINT

After you have poured the soufflé mixture into ramekins, run your thumb around the inside of the dish, just around the rim. This will help the soufflé to rise without sticking to the side of the dish.

Coconut and almond kulfi

Kulfi is the traditional ice cream of India, usually set in a conical mould and often decorated with gold or silver leaf for special occasions. This recipe is lower in fat than the original, which is based on whole milk. Serve this delicious iced confection after a simple curry, but it's rich, so serve small portions — a small glass is ideal.

500 ml (17 fl oz/2 cups) skim milk
125 ml (4 fl oz/1/2 cup) evaporated skim milk
100 g (3 1/2 oz/1 cup) skim milk powder
1 tablespoon custard powder, or use cornflour (cornstarch)
30 g (1 oz/1/3 cup) desiccated coconut
75 g (2 1/2 oz/1/3 cup) sugar*
40 g (1 1/2 oz/1/3 cup) slivered almonds
2 teaspoons finely grated orange zest
1 teaspoon vanilla essence

* Equivalent in powdered sweetener could be used.

1. Combine the skim milks, milk powder, custard powder and coconut in a saucepan. Stir continuously over low heat until the mixture boils and thickens.

2. Add the sugar, almonds, orange zest and vanilla and stir to combine. Remove from the heat and leave to cool.

3. When cool, pour the mixture into an ice cream machine and churn, following the manufacturer's instructions. Alternatively, pour into a shallow dish and freeze until the edges turn solid, then remove from the freezer and beat in an electric mixer. Refreeze until solid.

4. Serve in small portions with sliced mango or other fresh fruit.

SERVES 6
PREPARATION TIME: 15 minutes
+ 1–3 hours freezing time
COOKING TIME: 10 minutes

NUTRITIONAL
INFORMATION/SERVING:
13 g protein, 6.5 g fat (3 g
saturated fat), 30 g carbohydrate,
1.5 g dietary fibre, 130 mg sodium,
945 kJ (225 Cals)

A source of vitamins B2 and B3,
and also potassium, magnesium,
calcium and zinc.

SERVES 4
PREPARATION TIME: 10 minutes
COOKING TIME: 10 minutes

NUTRITIONAL
INFORMATION/SERVING:
2.5 g protein, 0 g fat (0 g
saturated fat), 33 g carbohydrate,
3 g dietary fibre, 5 mg sodium,
590 kJ (140 Cals)

A source of vitamins B2, B3, B6
and C, and also potassium.

Flaming bananas

This is a good weeknight dessert, which also works just as well with fresh peach or nectarine halves.

4 bananas, peeled and sliced lengthways
1 tablespoon soft brown sugar
1 teaspoon thinly sliced orange zest
60 ml (2 fl oz/¼ cup) orange juice
¼ teaspoon ground cinnamon
2 tablespoons rum or brandy

1. Preheat oven to 180°C (350°F/Gas 4). Place the sliced bananas in a shallow ovenproof dish.

2. Combine the sugar, orange zest, orange juice and cinnamon and dot over the bananas. Bake for 10 minutes.

3. Remove the bananas from the oven and place in a serving dish. Heat the rum or brandy in a small saucepan until it is warm, light it and carefully pour the flaming brandy over the bananas.

HINT

Stop apples, pears and
bananas going brown by
brushing cut surfaces with
a little lemon juice.

Fruity bread pudding

Bread puddings are usually high in fat but this low-fat version is excellent. Raw sugar has a little molasses added and is often used in baked goods to give a wonderful flavour and aroma. If you don't have any, use brown sugar.

2 tablespoons raisins
1 tablespoon whisky
8 slices of raisin bread, crusts removed
2 tablespoons raw (demerara) sugar
3 eggs
500 ml (17 fl oz/2 cups) low-fat milk
1/2 teaspoon vanilla essence

1. Soak the raisins in the whisky for at least 30 minutes.

2. Cut each slice of bread into four triangles. Place half the bread triangles in a greased ovenproof dish. Top with the raisins and sprinkle with half the sugar.

3. Preheat oven to 180°C (350°F/Gas 4). Beat together the eggs, milk and vanilla. Pour over the bread and raisins. Top with the remaining bread and sprinkle with the remaining sugar. Bake for 40 minutes, or until the pudding is set and the top is crusty.

SERVES 6
PREPARATION TIME: 15 minutes
COOKING TIME: 40 minutes

NUTRITIONAL
INFORMATION/SERVING:
10 g protein, 5.5 g fat (2 g saturated fat), 35 g carbohydrate, 1.5 g dietary fibre, 160 mg sodium, 985 kJ (235 Cals)

A source of vitamins B2 and B3, and also potassium, calcium, iron and zinc.

Lemon delicious

SERVES 4

PREPARATION TIME: 10 minutes

COOKING TIME: 30 minutes

NUTRITIONAL
INFORMATION/SERVING:
8.5 g protein, 2.5 g fat (1 g
saturated fat), 40 g carbohydrate,
0.5 g dietary fibre, 85 mg sodium,
900 kJ (215 Cals)

A source of vitamins B2, B3 and C,
and also calcium.

This low-fat version of an old favourite is wonderful on a cold evening. Substitute lime, grapefruit or orange for the lemon if desired.

1 teaspoon grated lemon zest
125 ml (4 fl oz/1/2 cup) lemon juice
115 g (4 oz/1/2 cup) caster (superfine) sugar
2 tablespoons self-raising flour
2 eggs, separated
50 g (13/4 oz/1/2 cup) skim milk powder

1. Preheat oven to 180°C (350°F/Gas 4).

2. Combine 125 ml (4 fl oz/1/2 cup) water, lemon zest, lemon juice, half the sugar, flour, egg yolks and milk powder in a blender and process until smooth.

2. Beat the egg whites until soft peaks form, then slowly add the remaining sugar and continue beating until stiff. Gently fold the egg whites into the lemon mixture and pour into a 16 cm (61/4 inch) round ovenproof dish. Place into a baking dish and pour hot water into the baking dish so it comes halfway up the side of the ovenproof dish. Bake for 30 minutes. Serve hot.

Passionfruit lime mousse

Served in tall glasses, this is a dessert for family or guests.

SERVES 4

PREPARATION TIME: 20 minutes
+ 4 hours setting time

COOKING TIME: nil

NUTRITIONAL
INFORMATION/SERVING:
6 g protein, 0 g fat (0 g
saturated fat), 15 g carbohydrate,
9.5 g dietary fibre, 60 mg sodium,
380 kJ (90 Cals)

A source of vitamins A, B1, B2, B3
and C, and also potassium,
magnesium and calcium.

2 teaspoons powdered gelatine
125 ml (4 fl oz/½ cup) boiling water
pulp from 8–10 passionfruit
2 tablespoons lime juice
3 egg whites
3 tablespoons sugar

1. Dissolve the gelatine powder in the boiling water. Stir in the passionfruit pulp and lime juice.

2. Beat the egg whites until soft peaks form, gradually adding the sugar. Fold into the passionfruit mixture and pour into individual glasses. Chill in the refrigerator for 2–4 hours to set.

HINT

Passionfruit have one of the highest levels of dietary fibre of any fruit. They make a healthy snack food and are easy to grow in the home garden.

Wholemeal lemon pikelets

Whip up these healthy pikelets for a Sunday afternoon treat.

300 g (10½ oz/2 cups) wholemeal (whole-wheat) flour, sifted
1 tablespoon caster (superfine) sugar
2 eggs, separated
375 ml (13 fl oz/1½ cups) skim milk
1 tablespoon lemon juice
1 teaspoon finely grated lemon zest
olive oil spray

1. Combine the flour, sugar, egg yolks, milk, lemon juice and lemon zest in a bowl and mix until smooth. Leave to stand for at least 15 minutes, or longer in the refrigerator if desired.

2. Beat the egg whites until stiff peaks form, then gently fold the egg whites into the flour mixture.

3. Spray a heavy-based frying pan with olive oil and heat. Spoon the batter into the pan, a tablespoon at a time, and cook until bubbles appear on the surface. Flip the pikelet over and cook the other side for 1 minute. Serve warm with whipped low-fat ricotta cheese or with a squeeze of lemon juice.

MAKES ABOUT 32 PIKELETS

PREPARATION TIME: 15 minutes + 15 minutes standing time

COOKING TIME: 15 minutes

NUTRITIONAL INFORMATION/4 PIKELETS: 6 g protein, 2 g fat (0.5 g saturated fat), 22 g carbohydrate, 4.5 g dietary fibre, 20 mg sodium, 555 kJ (135 Cals)

A source of vitamins B1 and B3, and also magnesium and iron.

Ricotta cheesecake

Halfway between a moist cake and a cheesecake, this recipe is delicious served with whole or puréed raspberries or puréed apricots. Use ricotta cheese from the delicatessen section of the supermarket, not the whipped low-fat variety found in small tubs.

3 eggs, separated
3 tablespoons sugar
500 g (1 lb 2 oz/2 cups) low-fat ricotta cheese
1 tablespoon honey
2 tablespoons plain (all-purpose) flour
2 teaspoons finely grated lemon zest
1 tablespoon lemon juice
250 g (9 oz/1 cup) low-fat natural yoghurt

1. Preheat oven to 160°C (315°F/Gas 2–3). Grease and line a 20 cm (8 inch) spring-form cake tin with baking paper.

2. Beat the egg whites in a bowl until soft peaks form. Add the sugar and continue beating until stiff. Gently tip the egg whites onto a plate.

3. Using the same bowl (no need to wash), combine the remaining ingredients and beat until smooth. Fold in the egg white mixture and pour into the prepared tin.

4. Bake for 40 minutes. Turn off the oven and leave in the oven to cool. Refrigerate until ready to serve, then remove from the tin and place on a serving plate.

SERVES 6
PREPARATION TIME: 15 minutes
COOKING TIME: 40 minutes

NUTRITIONAL
INFORMATION/SERVING:
15 g protein, 8.5 g fat (5 g saturated fat), 18 g carbohydrate, 0 g dietary fibre, 220 mg sodium, 925 kJ (220 Cals)

A source of vitamins A, B1, B2 and B3, and also calcium and zinc.

Apricot squares

MAKES ABOUT 48 SQUARES
PREPARATION TIME: 25 minutes
+ refrigeration time
COOKING TIME: 2 minutes

NUTRITIONAL
INFORMATION/2 SQUARES:
3 g protein, 2.5 g fat (0.5 g
saturated fat), 11 g carbohydrate,
1.5 g dietary fibre, 30 mg sodium,
310 kJ (75 Cals)

A source of vitamins B2 and E.

This recipe is great for any keen young chef because it doesn't require baking, but younger children will need help with the first step. Make fresh breadcrumbs in a blender or food processor.

140 g (5 oz/1 cup) chopped dried apricots
90 g (3¼ oz/¾ cup) sultanas (golden raisins)
125 g (4½ oz/½ cup) chopped pitted prunes
125 ml (4 fl oz/½ cup) orange juice
100 g (3½ oz/1 cup) skim milk powder
30 g (1 oz/½ cup) fresh wholemeal (whole-wheat) breadcrumbs
80 g (2¾ oz/½ cup) chopped almonds
2 tablespoons desiccated coconut

1. Combine the apricots, sultanas, prunes and orange juice in a saucepan. Bring to the boil, then turn off the heat, cover and leave to stand for 15 minutes.

2. Add the milk powder, breadcrumbs and almonds and mix thoroughly.

3. Sprinkle half the coconut over the base of a non-stick 25 x 18 cm (10 x 7 inch) shallow tin. Press the mixture into the tin and sprinkle with the remaining coconut, pressing it in well. Cover and refrigerate for several hours. Cut into small squares to serve.

Fruit slice

This is a good alternative to muesli bars. Children will have fun shaping the mixture and rolling it in the coconut.

180 g (6 oz/1 cup) pitted dates
125 g (4¹/₂ oz/1 cup) sultanas (golden raisins)
125 g (4¹/₂ oz/1 cup) raisins
75 g (2¹/₂ oz/¹/₂ cup) currants
90 g (3¹/₂ oz/³/₄ cup) chopped walnuts
30 g (1 oz/¹/₄ cup) sunflower seeds
2 tablespoons desiccated coconut
2 tablespoons lemon juice
1 tablespoon desiccated coconut, extra

1. Place the dates, sultanas, raisins, currants and walnuts into a food processor and process until chopped. Add the sunflower seeds, coconut and lemon juice and mix well.

2. Using wet hands, divide the mixture in half and shape into two logs. Lightly toast the extra coconut in a dry frying pan until light brown, then tip onto a plate. Roll the logs in the toasted coconut. Wrap in plastic wrap and refrigerate for several hours before cutting into slices.

MAKES ABOUT 48 SLICES
PREPARATION TIME: 20 minutes + refrigeration time
COOKING TIME: nil

NUTRITIONAL INFORMATION/2 SLICES:
1.5 g protein, 4 g fat (0.5 g saturated fat), 15 g carbohydrate, 2 g dietary fibre, 10 mg sodium, 410 kJ (100 Cals)

A source of vitamins B3 and E.

BAKING

Cakes and other sweet baked goods are fine to enjoy
occasionally — and they can be healthy, especially if you
keep the portions small.

Date loaf

A mixture of flours gives a better result when making gluten-free cakes.

MAKES 16 SLICES

PREPARATION TIME: 15 minutes
+ 20 minutes cooling time

BAKING TIME: 45 minutes

NUTRITIONAL
INFORMATION/SLICE:
2 g protein, 0.5 g fat (0 g
saturated fat), 22 g carbohydrate,
1.5 g dietary fibre, 145 mg sodium,
405 kJ (95 Cals)

A source of vitamin B3.

160 g (5^1/$_2$ oz/1 cup) chopped dates
1 teaspoon bicarbonate of soda (baking soda)
2 tablespoons honey
250 ml (9 fl oz/1 cup) apple juice
175 g (6 oz/1 cup) brown rice flour
35 g (1^1/$_4$ oz/^{1}/$_4$ cup) buckwheat flour
20 g (^{3}/$_4$ oz/^{1}/$_4$ cup) soy flour
2 teaspoons baking powder

1. Place the dates, bicarbonate of soda, honey and apple juice into a saucepan. Bring to the boil, turn off the heat and leave for 20 minutes to cool slightly.

2. Preheat oven to 180°C (350°F/Gas 4). Grease and line a 21 x 11 cm (8^1/$_4$ x 4^1/$_4$ inch) loaf (bar) tin with baking paper.

3. Sift the flours and baking powder into a bowl. Stir in the date mixture, then pour into the prepared tin and bake for 45 minutes, or until a skewer inserted into the middle of the loaf comes out clean. Turn out and cool before slicing.

Dried fruit and nut loaf

Here's an easy-to-make loaf that's great to pack for bushwalks or picnics. Pecans are a good source of healthy omega 3 fat.

MAKES 16 SLICES

PREPARATION TIME: 15 minutes

BAKING TIME: 1 hour

NUTRITIONAL
INFORMATION/SLICE:
5 g protein, 3.5 g fat (0.5 g
saturated fat), 27 g carbohydrate,
4.5 g dietary fibre, 255 mg sodium,
665 kJ (160 Cals)

A source of vitamins B1, B2 and B3,
and also potassium, magnesium,
iron and zinc.

50 g (1^3/$_4$ oz/^{1}/$_2$ cup) pecans
130 g (4^1/$_2$ oz/2 cups) processed bran cereal
120 g (4^1/$_4$ oz/^{3}/$_4$ cup) chopped dried fruit medley (apples, peaches, sultanas/golden raisins)
185 g (6^1/$_2$ oz/1 cup) soft brown sugar
225 g (8 oz/1^1/$_2$ cups) wholemeal (whole-wheat) self-raising flour, sifted
375 ml (13 fl oz/1^1/$_2$ cups) low-fat milk
2 eggs, beaten

1. Toast the pecans in a dry frying pan, tossing frequently so the nuts are browned, taking care they do not burn. Set aside to cool.

2. Meanwhile, preheat oven to 180°C (350°F/Gas 4). Grease and line a 21 x 11 cm (8^1/$_4$ x 4^1/$_4$ inch) loaf (bar) tin with baking paper.

3. Combine all the ingredients, except the pecans, in a bowl. Spoon into the prepared tin and press the pecans into the top of the mixture. Bake for 1 hour, or until a skewer inserted into the middle of the loaf comes out clean. Cool for 5 minutes, then turn out of the tin.

Apricot and almond loaf

The flavour of cardamom is wonderful in this loaf, but use cinnamon if preferred. This loaf keeps for several days in an airtight container.

200 g (7 oz) dried apricots
250 ml (9 fl oz/1 cup) orange juice
1 egg
125 ml (4 fl oz/^{1}/$_2$ cup) skim milk
2 teaspoons finely grated lemon zest
80 g (2^3/$_4$ oz/^{1}/$_2$ cup) roughly chopped almonds
45 g (1^1/$_2$ oz/^{1}/$_2$ cup) wheatgerm
150 g (5^1/$_2$ oz/1 cup) wholemeal (whole-wheat) self-raising flour, sifted
1 teaspoon baking powder
^{1}/$_2$ teaspoon ground cardamom or 1 teaspoon ground cinnamon

1. Preheat oven to 180°C (350°F/Gas 4). Lightly grease a 21 x 11 cm (8^1/$_4$ x 4^1/$_4$ inch) loaf (bar) tin.

2. Place the apricots and orange juice into a saucepan and bring to the boil. Cover and leave to stand until cooled slightly.

3. Combine the egg, milk, lemon zest, almonds, and apricots and orange juice in a bowl and mix well. Add the wheatgerm, sifted flour, baking powder and cardamom, tipping the wheat 'bits' from the sifter into the mixture.

4. Pour the mixture into the prepared tin and bake for 35 minutes. Turn out and cool before serving.

MAKES 16 SLICES
PREPARATION TIME: 15 minutes
+ 30 minutes cooling time
BAKING TIME: 35 minutes

NUTRITIONAL
INFORMATION/SLICE:
4 g protein, 3.5 g fat (0.5 g saturated fat), 13 g carbohydrate, 3.5 g dietary fibre, 105 mg sodium, 420 kJ (100 Cals)

A source of vitamins B1, B2, B3 and E, and also potassium, magnesium and calcium.

 HINT

If you don't have enough people to eat the whole cake or loaf, wrap individual slices and freeze them.

Low-fat chocolate cake

SERVES 8
PREPARATION TIME: 20 minutes
BAKING TIME: 35 minutes

NUTRITIONAL
INFORMATION/SERVING:
4.5 g protein, 1 g fat (0.5 g
saturated fat), 36 g carbohydrate,
2 g dietary fibre, 195 mg sodium,
710 kJ (170 Cals)

A source of potassium,
magnesium and iron.

A chocolate mud cake can have 80 grams of fat per slice, but this cake has just 1 gram. This cake is best eaten on the day of baking.

100 g (3^1/$_2$ oz/^{1}/$_2$ cup) pitted prunes
250 ml (9 fl oz/1 cup) apple juice, no added sugar
^{1}/$_4$ teaspoon bicarbonate of soda (baking soda)
125 g (4^1/$_2$ oz/1 cup) self-raising flour
40 g (1^1/$_2$ oz/^{1}/$_3$ cup) unsweetened cocoa powder
4 egg whites
115 g (4 oz/^{1}/$_2$ cup) caster (superfine) sugar
2 teaspoons icing (confectioners') sugar

1. Preheat oven to 160°C (315°F/Gas 2–3). Grease and line a 20 cm (8 inch) round cake tin with baking paper.

2. Place the prunes, apple juice and bicarbonate of soda into a saucepan, bring to the boil, turn off the heat, then cover and leave until cool. Transfer to a food processor or blender and purée until smooth.

3. Sift the flour and cocoa into the cooled prune purée and stir to combine.

4. Beat the egg whites until soft peaks form, then gradually add the sugar. Continue beating until stiff. Using a large metal spoon, fold half the egg whites into the prune mixture and then gently fold in the remaining egg whites.

5. Spoon into the prepared tin and bake for 35 minutes, or until a skewer inserted into the middle of the cake comes out clean. Cool on a rack. Transfer to a serving plate and just before serving, sift icing sugar over the top.

HINT

A healthy cake can be undone by a big blob of cream. Try thick drained yoghurt as a replacement. To make drained yoghurt, place a sieve lined with an absorbent cloth over a basin and fill it with 500 g (1 lb 2 oz/2 cups) low-fat vanilla yoghurt. Leave it overnight in the refrigerator to drain.

Seeded fruit loaf

MAKES ABOUT 16 SLICES

PREPARATION TIME: 15 minutes
+ 30 minutes standing time

BAKING TIME: 45 minutes

NUTRITIONAL
INFORMATION/SLICE:
4.5 g protein, 2.5 g fat (0.5 g
saturated fat), 16 g carbohydrate,
4 g dietary fibre, 115 mg sodium,
435 kJ (105 Cals)

A source of vitamins B1, B2, B3
and E, and also magnesium, calcium
and iron.

This healthy fruit loaf is an excellent way to add seeds to the diet. Seeds are highly nutritious, providing a rich source of vitamin E and many other vitamins and minerals.

65 g (2¼ oz/1 cup) processed bran cereal
45 g (1½ oz/½ cup) wheatgerm
375 ml (13 fl oz/1½ cups) skim milk
140 g (5 oz/1 cup) chopped dried fruit medley (apples, peaches, sultanas/golden raisins)
1 teaspoon vanilla essence
2 tablespoons dark brown sugar
30 g (1 oz/¼ cup) sunflower seeds
40 g (1½ oz/¼ cup) poppy seeds
150 g (5½ oz/1 cup) wholemeal (whole-wheat) self-raising flour

1. Place all the ingredients, except 1 tablespoon of the poppy seeds and the flour, into a bowl and leave for 30 minutes.

2. Preheat oven to 180°C (350°F/Gas 4). Grease a non-stick 21 x 11 cm (8¼ x 4¼ inch) loaf (bar) tin.

3. Sift the flour into the bowl, tipping the wheat 'bits' out of the sifter into the mixture. Mix well. Spoon into the prepared tin, top with the remaining poppy seeds and bake for 45 minutes. Turn out and cool before slicing.

HINT

Use baking paper to line cake tins and you won't need to worry about cakes sticking to the tin. It also saves added fat.

Wholemeal date scones

Date scones are an old favourite and are a perfect treat for afternoon tea. Dates have a high sugar content, so they provide enough sweetness here without the need for any added sweeteners.

2 teaspoons lemon juice
185 ml (6 fl oz/¾ cup) low-fat milk
300 g (10½ oz/2 cups) wholemeal (whole-wheat) self-raising flour
1 teaspoon baking powder
1 tablespoon reduced-fat dairy blend
80 g (2¾ oz/½ cup) chopped dates
milk, for brushing

1. Add the lemon juice to the milk in a bowl and set aside for 5 minutes until the milk thickens.

2. Preheat oven to 220°C (425°F/Gas 7).

3. Sift the flour and baking powder into a bowl, tipping the wheat 'bits' from the sifter back into the flour. Rub in the dairy blend using your fingertips (or this can be done in a food processor).

4. Add the dates and milk mixture and mix quickly to a soft dough. Turn out onto a floured surface, knead lightly and pat to a 2.5 cm (1 inch) thickness. Using a 5 cm (2 inch) cutter, cut the dough into 10 scones and place them on a greased baking tray, leaving about 1 cm (½ inch) between them. Brush the tops with a little milk so they will brown, and bake for 10–12 minutes.

5. Cool on a rack if you like your scones to have crisp edges, or wrap in a clean tea towel (dish towel) if you prefer them with soft edges. Split and serve with jam or low-fat spread.

MAKES 10
PREPARATION TIME: 15 minutes
BAKING TIME: 12 minutes

NUTRITIONAL INFORMATION/SCONE:
4.5 g protein, 1.5 g fat (0.5 g saturated fat), 22 g carbohydrate, 4 g dietary fibre, 250 mg sodium, 505 kJ (120 Cals)

A source of vitamins B1 and B3, and also magnesium and iron.

 HINT

All baked cakes and biscuits can damage teeth, so always brush teeth after eating them. If that isn't possible, at least rinse your mouth with water.

Apple and carrot muffins

Muffins are great as a snack and make lovely treats for a special breakfast picnic or packed lunches. Unlike most muffins, where the fat content can range anywhere from 10 to 20 grams of fat per serve, these have only 1.5 grams each. The muffins are best eaten on the day of baking.

1 large green apple, peeled and cored
1 large carrot
2 tablespoons dark brown sugar
2 eggs
250 ml (9 fl oz/1 cup) evaporated skim milk
1 teaspoon ground cinnamon
200 g (7 oz/1⅓ cups) wholemeal (whole-wheat) flour
2 teaspoons baking powder
45 g (1½ oz/½ cup) wheatgerm

1. Preheat oven to 190°C (375°F/Gas 5). Grease a 12-hole standard muffin tin.

2. Finely grate the apple and carrot using a food processor. Add the sugar, eggs and milk and whizz until well blended.

3. Sift the cinnamon, flour and baking powder into the carrot mixture, tipping the wheat 'bits' out of the sifter into the mixture. Add the wheatgerm and mix quickly, taking care not to overmix. (The mixture will be quite moist.)

4. Spoon the mixture into the prepared muffin tin and bake for 20 minutes. Cool in the tin for 5 minutes, then turn onto a rack. Serve the muffins warm.

MAKES 12
PREPARATION TIME: 15 minutes
BAKING TIME: 20 minutes

NUTRITIONAL
INFORMATION/MUFFIN:
6 g protein, 1.5 g fat (0.5 g saturated fat), 17 g carbohydrate, 3.5 g dietary fibre, 115 mg sodium, 440 kJ (105 Cals)

A source of vitamins A, B1, B2, B3 and E, and also calcium and iron.

Apple and carrot muffins and Zucchini and apple muffins

Zucchini and apple muffins

MAKES 12
PREPARATION TIME: 15 minutes
BAKING TIME: 20 minutes

NUTRITIONAL
INFORMATION/MUFFIN:
4 g protein, 9 g fat (1.5 g
saturated fat), 25 g carbohydrate,
1.5 g dietary fibre, 165 mg sodium,
825 kJ (195 Cals)

A source of vitamin B3.

Zucchini is another vegetable, like carrot, that can easily be incorporated into sweet muffins, adding lots of healthy vitamins and also keeping the batter moist. Use a food processor to grate the zucchini and apple to make preparation time shorter, and serve the muffins while they are warm.

250 g (9 oz/2 cups) self-raising flour
95 g (3¼ oz/½ cup) soft brown sugar
135 g (4¾ oz/1 cup) grated zucchini (courgette)
1 large apple, peeled, cored and grated
2 eggs
1 teaspoon vanilla essence
2 tablespoons macadamia oil or light olive oil
185 ml (6 fl oz/¾ cup) reduced-fat milk

1. Preheat oven to 190°C (375°F/Gas 5). Grease a 12-hole standard muffin tin.

2. Sift the flour into a bowl and stir in the sugar, zucchini and apple.

3. Beat the eggs with the vanilla, oil and milk and mix into the flour mixture, taking care not to overmix. Spoon the mixture into the prepared muffin tin and bake for 20 minutes. Cool in the tin for 5 minutes, then turn onto a rack.

HINT

It is important not to overwork the muffin batter or the muffins will turn out tough and rubbery. You only need to gently stir the mixture until it is just combined, preferably using a metal spoon.

Orange and carrot muffins

While most muffins rely on butter or oil to make them moist, these are made with carrot and puréed orange. Try to find seedless oranges if you can, so you can put the whole orange straight into the food processor; otherwise, you'll need to first cut the orange into quarters and remove any seeds.

2 oranges
1 large carrot, finely grated
2 eggs
90 g (3¼ oz/¼ cup) honey
185 ml (6 fl oz/¾ cup) low-fat milk
260 g (9¼ oz/1¾ cups) wholemeal (whole-wheat) self-raising flour
60 g (2¼ oz/½ cup) self-raising flour
1 teaspoon baking powder
1 teaspoon ground cinnamon
2 tablespoons sunflower seeds

1. Preheat oven to 190°C (375°F/Gas 5). Grease a 12-hole standard muffin tin.

2. Peel the oranges and place the orange flesh into a food processor of blender. Purée the oranges and then add the carrot, eggs, honey and milk. Mix well.

3. Sift the flours, baking powder and cinnamon into the orange mixture, tipping the wheat 'bits' out of the sifter into the mixture. Mix until just combined, taking care not to overmix. Spoon the mixture into the prepared muffin tin and sprinkle with sunflower seeds. Bake for 20 minutes. Cool in the tin for 5 minutes, then turn onto a rack. Serve warm.

MAKES 12
PREPARATION TIME: 15 minutes
BAKING TIME: 20 minutes

NUTRITIONAL INFORMATION/MUFFIN:
5.5 g protein, 2.5 g fat (0.5 g saturated fat), 25 g carbohydrate, 3.5 g dietary fibre, 240 mg sodium, 600 kJ (145 Cals)

A source of vitamins B1, B2, B3 and E, and also magnesium, calcium and iron.

 HINT

Use a food processor to grate carrots, apples or zucchini (courgette). This enables you to finely grate the vegetables or fruit, and makes preparation time much faster than grating by hand.

Almond bread

A finer form of biscotti, home-made almond bread makes a great gift. Tie them in cellophane and add a ribbon.

MAKES 40 SLICES

PREPARATION TIME: 20 minutes
+ 12 hours standing time

BAKING TIME: 30 minutes
+ 10–15 minutes

NUTRITIONAL
INFORMATION/2 SLICES:
3 g protein, 4.5 g fat (0 g
saturated fat), 11 g carbohydrate,
1 g dietary fibre, 10 mg sodium,
390 kJ (95 Cals)

A source of vitamins B2, B3 and E.

4 egg whites
115 g (4 oz/^{1}/$_2$ cup) caster (superfine) sugar
125 g (4^1/$_2$ oz/1 cup) plain (all-purpose) flour, sifted
155 g (5^1/$_2$ oz/1 cup) blanched almonds
^{1}/$_2$ teaspoon vanilla essence

1. Preheat oven to 180°C (350°F/Gas 4). Grease and line a 21 x 11 cm (8^1/$_4$ x 4^1/$_4$ inch) loaf (bar) tin with baking paper.

2. Beat the egg whites until soft peaks form. Fold in the sugar and continue beating until shiny.

3. Gently fold in the flour, almonds and vanilla. Spoon the mixture into the prepared tin, smooth the top, then bake for 30 minutes. Tip the loaf out and allow to cool completely. Store in an airtight container for at least 12 hours.

4. Preheat oven to 150°C (300°F/Gas 2).

5. Using a sharp knife, cut the loaf into very thin slices. Place the slices on ungreased baking trays and bake for 10–15 minutes, or until lightly browned, being careful not to burn them. Cool and store in an airtight container.

Mandarin cake

SERVES 12

PREPARATION TIME: 15 minutes
+ 45 minutes cooling time

COOKING TIME: 45 minutes
boiling, then 50–60 minutes baking

NUTRITIONAL
INFORMATION/SERVING:
6 g protein, 11 g fat (1 g
saturated fat), 17 g carbohydrate,
2 g dietary fibre, 60 mg sodium,
780 kJ (185 Cals)

A source of vitamins B2, B3 and E,
and also magnesium.

This variation on a traditional Middle-Eastern cake is ideal for those who must avoid wheat.

3 large or 6 small mandarins
4 large eggs
165 g (5¾ oz/¾ cup) sugar
200 g (7 oz/2 cups) ground almonds
1 teaspoon baking powder*

* Check the baking powder is gluten-free.

1. Place the whole mandarins in a saucepan, cover with water and bring to the boil. Continue to boil for 45 minutes. Leave to cool. Cut the mandarins open, remove and discard the seeds and place the pulp and skins into a blender. Process until smooth. There should be just over a cup of pulp.

2. Preheat oven to 180°C (350°F/Gas 4). Lightly grease and line the base and side of a 20 cm (8 inch) round cake tin with baking paper, leaving the paper overhanging the top of the tin.

3. Beat the eggs and sugar until thick and fluffy. Add the mandarin pulp, ground almonds and baking powder. Mix well and pour into the prepared tin. Bake for 50–60 minutes. The cake will fall slightly in the centre. When cool, use the baking paper 'handles' to lift the cake from the tin and slide onto a serving plate.

Date and apple loaf

This is a deliciously moist loaf cake that is made, surprisingly, without butter, sugar or eggs.

250 g (9 oz/1 1/2 cups) pitted dates, chopped
200 g (7 oz/1 1/2 cups) dried apples, chopped
450 ml (16 fl oz) orange juice
225 g (8 oz/1 1/2 cups) wholemeal (whole-wheat) flour
3 teaspoons baking powder
1 teaspoon ground cinnamon
1 teaspoon ground cardamom

1. Preheat oven to 180°C (350°F/Gas 4). Grease and line a 21 x 11 cm (8 1/4 x 4 1/4 inch) loaf (bar) tin with baking paper.

2. Place the dates and apples into a saucepan, add the orange juice, bring to the boil and cook for 1 minute. Remove from the stove, stir well and cool to lukewarm.

3. Sift the flour, baking powder and spices into the fruit mixture, tipping the wheat 'bits' out of the sifter into the mixture. Mix well, then spoon into the prepared tin and bake for 50–60 minutes, or until a skewer inserted into the middle of the loaf comes out clean. Turn onto a wire rack to cool.

MAKES 16 SLICES
PREPARATION TIME: 5 minutes
+ 15 minutes cooling time
BAKING TIME: 1 hour

NUTRITIONAL
INFORMATION/SLICE:
2.5 g protein, 0.5 g fat (0 g saturated fat), 29 g carbohydrate, 4.5 g dietary fibre, 100 mg sodium, 515 kJ (125 Cals)

A source of vitamin B3, and also calcium and iron.

HINT

Flour is sifted to lighten it and prevent it clumping in the mixture. When sifting wholemeal (whole-wheat) flour, tip the 'bits' in the sifter back into the mixture.

Banana and orange scones

Try to use macadamia oil if you can, as this oil has high levels of healthy monounsaturated fat and adds a subtle flavour. If using canola, check that it is fresh and has no 'fishy' aroma, as canola oil can turn rancid fairly quickly.

2 small ripe bananas
1 teaspoon finely grated orange zest
2 tablespoons skim milk powder
1 egg
2 tablespoons light olive oil, macadamia oil or canola oil
2 tablespoons orange juice
1/2 teaspoon ground cardamom
300 g (10 1/2 oz/2 cups) wholemeal (whole-wheat) self-raising flour
1 teaspoon baking powder
icing (confectioners') sugar (optional)

1. Preheat oven to 200°C (400°F/Gas 6).

2. Combine the bananas, orange zest, milk powder, egg, oil, orange juice and cardamom in a food processor. Alternatively, mash the bananas and mix well with the above ingredients.

3. Sift the flour and baking powder into the banana mixture, tipping the wheat 'bits' from the sifter into the mixture. Mix lightly to form a soft dough.

4. Put the dough on a floured board and pat out to a 1.5 cm (5/8 inch) thick circle. Using a 5 cm (2 inch) cutter, cut out 10 scones from the dough, re-rolling the scraps if necessary. Place the scones on a greased baking tray and bake for 12–15 minutes. Serve warm, sprinkled with a little icing sugar if desired.

MAKES 10
PREPARATION TIME: 15 minutes
BAKING TIME: 15 minutes

NUTRITIONAL INFORMATION/SCONE:
5 g protein, 5 g fat (0.5 g saturated fat), 21 g carbohydrate, 4 g dietary fibre, 255 mg sodium, 625 kJ (150 Cals)

A source of vitamins B1, B2 and B3, and also potassium, magnesium and calcium.

SPECIFIC DIETARY NEEDS

Sports nutrition

What you eat and drink won't turn you into an instant athlete, but sports people who eat poorly don't achieve their best performance. Depending on the type of activity, a sporting diet can be quite specific for any individual, but there are some general rules that apply to everyone.

Aerobic and anaerobic energy

The body gets energy from food by burning fats and glucose. The products of these reactions are carbon dioxide (which we breathe out), water, energy stored in adenosine triphosphate (ATP) and energy that is dissipated as heat.

Normally, combustion requires oxygen. Carbohydrates are unusual fuels for energy because they can provide short bursts of energy inside the body cells when oxygen is unavailable. This is called anaerobic oxidation and it comes into play when a large amount of energy is needed quickly, as occurs in sprinting or during a sudden explosive movement such as serving in tennis or lifting a heavy weight. Anaerobic activity does not last long because it leaves lactic acid in the muscle and this leads to rapid fatigue. Anaerobic energy is only used for physical activity that lasts less than 60 seconds.

Most of the energy produced in the body is aerobic energy — that is, it uses oxygen. Aerobic oxidation is much more efficient and is able to capture much more of the energy in the glucose molecule. Aerobic energy is used for any long or sustained physical activity.

Our ability to make the best possible use of anaerobic activity depends on the nature of muscle fibres. Some people inherit muscle fibres that fire better without oxygen. To some extent, a good sprinter is born rather than made. Training and technique are obviously still important for success.

Training also increases our ability to use aerobic energy. Fit people have more oxygen available for aerobic energy and they can keep exercising longer before they start to feel tired. Aerobic capacity is something that can be developed.

Sources of energy

Carbohydrate is stored in muscle as glycogen and the levels can be increased by training — as long as there is a good supply of carbohydrate. Athletes who train and eat plenty of carbohydrate can increase their glycogen stores greatly. This makes exercise easier and the more you exercise, the more muscle can be developed, although there are genetic and sex hormone influences — women will never develop as much muscle as men.

The body can also use blood glucose as a source of energy for aerobic activity. After meals, blood glucose increases. A small amount is converted to glycogen and stored in the liver from where it can be rapidly converted back to blood glucose if required. Endurance athletes rely on frequent replenishment of their blood glucose for energy. Sports drinks make this easy, as they supply fluid with sodium and potassium at the right concentrations for rapid absorption of the fluid from the stomach, and they also have the best concentration of glucose for rapid absorption into the bloodstream. Sports drinks are not needed for shorter or less strenuous activity.

With plenty of carbohydrate in the diet and plenty of glycogen in muscles, athletes can exercise for longer periods without feeling tired. Exercise also helps use up carbohydrate so it is not converted to body fat.

If muscle glycogen stores run out and there is no replenishment of blood glucose, an athlete will 'hit the wall'. This sometimes occurs in marathons and long-distance events and is hazardous because the brain will also be deprived of the glucose it needs to function properly. Muscles can burn some fat for energy, but this occurs only when there is also some glycogen present. You can think of it like a fire, with glycogen the kindling and fat as the large logs. You cannot burn a log unless you first get the fire going with kindling. Without glycogen, you cannot burn fat.

The ideal energy mix: fat or carbohydrate?

Under normal living conditions, the body uses a mixture of fat and glucose as its fuel. Exercise can change the fuel mix and some types of exercise can increase the amount of fat used for energy. The duration of the exercise also alters the fuel mix. This is important for anyone who is overweight.

For short bursts of activity, the fuel mix is almost 100% glycogen. For low to moderate intensity exercise, such as walking, running or swimming, a mixture of glycogen and fat are used, but the longer the activity proceeds, the greater the proportion of fat used in the fuel mix. Moderate exercise may be best for those who want to burn fat as their major energy source, but for most people who need to lose weight, any activity is desirable.

Training also increases the amount of fat used for energy. Untrained people accumulate lactic acid faster and therefore switch to using only carbohydrate for fuel. Trained marathon runners can make their precious carbohydrate stores last longer.

In most physical activity, the amount of glycogen stored in muscles is the limiting factor for exercise. Even

Good choices to provide healthy carbohydrates while travelling include bread rolls, fruit loaves (apricot or raisin are usually available), dried fruit and wholegrain crackers.

when using fat for fuel, some carbohydrate from muscle glycogen is also burned. Once the glycogen stores are empty, the body converts protein from muscle to glucose and fatigue then sets in. Low-carbohydrate diets are undesirable for anyone who wants to exercise.

Diet principles for athletes

- Drink enough fluid so that, apart from first thing in the morning, your urine is clear rather than yellow. The quantity of water you need will vary greatly according to your size, level of training and the weather conditions. There is no point in overdoing fluids, and sports drinks are only required for activities lasting several hours or for frequent events over the course of the day when it may not be possible to consume normal meals.

- Eat plenty of carbohydrate foods at each meal. Top choices include breads or cereals (preferably wholegrain), rice, pasta, polenta, couscous, potatoes and fruit.

- Keep fat intake moderately low by filling up on foods rich in carbohydrate and avoiding too many fried foods and fatty snacks such as biscuits, pastries, fast foods, chips and chocolate.

- Include foods such as fish, chicken, lean meat, cheese or eggs, but not so much that these protein foods crowd out the important carbohydrates.

- Make sure vitamins and minerals are adequate by eating plenty of fruits and vegetables, lean meat or a vegetarian alternative, and dairy products or fortified soy beverage every day.

In the average person's diet, high levels of fat tend to crowd out carbohydrates. Most people need to make an effort to cut back on fatty foods and instead include breads, cereals, grain foods such as pasta, rice, polenta, or couscous, as well as more fruit, potatoes and legumes. The bread should come with little or no fatty spread, the pasta with a sauce based on vegetables with seafood or lean meat rather than as a fatty lasagne, and rice is best steamed rather than fried. Potatoes themselves have no fat but chips and crisps are loaded with it.

Sugar is also pure carbohydrate, but is less desirable than other carbohydrates because it is so often found in fatty foods such as chocolate, cakes, biscuits, pastries, desserts and sweets. Sugary drinks contain artificial flavourings, colourings and preservatives. However, some sugar can be useful for endurance athletes who may need two to three times as many kilojoules as normal.

Training is usually designed to be strenuous enough to deplete muscle glycogen stores. Immediately after training, the body produces higher levels of insulin and more of an enzyme needed to convert glucose to muscle glycogen. In the 30 minutes or so following exercise, it is important to consume carbohydrates that can be rapidly converted to blood glucose, so that the extra insulin and enzymes can use this fuel to form more glycogen ready for the next day's training. Suitable carbohydrates have a high GI and include products such as sports drinks, watermelon and tropical fruits, sugary drinks, white bread, rice and crackers. Adding fats or proteins will slow down the rate at which the carbohydrate from these foods can be digested and absorbed. Those who go out for a walk or other mild exercise will not deplete their muscle glycogen and so do not need to look for high GI carbohydrate foods.

During training, the protein, vitamins, minerals and fibre required are easily obtained from a healthy choice of foods. Very few people need supplements. There is no evidence to support the use of extra amino acids or protein powders. Most of these are made up of skim milk powder, soy protein and extra vitamins. Athletes may perform better when they believe in various supplements, but this is usually a placebo response.

Carbohydrate loading

This technique was once popular with athletes as a way of storing extra glycogen in muscles. It consisted of depriving muscles of glycogen with a very low-carbohydrate diet and lots of exercise. This made the athletes exhausted. The next stage involved resting while consuming large quantities of carbohydrate. The muscle glycogen increased dramatically as a result.

Most athletes disliked carbohydrate loading as the exhaustion phase was unpleasant and the repletion phase made them feel heavy and bloated. Some also had disturbances to their heart rhythm.

These days, most athletes follow a high-carbohydrate diet all the time and rest from training a day or two before an event. The glycogen stores in a fit athlete by this method are almost as great and much more acceptable to athletes than the old carbohydrate loading technique.

Pre-event meal

Most of the glycogen in muscles comes from the carbohydrates eaten the day before an event. The food consumed on the day of an event will not influence these stores much. However, the food consumed before an event will influence the blood sugar and liver glycogen levels, and it is important to keep these normal as blood sugar controls the brain and nervous system and affects fine coordination and reaction times.

Features of the pre-event meal:

- Have it 2–3 hours before an event so you can digest the food and avoid a full stomach. (Note: rapidly growing children will need to eat a little closer to an event than this or they will feel hungry when the event begins.)
- Drink plenty of water. Diluted fruit juice is also suitable, but avoid anything but water (or a sports drink) in the hour before an event.
- Include carbohydrate foods, but avoid anything fatty. Suitable foods would be cereal with low-fat milk, pasta (but without a creamy rich sauce), rice, bread or muffins with jam or honey (avoid margarine or butter), potatoes (not chips) or fruit.
- Avoid excessive amounts of high-protein foods, especially those that also contain fat. Protein takes longer to leave the stomach than carbohydrate.
- Eat familiar foods that you like. Avoid any that you know give you wind.
- Avoid eating sugar or glucose in the hour before an event, as sugars can increase blood sugar levels, stimulate insulin and cause a more rapid loss of glycogen from muscles.

If you're walking for fitness, a pedometer is great for instant feedback. If your daily routine adds up to less than 10 000 steps (as is usually the case), go for a walk and gradually increase your daily steps until you reach this total.

Pregnancy and lactation nutrition

Pregnancy

The old saying that a pregnant woman is eating for two applies only to some nutrients, but not to kilojoules. The baby will take nutrients from its mother, so she must ensure that her supplies are adequate. However, the need for kilojoules does not increase as much as it was once thought.

Pregnancy does increase metabolic rate (which is why many pregnant women find they do not feel the cold as much as usual) and this increases kilojoule needs a little. However, most pregnant women reduce their physical activity because it is difficult to move as fast or as much as usual as they become bigger and bulkier. The drop in kilojoules expended for physical activity balances the increased needs of the higher rate of metabolism.

Because nutrient needs are higher but kilojoule requirements do not increase much, a pregnant woman needs foods that are of high nutritional quality.

Ideally, women should commence a top-quality diet some months before pregnancy so there are good reserves of all nutrients before facing the nutritional stress of supplying the needs of a baby. If the diet is not adequate during pregnancy, the baby has first call on scarce nutrients and it is the mother who is left with any deficiencies.

Nutrients needed in extra quantities during pregnancy

- protein
- vitamin A (only by a small amount; excess is harmful)
- all eight B group vitamins (thiamin, riboflavin, niacin, B6, B12, folate, pantothenic acid, biotin)
- vitamin C
- iron
- zinc
- copper
- chromium
- magnesium
- iodine

Most of these nutrients are already supplied in satisfactory quantities, with the exception of folate, iodine, and possibly iron.

Eating large servings of green vegetables would help provide folate, but in practice, the chances of this occurring are slim, so a supplement of folic acid (the synthetic form of folate) is usually recommended, preferably before pregnancy since the vitamin is needed from the moment of conception.

Recent studies show that iodine levels are often low and since this mineral is vitally important for the baby's brain development, an iodine supplement is advisable. Women who eat fish twice a week are unlikely to need iodine. A supplement containing 200–300 mcg per day is advisable. Taking twice this much is not advisable. Any woman who has a low level of thyroid hormone should be especially careful to keep to the recommended level of iodine supplements, as her body could absorb more and cause enlargement of the thyroid gland.

Omega 3s and mercury in fish

Fish and other seafood are an important source of omega 3 fats. During pregnancy, these fats are especially important as they pass through the placenta to the baby and play vital roles in the baby's brain and eyes. Eating seafood is therefore important during pregnancy.

Fish also concentrate minerals, including mercury. And mercury can be damaging to babies. Sea water contains mercury naturally and in some countries, pollution adds much higher levels. Fish from Australian waters mostly have low levels of mercury, but a few fish species have higher levels. These are not dangerously high, as occurs in some parts of the world, but they are sufficient for Food Standards Australia New Zealand to have issued guidelines for fish intake during pregnancy. These state that during pregnancy, women can:

- eat 2–3 serves a week of any fish or seafood not listed below

Or

- enjoy 1 serve per fortnight of shark (also called flake and often used in battered fish) or billfish (which includes swordfish, broadbill and marlin) and no other fish that fortnight

Or

- one serve per week of sea perch (also called orange roughy) or catfish and no other fish for that week

Listeria

Listeria is a bacteria that can be absorbed through the placenta and can be fatal to an unborn child. It is also harmful to newborn infants.

Foods such as raw meats, unpasteurized milk and raw fruit and vegetables can be contaminated with listeria, but most outbreaks of toxic reactions have been

associated with raw or unpasteurized milk, soft cheeses, contaminated vegetables or products such as pâté.

The main danger lies in foods that have been prepared and left sitting. Cooking usually kills the bacteria and freshly prepared foods are generally safe. To guard against listeria:

- Wash all fruit and vegetables before eating them.
- Do not eat any salad or cold meat that has been prepared or cooked 12 hours previously.
- Avoid prepared salads from salad counters.
- Avoid soft cheeses, such as ricotta, cottage, cream, brie and camembert.
- Avoid pâté.
- Do not eat raw meats or raw seafood.
- Do not drink unpasteurized milk or eat yoghurt or cheeses made with unpasteurized milk.

Listeriosis can occur without symptoms or it can be accompanied by flu-like symptoms such as fever and convulsions. Diarrhoea and vomiting may also occur. Any pregnant woman who has these symptoms should contact her doctor. (Note that morning sickness is not due to listeria.)

Drinks

Water is fine during pregnancy. Alcohol should be avoided as it crosses the placenta and can easily damage the developing baby's brain and nervous system. Studies do not show any deleterious effects from an occasional glass of wine, but as it is always easier to have a second glass after the first, the usual advice is to avoid alcohol.

There are doubts about the safety of large quantities of coffee during pregnancy but no evidence to suggest that 1–2 cups a day is harmful. Tea appears to have no harmful effects, however some herbal teas are not considered safe during pregnancy. Raspberry leaf tea is sometimes recommended as being good for the uterus, but some research indicates that this tea causes the uterus to contract and this could, theoretically, cause an abortion. It is probably best avoided. Other herbal teas that should not be used include comfrey tea, juniper, pennyroyal, sage, senna and yarrow. The safety of ginseng is also unknown although most ginseng products contain so little gingseng that they are unlikely to do much harm.

Constipation

Many pregnant women become constipated. Extra fibre from wholegrain cereals and breads, legumes and larger servings of vegetables and fruits will usually help. Iron tablets sometimes cause constipation. If this occurs, ask your doctor to recommend a different type of iron tablet.

Weight gain

It is hard to get weight gain right in pregnancy. Too little weight gain may harm the baby; too much extra weight may be a problem for the mother after the baby is born. A high weight gain during pregnancy may also increase the risk of gestational diabetes and this then increases the chance the mother herself, and possibly also her child, will develop type 2 diabetes at some stage in life. In general, aim for a weight gain of 10–13 kg (22–28 lb) for the whole pregnancy. This may not be distributed evenly and many women find they do not gain much weight at all during the last month or so. As a general rule, weight gain of 2 kg (4^1/$_2$ lb) for the first 3 months and then 1–2 kg (2–4^1/$_2$ lb) a month is recommended.

Some people tell pregnant women not to worry about how much weight they gain. This can be a problem in later life and many overweight women report that their weight problems began with very large gains during pregnancy. Other women struggle to keep their weight gain very low during pregnancy. This is foolish as it increases the risks to the baby before birth, and studies also show that when women gain too little weight during pregnancy, their children have a much higher risk of diabetes and cardiovascular problems later in life.

Morning sickness

The nausea and vomiting that can occur in the first few months of pregnancy are caused by hormonal changes associated with the pregnancy. Some women never feel sick; others find the first 3 months consists of endless visits to the bathroom. Most morning sickness passes by 3 months.

Even when you feel nauseated, it is better to eat something. Dry foods are best — a piece of unbuttered toast, a couple of cracker biscuits, some boiled rice or a piece of fruit may help. Many women find it best if they eat one of these foods before they get up in the morning. It is also best to eat small frequent snacks throughout the day rather than large meals.

Cravings

Some pregnant women crave particular foods during pregnancy. There is no evidence that these cravings represent any physiological inner wisdom. They are more likely to be psychological in origin. If you feel like strawberries at 3 a.m. or pickles with breakfast, go ahead and have them. If, however, you feel like eating a whole box of chocolates or heaps of pastries, try to talk yourself out of the urge to indulge in large amounts of fatty foods. If you want to eat dirt or chalk or some other non-food substance, resist the desire — it could be dangerous.

Lactation

Breast-feeding is a great gift for every child. Current recommendations are to breast-feed babies for the first 6 months, with no other foods or liquids to be given. Babies grow best on just breast milk and studies show that breast-fed babies are less likely to become overweight in later life and are also less likely to develop allergies, as long as no other foods are given for the first 6 months. From 6–12 months, continue breast-feeding but add other foods.

When feeding a baby, the mother needs higher levels of many nutrients, but also more kilojoules than usual. This is easier than during pregnancy, when the extra kilojoules are not usually needed. While breast-feeding, you simply eat more of the nutritious foods.

Most women find they are hungrier than usual once breast-feeding is established. However, it's still important to listen to your body and eat only if you are hungry. Not everyone needs more food. Most women gradually lose weight while breast-feeding, but a few find their increased appetite leads them to eat too much and they gain weight. The best idea is to eat more, but not so much that you gain weight.

Magazines often run stories of how celebrity mothers have lost all the weight they gained during pregnancy. They don't tell you that the woman has a nanny and a personal trainer who ensures she exercises rigorously. Weight falls gradually over 3–4 months after the birth of a baby, but it is not unusual for it to take 6 months before you are back to your pre-pregnant weight. By all means, avoid eating junk food and too much fat or sugar, but don't follow any strict diet when you are breast-feeding or you may lose your milk.

If you are tired, you may find your breast milk supply is affected. Try to get enough rest, to include some exercise (take the baby for a walk), eat only healthy foods and try some relaxation techniques. If your milk supply does decrease, the best way to build it up again is to let the baby suck more frequently. Forget the housework for a while, or ask a family member or a friend for help so you can spend more time feeding the baby and relaxing. The milk supply will quickly re-establish itself.

If your new baby won't stop crying, ask a friend or neighbour to take the baby for a walk. Take a relaxing warm bath and when the baby returns, you'll be more able to cope.

Vegetarian diet

There are two major types of vegetarian diet:

- lacto-ovo diet, which includes milk, yoghurt, eggs and cheese
- vegan diet, with no animal products

From a nutritional viewpoint, either of these diets can be adequate. In practice, however, it is much easier for a lacto-ovo vegetarian diet to supply enough nutrients because of the high concentration of nutrients in dairy products and eggs. A vegan diet needs much more care to ensure all nutrients are present in adequate quantities, and some small children may have difficulty eating the quantities and varieties of foods needed.

Studies show that those who follow a healthy vegetarian diet have less heart disease, high blood pressure, type 2 diabetes and some types of cancer. Such a good report card depends on having a *healthy* vegetarian diet.

Some people adopt a partial vegetarian diet where they avoid red meat, but eat fish and free-range or organic chicken. This is a healthy way to eat and has no nutritional problems. But a diet that just omits meat and makes no substitutions may lack some nutrients. Meat needs to be replaced by legumes and a range of grains, seeds and nuts. If a wide range of such foods are included, the vegetarian diet can be adequate and may be healthier than that of meat eaters.

A healthy vegetarian diet needs to include a regular intake of legumes, nuts, seeds, grains and cereal foods, a range of vegetables, plus eggs, dairy products or soy substitutes. A lentil burger once a month is not enough!

About one in four teenage girls and a smaller number of boys shun meat, at least sometimes. The odd piece of bacon on a pizza may escape their scrutiny, but 'a lump of dead animal' is usually off the menu. As well as revulsion at the idea of killing animals, some adopt a vegetarian diet because they think it will help them stay slim.

Overall, long-term vegetarians tend to be a little slimmer than meat eaters, but that is usually because they're more health conscious overall. When teenagers choose a vegetarian diet with lots of chips, chocolate, cheese, crisps, cream and cola, it is unlikely to do much for their waistline — or their health.

Most of the world's population is vegetarian. This is not usually by choice but because of economic considerations. In many places where there is no refrigeration, legumes, grains, nuts and seeds as well as fruits and vegetables will keep well, whereas flesh foods would go bad.

Many people worry about the protein in a vegetarian diet. As mentioned on page 14, this is not a problem and there is no difficulty getting enough protein without animal foods.

Potential problems and how to avoid them

Vitamin B12

Vitamin B12 is vital for the growth and functioning of the nerves and brain cells. It is found only in animal foods — meat, poultry, fish, eggs and dairy products — so a vegan diet will lack this important vitamin.

Mushrooms may absorb a small amount of vitamin B12 from the compost in which they are grown, but the quantity is far less than even a small child needs. Claims that comfrey or spirulina contain vitamin B12 ignore the fact that the type of B12 in these products can't be absorbed by the body. All vegans need a vitamin B12 supplement. This is very important during pregnancy and lactation, and for children. Vitamin B12 deficiency can cause permanent damage to the spinal cord and brain.

Low levels of iron or very high doses of vitamin C also reduce the amount of B12 that can be absorbed. The solution is to:

- include milk, yoghurt, cheese, eggs or fish
- choose soy products that have added B12
- take a B12 supplement

Iron

A vegetarian diet does not cause iron deficiency but a poorly chosen vegetarian diet can make it worse. Iron is needed for making red blood cells and children have high requirements because their blood volume must increase as they grow. Teenage girls also lose iron with menstrual bleeding and need more iron than teenage boys.

The haem iron in meat, poultry and fish is better absorbed than the non-haem iron in green vegetables, legumes, wholegrain products, eggs or foods with added iron. The solution is to:

- eat legumes, green vegetables, wholegrains, oats, wholegrain bread) and tofu every day
- always include fresh fruit or vegetables at every meal as their vitamin C increases the absorption of non-haem iron

If you are prepared to include a small amount of fish in your diet, this will increase absorption of non-haem iron from a meal.

The body can store enough vitamin B12 to last for many months, or even years, but a lack of the vitamin allows irreversible changes to occur in the spinal cord.

Calcium

Vegans and those who avoid dairy products often have a low calcium intake. This is easily solved by:

- using soy or rice beverages that have calcium added to a level of 130 mg per 100 g
- a calcium supplement
- regular use of tofu that is set with a calcium salt rather than one set with nigari. (Nigari is a setting agent that is extracted from seaweed and sea water and consists mainly of magnesium chloride)

Do not rely on sesame seeds for calcium, as they have much less than some people think and their calcium is not well absorbed. It is also important to ensure that part of the skin (arms, face) is exposed to sunlight, as this allows production of vitamin D, which is essential for calcium to be absorbed.

Zinc

Seafood and meat are rich sources of zinc, which is more easily absorbed by our bodies than the zinc in plant foods. If zinc intake is low, the body will gradually absorb more, but in the early stages of a vegetarian diet it's important to include plant foods that are rich in zinc. If seafood is acceptable, include it regularly as it is a good source of zinc. Other ways to increase zinc intake include:

- add wheatgerm to porridge or cereal
- use pepitas (pumpkin seeds), sunflower seeds, soya beans, green peas, legumes, muesli and wholemeal (whole-wheat) pasta
- regular consumption of dairy products

Feeding fussy eaters

Even before they turn one, children have discovered that the best way a small person can have power over a larger person is to refuse to eat. When you have invested time, effort, money and love into preparing food that children reject, it is difficult not to react. But whether the reaction is obvious concern, gentle cajoling or scolding, the more you react, the more the child will reject the food. This is a game for children and they always win, because no matter how hard you try, you can't force a child to eat.

Some foods are more likely candidates for rejection than others. Vegetables come top of most children's hit list, partly because their lack of sweetness doesn't appeal to most young palates. Some reject any foods that need to be chewed, possibly because soft baby foods have ruined the natural reaction to chew as soon as teeth erupt. Parents' likes and dislikes also play a role and some children pick up the greater status accorded to their father's preferences. Sometimes, if daddy rejects a food, that food is not served to the family, whereas if mummy doesn't like something, she is still expected to prepare it for those who do. It is worth noting that no healthy child ever starved when food was available.

Children who are breast-fed by a mother who eats a variety of different-flavoured foods will have already learnt that not every meal tastes the same. These babies then accept a greater range of flavours once they begin to eat solid foods. Babies fed formula don't have this experience and tend to expect more sameness in the flavours of foods. If the child is then given bland-tasting baby foods, they are likely to be very timid eaters as far as flavour is concerned.

Prepared baby foods also have a smooth texture and even the junior varieties often just have a few lumpy bits. Infants who get used to eating these foods often won't chew other foods and develop a preference for bland-tasting soft foods.

Some of children's fussiness about eating comes from our society's habit of giving children special foods. When children just eat smaller portions of whatever food the adults are eating, problems of rejecting food are much less common.

Toddler tantrums

Eating problems commonly occur in a child's second year of life. At this stage they are learning to walk and talk and just when they are doing something that seems exciting, meal time arrives. Many signal their dislike of the interruption by refusing to eat the meal.

This is also a stage where their growth rate is lower than during their first year and they don't need to gain much weight. Relative to their size, they therefore do not need to increase their food intake as they did during their first year.

After eating very little at a meal, the toddler will then feel hungry between meals. If given sweet or savoury snacks, this can seem like much more fun than eating meat and vegetables, so they repeat the behaviour.

Most problems with food occur at dinner. By then, the child is tired and often irritable — although they don't understand this. But having finished running around for the day, their need for energy decreases, so eating is less important. Some have already eaten enough during the day, especially if they have been snacking.

The solution for fussy eaters

The best way to get children to eat is to take as little notice of their behaviour as possible. This is difficult, but no harm will come to them if they eat very little for a few days. Nor will a toddler who hasn't eaten dinner necessarily wake in the night from hunger the way a small baby would.

The 'empty plate' technique often works well for children between the ages of 18 months and 5 years. It works like this: when everyone is seated at the dinner table, place plates of food in the centre and give everyone an empty plate. If you are alone with a toddler, you may need to invite family or friends. Tell the fussy eater you will help serve her anything she would like, and then ignore the child. Encourage everyone to help themselves and if the fussy eater chooses nothing, say nothing. Sitting watching others eating and enjoying a meal, the child with the empty plate will feel left out and will eventually decide to join in. This may take several days.

Ask young children to help you in the supermarket. Even young children can put mushrooms into a bag or pick up a cucumber or some carrots for the shopping trolley.

When children grow vegetables themselves, they are much more likely to eat them. If you have a garden, sow some carrot seeds, grow green beans, beetroot and lettuce. Pick and eat the vegetables while they are young and sweet. If you don't have room for a garden, grow cherry tomatoes in a pot and lettuce in ice-cream containers.

If the child wants nothing and then wants to leave the table, you may decide to allow this to happen after a few minutes. But you must make it clear that this is the meal and there won't be any other food until the next meal. You must also stick to this, even though there will probably be tears and tantrums later when the child wants a snack. The method works and a few days of misery is better than months (or years) of living with a fussy eater.

The following technique has been tried successfully in child care centres. The carers put the food on a low table, give each child a plate and then ask the best eaters to make their selections first. The other children follow like little lambs, often eating foods their parents swear they won't eat.

Snacks

In theory, there is nothing wrong with dividing the day's food into small meals and snacks. In practice, if the snacks are sweet and the meals include vegetables, most children will start hanging out for more snacks and will have little appetite for meals. However, some children are so active that they may need to eat more frequently than three meals for the day.

Snacks should be healthy. Biscuits, chips, muesli bars, cakes, lollies and soft drinks are best reserved for parties and should not be seen as everyday foods. Healthy snacks include:

- fresh fruit
- yoghurt — preferably low-fat natural yoghurt, with vanilla essence or fruit added, if desired
- toast or bread, or toasted English muffins, preferably wholemeal (whole-wheat) or wholegrain, with a thin scrape of spread. Most children will happily eat a slice of plain bread.
- nuts — for older children only, as small children risk choking on nuts, especially peanuts

This list may seem short, but there is a wide variety of fruits and many different kinds of breads available, and we need to avoid giving children sweet or salty snack foods. These are the foods that are contributing to childhood obesity. The carbohydrate in sweet foods, crackers and crisps also creates food for bacteria that cause dental decay.

Drinks

The ideal drinks for children are milk and water. After age two, the milk should be reduced-fat. Children who drink large quantities of full-cream milk (usually from a bottle) in their second year of life often have no appetite for other foods. Milk on cereal at breakfast and a glass of milk at lunch and dinner is enough milk for a child.

Fruit juices are fine occasionally, but no more than a small quantity once every few days. Children who become accustomed to having juices, cordial or soft drinks take in kilojoules that should be coming from food. Fruits are better for children than juices.

Treats

There is nothing wrong with an occasional treat. A treat used to be something that was enjoyed perhaps once a week. When children demand treats several times a day, something has gone wrong. In some cases, working mothers feel guilty and provide their children with treats to eat as a way of expressing their love — it is much better to spend some time reading to a child or playing a game or going for a walk together than to show your love with junk food. From the start, try to make treats something that the family enjoys together occasionally. By the age of four, most children will enjoy cooking and this may be a time to spend an occasional rainy day cooking a cake or some other special occasion food.

Once children attend pre-school or school, get together with the parents of your children's friends and agree that none of you will put junk food in your child's lunchbox. This will remove the whinge from a child that he or she is the only one who doesn't have junk food. Some governments have made it mandatory for schools to sell only healthy foods in the school canteen and this is a big help.

Parties are a time for indulgences and there is no reason why a birthday cake and other treat foods can't be served at parties.

Diabetes

Type 2 diabetes was once called 'adult-onset' or 'mature-age' diabetes because it occurred mainly in people over the age of 60. The name change was needed because type 2 diabetes now occurs in all age groups, including children as young as 10. The incidence of type 2 diabetes has tripled in Australia over the last 20 years and similar increases are occurring in most other countries as people grow fatter and take less exercise.

Diabetic diets have changed as research proceeds. Years ago, the major advice for people with diabetes was to cut back on carbohydrates as much as possible (not a grain of sugar was to be consumed), although fat and protein were considered harmless and were therefore encouraged. People with diabetes would happily eat cream (35% fat, mostly saturated) but would not touch ice cream (10% fat, mostly saturated) because it contained sugar.

By the 1960s and 70s, the realization that people with diabetes were at high risk of cardiovascular disease led to prescriptions for very low-fat diets, with instructions to include carbohydrate foods at each meal and between meals, usually as plain biscuits. All carbohydrate foods had to be weighed and there were long lists of foods, including vegetables, ranked according to their carbohydrate level. Carbohydrates were described as 'complex' (starches) or 'simple' (sugars). Complex carbohydrates were preferred, although fruits (which contain only sugars) were also promoted.

Recent recommendations are based on much better evidence and those with diabetes are now advised to follow the healthy diet recommended for the whole population, that is:

- low in saturated fat
- high in vegetables, fruits and grain products (preferably wholegrains)
- moderate quantities of lean meat, reduced-fat milk, cheese and yoghurt
- small quantities only of added sugar, fats and alcohol

This type of diet is designed to achieve optimal body weight, especially if combined with physical activity.

The diabetic diet is also being further refined with greater emphasis on the types of fat and the glycaemic effect of different carbohydrate foods.

Fat

Evidence against saturated fats continues to strengthen, as they are implicated in cardiovascular disease, some cancers and dementia.

Most people are aware they should choose lean meat and reduced-fat dairy foods, but saturated fats now extend well beyond animal fats. Almost half of our saturated fat now comes from vegetable oils, which have been hydrogenated or blended with palm kernel oil (a highly saturated vegetable fat) for use in snack foods, crackers, sweet biscuits, cakes, pastries, crumbed or fried coatings, chips, confectionery, sauces, spreads and takeaway foods.

For the average adult, total saturated fat intake for the day should not exceed 15–20 g. A single serve of many restaurant and takeaway meals and some snacks have more than that, so home cooking of low-fat foods is very important.

In theory, unsaturated fats are not a problem for those with diabetes. In practice, since all fats contribute 37 kilojoules per gram, too much of any kind of fat is undesirable for those who are overweight, unless they reduce their consumption of kilojoules from other foods. A meal of Mediterranean-style vegetables or salad with olive oil would be fine, but adding lots of olive oil to everything you eat will add too many kilojoules.

Those with diabetes should:

- keep saturated fats low by avoiding fatty meat, dairy fats and processed vegetable fats.
- choose monounsaturated fats for preference (nuts, olive, canola and macadamia nut oils, and avocado). Use sparingly where weight loss is needed and in slightly larger quantities when weight is stable. For those who may need to gain weight, these fats are safe as they will not increase cholesterol or triglyceride levels.
- increase omega 3 fats by eating fish or other seafood twice a week.

If a serving of any food has at least 6 grams of dietary fibre, its sugar content is unlikely to be a problem, as fibre slows down the rate at which sugar is released from the food.

Glycaemic index

Dietary guidelines in most countries recommend most people eat more breads and cereals, and specify they should preferably be wholegrain. This advice also applies to those with diabetes. Claims that populations have been growing fatter since dietary guidelines were first developed ignore the fact that few people have put the guidelines into practice. Consumption of bread and wholegrain cereals has decreased in most countries and most people fail to eat enough dietary fibre.

However, carbohydrate consumption has risen from an increasing intake of soft drinks, confectionery, snack foods, biscuits, cakes, fast foods and takeaway meals, and mixed dishes such as pies, pizza and pasta with fatty sauces. Cutting back on these foods makes good sense, especially as most cause a large rise in blood glucose.

The concept of glycaemic index (GI) was first described in Canada in 1981, and has importance for those with diabetes. GI values have been determined for some foods by comparing how much blood glucose rises after eating a food containing carbohydrate compared with the blood glucose response to an equal quantity of straight glucose. In the United States (and on the internet), some GI tables compare the response with white bread, but as the GI of bread varies according to the flour, the additives used and the baking method, comparisons with glucose are more suitable.

The GI has been described on page 17. Foods with a low GI value are converted to blood glucose more slowly than those with a higher GI. Lower GI foods are usually preferable for those with diabetes, but advertisements and articles in some popular magazines often distort the facts about GI.

In most cases, foods high in dietary fibre have a lower glycaemic index. However, this does not apply to packaged wholemeal (whole-wheat) bread where the fibre may be high, but so is the GI. This is because packaged wholemeal bread is made from white flour combined with wheat bran and wheatgerm and the recombination does not reproduce the slow digestion that occurs with breads made from stoneground wholemeal (whole-wheat) flour. Other breads with a low GI include wholegrain loaves (with 'bits'), breads made without rapid dough risers (which are common in many packaged breads) and genuine sourdough loaves. Rapid dough risers used in many large bakeries force the bread dough to rise in a few minutes and this changes the nature of the starch granules and causes them to break down to glucose faster in the intestine.

The glycaemic load (GL) is preferred by some as it takes account of the quantity of carbohydrate in a serving of a food, as well as its GI.

Practical guidelines for using GI

- Only foods that contain enough carbohydrate to affect blood glucose (at least 10 g per serve) can have a GI — for example, it is not valid to say that broccoli, spinach or salad vegetables have a low or high GI as they have very low levels of carbohydrate.

- The overall nutritional value of the food is still of major importance — for example, it is not valid to recommend chocolate over carrots because chocolate has a lower GI. Always consider the nutritional value of a food first, then the GI.

- The GI should only be used to compare foods of similar composition within food groups — for example, it is valid to compare one kind of bread or cereal with another bread or cereal, but not valid to compare the GI of ice cream and wholemeal bread.

- GI values are derived from the average blood glucose response of about 10 volunteers. The values are only valid to within 10 to 15 GI points, so there is no validity in choosing a food with a GI value of 72 over one with a GI of 75.

- The GI is influenced by fat and protein levels — for example, toasted muesli with a higher fat level may have a lower GI than natural muesli. This does not make the higher fat toasted muesli preferable to the natural product.

- Most meals consist of a variety of foods and have an overall GI according to the contribution made by each food. For example, adding milk (low GI) to a breakfast cereal with a moderate GI will lower the GI of the combination.

- There are anomalies with GI — for example, sugar has an intermediate GI but boiled sweets have a high GI. No one yet understands some of these aspects, but they show that although GI is important, it does not address all issues.

A note on sugar

The World Health Organization recommends that added sugar should contribute no more than 10% of the day's kilojoules. This is less than many people currently consume. For those with diabetes, sugar need not be eliminated, but only small quantities should be included, preferably from foods that provide other important nutrients and have a low or moderate GI. Low-fat sweetened yoghurt would be a better choice than a slice of cake or a biscuit. It is also more important to reduce saturated fat than sugar. In practice, reducing saturated fat will also reduce sugar consumption since the two are often found together in foods such as biscuits, cakes, desserts and confectionery.

Allergies

Allergies and intolerances

Food allergies occur if the body's immune system reacts adversely to a protein in food and makes antibodies to it. Next time the person consumes even a small quantity of that protein, the antibodies fight it, causing an allergic reaction which can be severe enough to require urgent medical attention.

The most common causes of food allergies are cow's milk, soy, eggs, seafood and nuts. Allergies almost always begin in childhood and are related to the child's immature digestive system failing to digest particular proteins. By age three or four, most children will have grown out of allergies to cow's milk and eggs as their digestive system matures and can break down the proteins to smaller units, which do not cause any reaction. Allergies to nuts and seafood may last throughout life and only about 20% of children with peanut allergy outgrow the problem.

Symptoms of food allergy include eczema, hives, vomiting, diarrhoea, severe asthma, swelling of the lips, tongue and throat, and in extreme instances (fortunately rare), there may be anaphylactic shock with difficulty in breathing. If not treated quickly with adrenalin, such severe reactions can be fatal. Blood tests can diagnose this type of severe allergy, known as IgE, and the usual culprits are peanuts, tree nuts and shellfish. Most people with an allergy to peanuts, tree nuts (such as almonds, brazil nuts, walnuts, pistachios and cashews), or shellfish will not have such a severe reaction, but as we cannot always predict the reaction, those with any of these allergies need to avoid these foods.

Peanuts are not really nuts, but legumes. Once rare, peanut allergy now occurs in approximately 1 in 100 children in countries such as Australia and the United States, but is rare in China, where peanuts are generally consumed in much higher quantities. Allergists suspect the way we dry-roast peanuts at high heat may increase problems, and some suspect it may be the particular types of peanuts we grow.

With adverse reactions to milk, wheat, soy, egg white, tomato, corn, chocolate, oranges, strawberries and garlic, symptoms may occur from 12 to 48 hours later and may be related to the quantity of the food consumed.

Food sensitivities

Food sensitivity (or food intolerance) occurs when a particular dose of a food chemical (added or natural) triggers an adverse reaction. The body's immune system is not involved but symptoms may be severe and include headaches, hives, eczema, stomach cramps or other gastrointestinal symptoms. There is controversy over whether food sensitivities also cause behavioural and mood changes. These are difficult to define and are mostly due to causes other than food. Unlike food allergies, where even a small amount of the ingested substance may cause a reaction, with intolerances, a small dose of the offending chemical may not produce a reaction.

Unlike allergies, food sensitivities do not involve antibodies and can't be reliably diagnosed with blood tests. The only reliable way to diagnose food sensitivities is with an elimination diet, which excludes all foods known to cause sensitivities. Machines that supposedly diagnose food allergies and sensitivities are notoriously inaccurate and such tests are worthless.

With many allergies and intolerances, it can be difficult to know which foods are safe. Fortunately, food labels must now list all ingredients and it is important to read them carefully. Many food companies now state 'may contain traces of peanut' if any peanut products are made in the same factory. This can be confusing, but since traces of peanuts can be left on machinery or surfaces in the factory, those with a severe allergic reaction need to avoid such foods.

It is generally considered advisable for all children to avoid peanuts until they are 3 years old. The website http://www.foodallergy.org is a reliable source of information for peanut allergy.

If your child has an allergy to any food, or to insect stings, make sure their school or pre-school knows and has access to an Epipen, which can quickly counteract an anaphylactic reaction, should it occur.

If you have coeliac disease, tell the staff when making a booking at a restaurant. Also, products such as soy sauce, cornflour (cornstarch) and various desserts may contain wheat, so check the ingredient list on all food labels when shopping.

Coeliac disease

Coeliac disease is a hypersensitivity to one or more of several proteins found in gluten, which occurs in wheat, rye and barley. Some people also have an adverse reaction to oats. The intestine is lined with millions of small projections called villi, which help in the digestion and absorption of nutrients. In coeliac disease, the cereal grain proteins damage the villi and if the damage is severe, nutrient deficiencies may occur.

The nutrients most likely to be affected include lactose, calcium, folate and iron, and in some cases, a deficiency of iron or the early onset of osteoporosis may lead to the initial diagnosis. Once all gluten from wheat, rye and barley is totally removed from the diet, the villi will gradually recover and nutrient absorption will return to normal.

Oats do not contain gluten, but they are often contaminated with wheat or rye and, for this reason, many people with coeliac disease are advised to avoid them. Uncontaminated oats may be suitable for those with coeliac disease, but this needs to be checked with the gastroenterologist who makes the initial diagnosis, as some people with coeliac disease also have a reaction to another protein in oats.

Coeliac disease is not a true allergy. Certain blood tests can provide clues about coeliac disease, but proper diagnosis can only be made by examining a piece of tissue from the small intestine. This involves an endoscopic examination by a gastroenterologist.

Wheat allergy may occur as a separate condition to coeliac disease and may cause symptoms such as eczema or asthma but does not necessarily damage the lining of the intestine as occurs in coeliac disease.

Coeliac disease can arise at any age. Many experts believe it is more common if infants are given cereals too early. This was one factor in current recommendations that babies should have only breast milk or formula for their first 6 months.

In the past, coeliac disease was diagnosed mainly in children who had frequent diarrhoea, poor growth and muscle wasting. With a damaged intestine, these children could not absorb fats or sugars and the first (wrong) diagnosis was that their basic problem was an intolerance to fat.

Adults with coeliac disease may have diarrhoea and lose weight, or their weight may be normal but they may be constantly tired, anaemic or develop osteoporosis. A small number may have a blistery, itchy rash or frequent outbreaks of severe mouth ulcers. Since most of the symptoms of coeliac disease can have other causes, accurate diagnosis is vital.

No one knows the prevalence of coeliac disease, but newer methods of diagnosis are uncovering many more cases among adults, and experts estimate it may affect as many as one in every 300 people. If you suspect wheat allergy or coeliac disease, make sure you go to a doctor who can properly diagnose the condition. Many people are wrongly diagnosed with wheat allergy on the basis of a VEGA test, which measures electromagnetic conductivity in the body, or tests of muscle strength when wheat is placed in a vial in front of them, or equally spurious tests where a filter paper is placed over the skin of the forearm and the pulse measured while a bright light is shone through the ear lobe or back of the hand.

When gluten is removed from the diet, symptoms usually clear up promptly, but once diagnosed, a lifelong gluten-free diet is essential to reduce damage to the intestine. Frequent damage can reduce the absorption of calcium and iron and also increase the incidence of lymphoma, a rare type of cancer.

At the time of diagnosis, especially in children, there may be an associated intolerance to lactose, the sugar in milk. Some people think the problem with lactose means milk must be permanently rejected, but when gluten is removed, the intestine recovers and lactose tolerance returns, usually within weeks.

Eliminating wheat

Wheat is the most widely used grain in the world. If the germ and bran are present (as is the case with wholemeal, wholegrain and whole-wheat products) it is highly nutritious, providing protein, B complex vitamins, vitamin E and many minerals.

Wheat is also used in healthy foods such as bread (including most rye breads), pasta, many breakfast cereals, tabouleh and couscous, and also in buns, cakes, biscuits, crackers, crumbed or coated foods and as a thickener for sauces and custard. Without wheat, eating out becomes especially difficult with no pizza, pies, hamburgers, battered or crumbed fish, barbecued stuffed chicken, spring rolls, hot dogs, pasta, sauces, coatings, croissants or pastries.

Processed foods may also contain gluten or wheat derivatives. Soy sauce, for example, may contain wheat, and it is also present in some thickeners, maltodextrins, hydrolyzed vegetable protein, malt or malt extract. Fortunately, food labels are now helpful, with companies obliged to state if their thickeners come from any gluten-containing grain.

There is no wheat (or gluten) in fruits, vegetables, fresh meat, fish and other seafood, poultry, eggs, nuts, seeds, milk, genuine yoghurt and cheese. Wine is fine, but those on a gluten-free diet will need to avoid beer because it is made from barley. A beer that is guaranteed gluten-free is now available.

To replace wheat, suitable products include those made from rice, corn (also called maize), millet, buckwheat, soy, chickpeas, potato, sorghum, sago and arrowroot. As gluten gives structure to bread, gluten-free breads tend to be heavy and scone-like. Rye breads contain gluten and so are unsuitable for those with coeliac disease. Spelt, one of the oldest cultivated forms of wheat, makes delicious bread but, contrary to some claims, it is just as harmful for those with coeliac disease as regular wheat.

Extra servings of legumes, vegetables and fruits, as well as permitted grains will make up for the nutrients previously provided by wheat.

No dairy?

A small percentage of children are allergic to the protein in cow's milk. Many are also allergic to the protein in goat's milk and also soya beans and soy beverages. Most grow out of this allergy by the age of three or four when their intestine matures and is able to break down the offending milk protein into its harmless component, amino acids. If a child is allergic to milk protein during these early years, they need to avoid milk, cheese, yoghurt and ice cream.

Throughout the world, many people develop an intolerance to lactose, the sugar found in the milk of all mammals, including cows, goats and sheep. People in Middle Eastern and Asian countries and indigenous Australians are commonly affected, and those from Mediterranean countries may also develop an intolerance to lactose as they age. The symptoms include excessive wind, bloating, pain and diarrhoea. Lactose intolerance is not an allergic reaction, but develops because the body stops producing enough lactase, the enzyme produced to digest lactose. There is rarely any need to avoid all lactose, and many studies show that small amounts of lactose do not cause problems. Cheese contains virtually no lactose and is not a problem. Yoghurt is also usually well tolerated since the bacteria that thicken the yoghurt also partially digest the lactose. With regular cow's or goat's milk, quantities of half to one cup generally cause few problems.

For children with an allergy to milk protein (and also for the small number of adults who continue to have an adverse reaction to milk protein), other sources of calcium are important. These could include soy, rice or oat beverages that have calcium added to the same level as milk (at least 120 mg/100 ml). Other sources of calcium are listed on page 26.

If you are in doubt about how to ensure your diet is healthy or whether some health claim is true, see a registered dietitian who can go through your eating pattern and suggest appropriate substitutes to provide all the nutrients you need for good health.

Index

Quick and easy index

Vegan index

Vegetarian index

Gluten-free index